THE SOCIAL DIMENSIONS OF
MENTAL ILLNESS, ALCOHOLISM,
AND DRUG DEPENDENCE

CONTRIBUTIONS IN SOCIOLOGY

Series Editor: Don Martindale

Contributions in Sociology, Number 9

THE SOCIAL DIMENSIONS OF MENTAL ILLNESS, ALCHOHOLISM, AND DRUG DEPENDENCE

DON MARTINDALE AND EDITH MARTINDALE

GREENWOOD PUBLISHING COMPANY

WESTPORT, CONNECTICUT

Library of Congress Catalog Card Number: 72–133499
ISBN: 0–8371–5175–9

Greenwood Publishing Company
A Division of Greenwood Press, Inc.
51 Riverside Avenue, Westport, Connecticut 06880

Printed in the United States of America

FOR RUTH L. BOWMAN AND
GERTRUDE E. CAMMACK

CONTENTS

PREFACE

The three great problems that all men must solve if their collectivities are to persist are the mastery of nature, social control, and socialization. The mastery of nature is accomplished in a wide variety of economic and scientific-technical groups; social control is accomplished in governmental, political, legal, law enforcement, and military groups; socialization is accomplished in families, and educational, religious, welfare, and health institutions.

Socialization in its most comprehensive sense comprises all those collective actions by which events and activities which are not social in themselves are transformed into social form.

The human individual, for example, is not born social. He has no instincts for being social in any special way. At birth he cannot speak a word in any language. He is, however, dependent to an unusual degree and could not survive without the help of other humans. They will transform him into a particular kind of social being, equipped with knowledge, skills, value systems and norms.

While the transformation of the feelings, ideas, and skills of the human individual into a form that adapts him to a particular system of social life is the primary work of socialization, there are other phenomena which also are best viewed as socialization problems. Accidents and illnesses are not in themselves social. Characteristically, both impair the individual's capacity to carry on routine social tasks. If, however, an individual's accidents and illnesses are defined as occasions for the assistance of other persons, they initiate new forms of social activity. Human life is enriched in the process of extending and receiving aid. Similarly, man is capable of raising questions about various transroutine matters such as death, the nature of the world, and the origin and destiny of all life. When these questions are brought within the compass of social life and made the occasions for new types of collective action, the range of life is once more extended and deepened.

In almost all forms of traditional society, two properties tend to characterize the socialization institutions: first, they tend to form a close-knit complex, and second, they constitute the most conservative sphere of collective life. The socialization complex saves, stores, cherishes, and transmits the social heritage. It is the great slow flywheel of the social engine. It is slow to start and its momentum makes it hard to stop. This has also been true of contemporary society: family, education, religion and health institutions have tended to bear close relations to one another. Furthermore, these areas have presented the greatest resistance to change. In the continuing conflict between the federal government and local interests, for example, some aspect of proposed change in the socialization complex is almost always the issue.

The great changes in contemporary society have had their points of gravity in the spheres of mastery of nature and social control. Both of the great systems of economic and political life of the contemporary world, capitalism and socialism, have centered on economic-technological and political institutions. Structurally, the modern world is characterized by the emergence of the large-scale organization, which first appeared in the economic and political spheres.

But in the long run, one cannot transform one sphere of life without forcing adjustments in others. A few of the more familiar ways in which changes in the economic and political sphere have consequences for socialization may be detailed by way of illustration. For example, the family has lost much of its former socializing functions. Many functions formerly performed in the home have been taken over by industry—textile and clothes manufacture, food processing, the manufacture of household items, and so on. In time women followed their former jobs and increasingly acquired economic and political equality with their mates. Not very long ago, much theoretical and practical education was in the hands of the family. The range of universal public education expanded, with ever larger numbers finding it essential to finish high school and then finding it essential to finish college. Meanwhile, with more women working outside the home, there has been a major tendency to develop preschool education. The changed situation of women and children is a major factor in the decline of the patriarchal family and the rise of the democratic family.

Child labor legislation removed children from the laboring force, reinforcing the impulse toward more education and incidentally sharpening the generation gap. The rise of large-scale organization in business, industry, and government drew the work force to these centers. The average family in America moves once every five years. The family remains less and less in the context of a single local community. The ties of the family with any particular religious group, school, or medical complex are continuously subject to change. Through such moves, the family becomes less able to support dependent members. Meanwhile, more and more individuals find a tiny niche in great organizations over which they have virtually no control. All such changes, and hundreds more, tend to shatter the old type of socialization complex.

It is hardly surprising under the circumstances that the sphere of socialization has been undergoing dramatic changes. The large-scale organization has made its appearance in the hospital and medical clinic, in education, even in religion. The family has abandoned or has been deprived of many of its former socialization functions, as is dramatized by the controversy over sex education in the grade schools. Welfare institutions have shifted in considerable measure out of the sphere of religion or private charity to' the state and national level. And, finally, the whole field of mental illness has been in transition.

Since World War II, the problem of mental illness has been defined in national terms. The declining capacity of small, cramped, and mobile urban families to keep mentally ill members at home has increased the pressure on mental institutions. Meanwhile, the old types of insane asylum have become unacceptable. At the same time that increased pressure has developed to place mentally ill individuals outside the home, transformations of the mental hospital into a therapeutic rather than a custodial institution have taken place. The rise of the theory and practice of the therapeutic community has dramatized this tendency. County welfare departments have developed whole new aftercare services for the mentally ill in response to these developments.

Modern chemistry has made available a wide variety of new drugs. Modern business and industry have made available an endless supply of alcoholic beverages. Meanwhile, the average individual is becoming atomized and is beginning to find himself in situations over which he has diminishing control. The generation gap has sharpened, and large numbers of young people find themselves in situations of tension with their elders and with the "establishment." Racial and ethnic minorities are in revolt. When the external avenues of the individual's self-expression are blocked, when he finds himself less and less in a social context that gives significance to life, he may be inclined to make his personal experience more gratifying through the use of alcohol and drugs. The problems of alcoholism and drug dependence have taken on new contours.

In short, in the post-World War II period, the problems of mental illness, alcoholism, and drug dependence have assumed a new and more critical form. From the national government to the smallest locale, the American community has been galvanized to new awareness of these problems. The therapeutic resources of the community are being explored with new intensity. Theories of mental illness, alcoholism, and drug dependence are undergoing brisk evolution.

Two conflicting theories of mental illness, alcoholism and drug addiction and their necessary solutions are ascendant today. One group defines them primarily as problems of social control; the second defines them primarily as problems of socialization. In the measures taken to solve the problems they pose, this same division manifests itself between those who define mental illness, alcoholism, and drug dependence primarily as forms of illness, to which therapeutic procedures are most appropriate, and those who view these problems as forms of deviance or delinquency, requiring a variety of legal and police controls.

In the following pages we review the nature and extent of these problems and explore at some length the therapeutic procedures for dealing with them. We offer evidence for the position that they are best viewed as problems of socialization rather than as problems of social control. We develop the theory that the common element in mental illness, alcoholism, and drug dependence is a failure of socialization.

ACKNOWLEDGMENTS

For an understanding of the problems of mental illness, alcoholism, and drug dependence, the authors owe much to the personnel of the Ramsey County Probate Court of Minnesota, the St. Paul-Ramsey Hospital, St. Paul, Minnesota, the Minnesota Department of Public Welfare, and various other services and agencies which deal with these problems in Minnesota. Among the persons working in and out of the the Ramsey County Probate Court whose judgments, decisions, and actions have thrown much light on the legal aspects of these problems are: the Honorable Andrew A. Glenn, probate judge; George E. Anderson, referee in probate; the Honorable Robert Chial, U.S. commissioner and probate court reporter; James F. Finley, court commissioner; Frank J. Danz, attorney; Helen Dady, clerk; and Mrs. Mae Berg, deputy sheriff for Ramsey County.

Many of the psychological and psychiatric aspects of the problems of mental illness, alcoholism, and drug dependence have been clarified for the authors in the course of work with the personnel of the St. Paul-Ramsey Hospital, St. Paul, Minnesota. Particularly valuable have been the insights provided by Richard R. Teeter, M.D., chief of psychiatry; James C. Kincannon, Ph.D., clinical psychologist, Alcohol and Drug Addiction Unit; and Matt Vacha, counselor, Alcoholic and Drug Addiction Unit.

Various social work aspects of the problems have been clarified for the authors by former and current members of the Minnesota Department of Public Welfare, particularly Miss Winnifred Malmquist, supervisor, patient transfers, and by members of the Ramsey County Welfare Department, including: James W. Edmunds, executive director; Robert Boyer, assistant director; James L. Plumbo, supervisor, intake services; Miss Ruth L. Bowman, former executive director; Miss Alice Colter, former psychiatric social worker; and Miss Gertrude E. Cammack, former supervisor of child welfare services.

The personnel of various other services and agencies have also over the years illumined other aspects of the facilities and procedures for dealing with the mentally ill, alcoholics, and drug addicts. Particularly important have been: Walter Gardner, M.D., psychiatrist and board member, Ramsey County Mental Health Center; Richard M. Lynch, executive director, State of Minnesota Commission on Alcohol Problems; David C. Hancock, executive counselor, Alcoholism Information Center, St. Paul, Minnesota; John L. Wakefield, veteran service officer, Ramsey County, Minnesota; and Richard J. Kaess, assistant veteran service officer, Ramsey County, Minnesota.

Finally, we are indebted to Mrs. Linda Weinraub for her assistance on the chapters on drug abuse and alcoholism and perceptive work on the manuscript as a whole, and to Mrs. Helen Keefe for her yeoman service in typing the manuscript.

DON MARTINDALE
EDITH MARTINDALE
September 1970

THE SOCIAL DIMENSIONS OF MENTAL ILLNESS, ALCOHOLISM, AND DRUG DEPENDENCE

1

CONTOURS OF THE CONTEMPORARY PROBLEM OF MENTAL ILLNESS

Mental illness in the present context is taken to be a psychically based behavioral disorder of sufficient seriousness to impair the routine social functioning of the individual. No one reviewing the problems of mental illness at the present time can afford to ignore the challenge of Thomas Szasz that "mental illness is a myth," and his argument that the view that a person may be mentally ill "is scientifically crippling." [1]

The damage done by the concept of mental illness according to Szasz is that

it provides professional assent to a popular rationalization, namely, that problems in human living experienced and expressed in terms of bodily feelings or signs (or in terms of other "psychiatric symptoms") are significantly similar to *diseases of the body*. It also undermines the principle of personal responsibility, upon which a democratic political system is necessarily based, by assigning to an external source (i.e., the "illness") the blame for antisocial behavior. [2]

From this last formulation Szasz appears to bring the notion of mental illness within the compass of the notion of "ma-

3

lingering." Apparently, in communist countries the notion of mental illness is also thought to undermine the principle of personal responsibility, upon which an authoritarian political system is based. According to Szasz, "The concept of malingering is very much in vogue in Russia, whereas in Western countries it has largely been displaced by the concepts of hysteria, neurosis, and mental illness." [3]

One cannot help but wonder whether the attitude toward mental illness shared by Szasz and the Russians does not bear some similarity to the attitude of the German Dr. Bautze toward Czech army recruits in the novel *The Good Soldier Schweik*. Dr. Bautze, chairman of the medical board, stood for no nonsense and regarded every complaint as a fraudulent attempt to avoid military service.

> Within ten weeks of his activities he weeded out 10,999 malingerers from 11,000 civilians and he would have collared the eleven thousandth man, if at the very moment when Dr. Bautze yelled at him "Kehrt euch [About face]!" the unfortunate fellow had not had a stroke.
>
> "Take this malingerer away," said Dr. Bautze, when he had ascertained that the man was dead. [4]

Szasz argues that the physical symptoms of mentally ill persons may be conceived as a specialized "language," by which the individual seeks to make contact with his environment. "The language of illness—and of social deviance, too—constitutes the last, and perhaps the firmest, bastion on the grounds of which the unsatisfied and 'regressed' man can make a last stand and claim his share of human 'love.' " [5]

What is called mental illness, in Szasz's view, is a specialized game the individual plays. The treatment of mental illness consists of persuading the individual to play the games of the majority of the persons around him.

The incontrovertible fact in "mental illness," however one prefers to designate it, is that the routine social functioning of the individual is so seriously impaired that the lives of others involved with him are also distorted. In some cases and in some forms of mental illness, physiological factors appear to be a component. At least in these cases mental illness would appear to be in part a medical problem. But over and beyond this, the assimilation of the problem of mental illness to the problems of health and disease rather than to magic, religion, or criminal behavior has been a progressive rather than unprogressive development. For this reason, the practice will be followed in the present work of retaining the term mental illness and conceiving of it as a psychically based behavior disorder of sufficient seriousness to impair the routine social functioning of the individual.

The extent to which mental illness has organic foundations is of secondary significance for the present definition, although this has important bearing on the treatment of mental illness and on the prospects for eventual full return to the community. Furthermore, what may be included in the category of mental illness has many features that overlap other categories of social problems, such as mental retardation, alcoholism, and drug addiction. Mental retardation may be complicated by psychic disorders; alcoholism and drug addiction may be intertwined in a complex cause and/or effect with mental illness.

The stress in the above definition of mental illness is placed on behavior and on the individual's capacity for entering into routine interaction with other individuals. Typical definitions of mental illness, or insanity, may be illustrated by the following:

> Insanity. This term ordinarily connotes more or less severe unsoundness of mind. Though its loose usage is almost synonymous with mental disease, scientifically the term should only be applied to the mental condition of an individual who, through socially inefficient conduct, has to be placed under supervision and control.[6]

> Mental disorder can be divided into the organic and the functional, the latter being primarily of interest to social scientists. Mental disorder may be defined statistically, clinically, in terms of middle class values, and in terms of residual norms and societal reaction. Because of definition the extent of mental disorder is difficult to determine.[7]

The line between mental illness and mental retardation is the presence in mental retardation of a deficiency rather than a potentially correctable disorder.[8] It is, however, possible that at times behavior treated as deficiency may actually be disorder, and that the mentally retarded may possess disorders as well as deficiencies. Alcoholism and the use of drugs introduce temporary behavioral disorders which often counterfeit mental illness, but which vanish when the individual is not "under the influence." Alcoholism and drug addiction, of course, may be caused by real or incipient mental illness. But for long periods in the course of alcoholism [9] or drug addiction [10] the individual may be able to carry on fairly satisfactorily routine social interaction. Alcohol and drug addiction, however, may quite evidently terminate in mental illness of either a functional or organic type. In any case, the reasons are clear for treating the core of mental illness as a behavioral disorder and recognizing both its difference from and close affinity with a variety of other problem circumstances.

HISTORICAL PERSPECTIVES

We have no way of estimating the frequency of mental illness among prehistoric people. The potential for mental illness among primitive man would in some respects have been much the same as for modern man, since men have had the identical gene structure for the last 60,000 years. On the other hand, life was short and society was far more simple, reducing its potential incidence. Also, attitudes toward mental illness may have differed; among some primitive peoples, certain forms of insanity were looked upon as gifts from the gods, and the afflicted were held in great esteem, often becoming powerful shamans or medicine men.

Primitive man had to rely on simple lore and his intuitions when members of his family or tribe became ill. Wounds were soothed with leaves or mud, thorns were extracted with a sharpened stick, abrasions were moistened with his own saliva. When these remedies failed he appealed to the medicine man of the tribe to rid him of the bad spirits which had invaded his body, for health and disease was looked upon as a battle between good and evil spirits.

The fact that primitive man was concerned about mental illness and attempted to treat it is evidenced by skeletal findings. Neolithic man performed skull trepanation to alleviate brain disorders. In the literature of Babylonia and Assyria (after 3000 B.C.), individuals afflicted with hysteria, delirium, and epilepsy were thought to be possessed by demons. Early Greek mythology frequently refers to episodes of hallucinations, demon-produced madness, and frenzy.

During the Greco-Roman period (580 B.C. to A.D. 1300), sometimes called the Hippocratic period, the philosopher-physician emerged as the dominant figure in treatment of disease. The source of intellectual activity was thought to be centered in the brain; mental diseases were related to disturbances in the brain. According to one popular theory of "humoral pathology," delirium and epilepsy were caused by a retention of fluids in the brain.

Human dissection as well as animal vivisection were performed, with some resultant tendency to draw a distinction between organic and functional disorder. Aristotle (384–322 B.C.) is credited with the development of comparative anatomy and embryology; Herophilus (335–280 B.C.) founded neuroanatomy; and Galen (A.D. 130–210) studied experimental neurology. Aretaes (second century A.D.) described the symptoms of hysteria, apoplexy, and epilepsy; he felt there was a relationship between mania and melancholia.

Among the various practices employed to treat mental diseases were purging and bloodletting. Flogging, starvation, torture, and restraint by use of chains were recommended by Celsus (first century A.D.). In contrast to such brutal measures, Soranus of Ephesus (second century A.D.) prescribed more humane treatment for the mentally ill, such as housing them in clean, well-lighted rooms with regulated temperatures; his patients were afforded sympathetic, tolerant care. The mentally ill among the poorer classes and slaves in Greece and Rome, however, received little care and often were put to death to alleviate the public burden.

In 1408, Fray Gope Gilaberto founded the first asylum in Europe for the care of the mentally ill at Valencia, Spain. This was followed by the establishment of other asylums in sixteenth-century Europe. But primitive notions of demonic possession persisted and rites of exorcism were performed by priests, to whom the mentally ill were brought for treatment.

The theory that organic causes were responsible for mental illness, according to acquired congenital and hereditary types, was advanced by Felix Plater (1536–1614). Francis Willis (1621–1675) presented the first clinical description of general paresis. Thomas Sydenham (1624–1689), the father of clinical medicine, formulated the first clinical description of hysteria.

Franz Joseph Gall (1758–1828) and Johann Kaspar Spurzheim (1776–1832) attempted to establish scientifically the controlling centers of bodily function in the brain. In their opinion, the brain was a composite organ consisting of many systems, each controlling a separate body function. Mental illness was assumed to represent an impairment of a brain center.

The first hospital devoted solely to the care and treatment of the insane in the western hemisphere was built by Bernardino Alvarez in 1566 at San Hipolito in Mexico.

During the colonial period in America, the mentally ill were treated with indifference or punished by means of stocks, whipping posts, or pillories.[11] At the time of the Salem witch-hunts, the mentally ill were considered agents of Satan and were hanged or tortured. In some localities they were driven out of town, left to wander about naked, or treated as vagrants. Frequently they were confined to the workhouse along with the paupers to work for their keep.

The first hospital in America to accept, along with other patients, those afflicted with mental diseases for the purpose of treatment and cure was the Pennsylvania Hospital at Philadelphia, completed in 1756. Benjamin Franklin was among its founders. Although the treatments employed (bleeding, purging, restraints by use of chains) were harsh and brutal by contemporary standards, they represented for that time a new approach in the treatment of the mentally ill. In 1773, an asylum was opened at Williamsburg, Virginia, the first erected in the United States solely for the treatment of mentally ill patients.

The first physician in America to study the problem of mental illness from a scientific viewpoint was Dr. Benjamin Rush (1745–1813), who joined the staff of the Pennsylvania Hospital in 1783. He wrote the first general treatise on psychiatry in America, *Medical Inquiries and Observations Upon Diseases of the Mind*. Published in 1812, this book was the only one of its kind available to students and practitioners of medicine for seventy years. Rush's method of treatment consisted mainly of purgatives, bloodletting, and emetics. Two of his inventions used as forms of shock therapy were the "gyrator," which, based on the principle of centrifugal action, increased circulation in the brain, and the "tranquilizer," a strong armchair intended to reduce the pulse by lessening motor activity.

During the same period that Rush was active in America, various continental doctors were changing the approach to mental illness. Philippe Pinel (1745–1826), a Parisian physician, was appointed in 1793 to the Bicêtre in Paris. At that time, male lunatics were restrained by chains shackled to the floor and walls and whipped by the attendants, many of whom were convicts. Pinel was outraged at such brutality; determined to free the mentally ill from their chains, he sought to institute a form of treatment based on tolerance and kindness. After receiving the permission of the Commune, he abolished the use of chains as a form of restraint at the Bicêtre. A few years later, he did the same at the Salpêtrière, an asylum in France for female lunatics. Pinel's essay *Traité médico-philosophique sur l'aliénation mentale ou la manie* [*Medico-philosophical Treatise on Mental Alienation*], published in 1801, set forth his theories on the humane treatment of the mentally ill. Pinel advocated the moderate use of drugs and placed the main emphasis on humane treatment.

Another proponent of humane treatment was William Tuke

(1732–1822), a Quaker and merchant who lived in York, England. His efforts resulted in the establishment in 1796 of The Retreat at York, where patients were allowed considerable personal freedom, and some of whom were even employed in industry. Restraints were reduced to a minimum.

In France, Jean Etienne Dominique Esquirol (1772–1840) advanced the humanitarian treatment advocated by Pinel. Esquirol's textbook on psychiatry, *Des maladies mentales,* was published in 1838. Another Frenchman, Guillaume Ferrus (1784–1861), was instrumental in the founding of a number of asylums in France, in which the criminals and lunatics were kept in separate quarters. The separation of criminality and mental illness was strongly advanced.

The establishment of institutions in the United States for the care and treatment of the mentally ill was in great measure due to the efforts of Dorothea Lynde Dix (1802–1887), a former school teacher. She toured almshouses, asylums, and jails and found their conditions deplorable. Inmates were confined to filthy cells, bound with chains, and accorded brutal treatment. As a result of her crusading efforts in the United States, Canada, and the British Isles, thirty-two hospitals were built. In America alone, twenty states built new hospitals or expanded their facilities largely at her stimulus.

In 1832, Massachusetts became the first state in New England to build a mental hospital. Its first superintendent, Dr. Samuel B. Woodward (1787–1850), had been instrumental in founding the Retreat for the Insane at Hartford, Connecticut. Woodward believed that alcoholics required special medical care and set forth his ideas on this subject in his book *Essays on Asylums for Inebriates,* published in 1838.

The relationship between legislation and insanity was of particular interest to the American psychiatrist Isaac Ray (1807–1881), who published, in 1838, the first book in the English language on this subject, entitled *Treatise on the Medical Jurisprudence of Insanity.* Dr. Ray was appointed medical superintendent of the State Hospital for the Insane at Augusta, Maine, in 1841.

The humane treatment of mental patients became widespread in the latter part of the nineteenth century due to several factors. The number of hospital attendants increased, and they were beginning to be professionalized through courses set up for their training. At some institutions, patients were provided with private rooms—if they were violent, their rooms were padded.

In 1841, female nurses were assigned to care for male patients at the Asylum in Gloucester. Florence Nightingale's experience in the Crimean War of 1854, followed by her crusading efforts in Great Britain, led to the creation of training schools for nurses. The first training school for nurses in an American mental hospital was established in 1882 by Dr. Edward Cowles at McLean Asylum.

The work of Emil Kraepelin (1856–1926), a German professor of psychiatry, profoundly influenced the development of psychiatry and the treatment of the mentally ill in the United States. He is still regarded as one of the foremost systematizers of mental illnesses. He employed the natural history method of studying mental disorders, following each individual case from its first symptom to the end. He developed a new classification of mental diseases. In 1898, he described dementia praecox, a type of insanity which develops in the young adult. In 1911, Eugene Bleuler (1857–1939), another German professor, modified some of Kraepelin's ideas about the disease and called it schizophrenia.

The founder of psychoanalysis, Sigmund Freud (1856–1939), had significant influence on the understanding and treatment of mental illness. Freud studied in Paris with J. M. Charcot, a French neurologist who encouraged him to pursue his research on hysteria. Later Freud developed the method of free association to bring to light buried memories which he felt were the cause of neurosis. (Hypnosis had already been employed to accomplish this in the treatment of hysteria.) Freud also used the method of dream interpretation to help resolve hidden conflicts in the disturbed patient.

The mind, in Freud's opinion, consists of three levels: the conscious (ego), preconscious (superego), and subconscious (id). Through free association, the patient was encouraged to talk at random about events in his life, thus bringing to the conscious level painful experiences which had been repressed in the subconscious level. Quite apart from the controversies between different branches of psychoanalysis and between psychoanalysis and other psychological and psychiatric theories, Freud and his one-time associates, Alfred Adler (1870–1937) and Carl Gustav Jung (1875–1961) helped sharpen the distinction between organic and functional mental disease.

In the late nineteenth and early twentieth centuries in the United States, significant developments in medicine and social work led to improved treatment for the insane. The Pathological Institute of the New York State Hospitals was founded in 1895 to conduct psychiatric research. Dr. Ira Van Gieson, a neuro-pathologist, was its first director. Dr. Adolph Meyer (1866–1950), who succeeded Dr. Van Gieson in 1902, inaugurated a training course for staff doctors in the clinical department at the institute.

The collaboration of psychiatry and social work resulted from Dr. Meyer's efforts. Mental disorder, in his opinion, was a maladjustment of the whole personality of the individual. He placed great stress on securing case histories of patients and encouraged visits to the patient's home, relatives, and employer for background information on possible precipitating factors of the illness. This function was gradually taken over by social workers, who now serve as an integral part of the "team" in mental hospitals throughout the country. During this period, the aftercare movement was established in the United States to provide discharged mental patients with adequate medical, financial, and moral support in the community. The first social worker to provide aftercare services was Miss E. H. Horton, appointed by the Manhattan After-Care Committee in 1906.

The National Committee for Mental Hygiene was formed in 1908 through the efforts of Dr. Adolf Meyer, Clifford Beers, and other dedicated persons. Earlier the same year, Beers, a former mental patient, published his book, *The Mind that Found Itself,* based on his personal experiences in three mental institutions. One of the charter members of the committee was the eminent psychologist William James. Some of the objectives of this committee were: to protect the public mental health; to raise standards of care for the mentally ill; to promote the study of mental diseases; to seek the aid of the federal government; to coordinate existing agencies; and to help establish similar committees in each state.

The National Committee for Mental Hygiene was of invaluable assistance to the United States government during World War I by helping to set up a program for recognizing and treating members of the armed forces afflicted with war neurosis. Dr. Thomas W. Salmon (1876–1927), who was recommended by the committee, headed up this program. In spite of many obstacles, Dr. Salmon was able to organize psychiatric, medical, and social services within the military structure, thus improving the efficiency of the armed forces. His methods were so effective that they were used during World War II and the Korean War and influenced the development of psychiatry in the United States.

RECENT TRENDS IN MENTAL ILLNESS

During the last three decades, there have been changes in the administration policies of mental hospitals, the development of more intensive aftercare programs, the appearance of training programs for nurses, psychiatric aides, and social workers working with the mentally ill, increased salaries and better working conditions for personnel in mental hospitals, congressional allocation of federal funds for development of community mental health centers, mental health education and research, and the passage of commitment legislation to protect the rights of the patient.

More professional personnel are entering the field of mental health; halfway houses have been established on hospital grounds as places where improved patients can live prior to provisional discharge; hospital and medical insurance plans have expanded their coverage to include psychiatric care for both inpatients and outpatients; psychiatric wards have been developed in general hospitals to provide for the care of mentally ill in their own communities.

Custodial care has been replaced to a considerable extent by active treatment. The use of psychotropic drugs now permits the patient to return sooner to an active life in the community. The use of restraints, isolation of unmanageable, noisy patients, and locked doors have been largely replaced by the tranquilized ward.

More and more, mentally ill persons are being treated on an outpatient basis. The National Institute of Mental Health defines an outpatient psychiatric clinic as

> an administratively distinct unit in which a psychiatrist is in attendance at regularly scheduled hours and takes medical responsibility for all patients in the clinic. Also *included* are facilities in which there is a budgeted, but temporarily vacant, position for a psychiatrist. *Not included* are private clinics in which patient fees are retained by individual staff members, and the outpatient psychiatric clinics of the Armed Forces. Psychiatric day-night services with a regularly scheduled psychiatrist also are excluded.[12]

A mental hygiene clinic of the Veterans Administration is defined as "A separate unit in which a psychiatrist is in attendance at regularly scheduled hours and takes the medical responsibility for Veterans with service connected psychiatric disabilities." [13]

As of June 30, 1967, there was in the United States a total of 2,259 outpatient psychiatric clinics, an increase of 58 percent over the number reported in 1959. Included in this total of 2,259 clinics were sixty-eight mental hygiene clinics of the Veterans Administration. These clinics in 1967 provided treatment services for an estimated 1.354 million individuals; 33 percent of these were children under eighteen years of age and 67 percent were adults. New admissions to these clinics amounted to 49 percent, while patients carried over on the clinic rolls at the beginning of the year totaled 45 percent; 6 percent were readmissions. Clinics of the Veterans Administration treated about 9 percent of the total patients receiving care in 1967.[14]

Until ten to fifteen years ago, state and county mental hospitals served primarily as custodial institutions for mentally ill and senile patients who were incapable of functioning in society. Patients once admitted on a voluntary or involuntary basis often remained in these hospitals for as long as thirty or forty years. Some patients, admitted at the age of twenty or twenty-five, lived in the hospital until they died at the age of eighty or ninety. Their relatives were reluctant to accept them back into their homes, afraid of their bizarre behavior, ashamed to admit that one of their kin had a mental disease, or unwilling to assume the responsibility of caring for patients in their own homes.

In response to the development of the tranquilizing drugs and new therapeutic techniques, the state and county mental institutions are changing from custodial to treatment hospitals. Patients are being discharged earlier, as shown by recent studies. At least seven out of ten patients in mental hospitals are discharged as totally or partially recovered. In some states 75 percent of the newly admitted patients are discharged from the hospital within the first year. Some 80 percent of schizophrenic patients, 65 percent suffering from involutional psychosis, and 75 percent afflicted with manic depressive psychosis are being released within the first year.

As of June 30, 1967, there were 426,009 resident patients in state and county mental hospitals in the United States. Since 1955, when the total resident population numbered 559,000, there has been a steady decrease amounting to 24 percent in this twelve-year period.[15]

Helping to bring about this sharp decline in patient population have been the new aftercare programs linking hospital with community, public acceptance of the mentally ill as persons requiring tolerance and sympathy rather than isolation and rejection, and the development of nationwide community mental health centers made possible in large measure through the passage of the Mental Health Act of 1963.

While the total number of patients in state and county hospitals has been declining, the net admissions and releases have been rising. In 1955, net releases totalled 126,498 while in 1967 there were 335,737 net releases. Since the mid 1940s the number of patients admitted to state and county mental hospitals has been steadily increasing. Total admissions in 1967 numbered about 349,000 patients. By June 30, 1967, there were 219,000 full-time personnel providing care for mental patients in 304 state and county hospitals in the United States. The cost of treating these patients has been rising each year. In 1967 the total expenditure was $1,415,480,302, which amounted to $4.84 a day for the care of each patient under treatment.[16]

What types of mental disorders are being treated in our state and county mental hospitals? Statistics in 1965 indicated that schizophrenic reactions, alcoholism disorders, and mental diseases associated with the aged constituted the majority of first admissions. Schizophrenics, mostly in the fifteen to forty-five age group, were the largest porportion (18 percent) of first admissions. An additional 16 percent of first admissions consisted of patients with senile brain disease and cerebral arteriosclerosis. One-half of the resident patients suffered from schizophrenia, one-fourth from chronic brain disorders. Among the resident patients and first admissions, more men were diagnosed as having alcoholic disorders and brain disorders associated with syphilis and mental deficiency, while more women had psychotic and psychoneurotic disorders. Among children under age fifteen admitted for the first time, 45 percent were diagnosed to have personality disorders and another 17 percent were diagnosed as schizophrenic reaction.[17]

The state mental hospital is no longer being used as the primary treatment center for individuals suffering from mental illness. Twenty years ago, three out of every four mental patients were cared for in state hospitals. In 1965, only one mental patient in every five was receiving psychiatric care in state hospitals.

What facilities are there for the treatment of the mentally ill at the community level? Outpatient care by private psychiatrists or treatment in community mental health clinics is helping to reduce the patient population in our institutions. Another resource is the general hospital with special psychiatric facilities. In the year ending April, 1965, general hospitals treated 600,000 mentally ill patients. Of the 3,183 general hospitals admitting mental patients in 1966, about 1,046 hospitals had special psychiatric wards or treated the mentally ill on general wards. The remaining 2,137 hospitals treated the mentally ill on an emergency basis, as well as for evaluation and diagnosis. In 1965, the 467 general hospitals with special psychiatric wards were responsible for 81 percent of all psychotic discharges from general hospitals.[18]

Many patients suffering from mental illness would rather be treated in their local community hospital than be sent on a voluntary or commitment basis to the state or county hospital, sometimes located several hundred miles away from home. At the community hospital, anxious spouses or parents can visit the patient daily and consult with the professional staff, and most importantly, the patient's tie with his normal way of life in the community can be maintained.

Other resources for treating the patient in the community are the mental health center and the day-night hospital. More than half of the community mental health centers being developed through passage of the 1963 and 1965 Community Mental Health Center legislation are associated with a psychiatric ward of a general hospital. By 1966, there were 175 day-night hospital programs treating mental patients in the United States.[19]

During 1966, approximately 19 million (one out of ten) people suffered from mental or emotional illness that required treatment. About half a million children were mentally ill, most of them suffering from schizophrenia; very few of these children were receiving treatment. About 3.921 million Americans received treatment for mental illness in 1965, as illustrated in Table 1.

Of the 531 public and private hospitals for mental disease, 326 were run by state and local governments. There were 2,000 psychiatric clinics in the United States at the close of the year

TABLE 1

DISTRIBUTION OF MENTAL PATIENTS RECEIVING
TREATMENT IN THE UNITED STATES (1965)

TYPE	No. of Patients (in thousands)
State and county mental hospitals	807
Private mental hospitals	110
General hospitals	600
Outpatient clinics	950
Psychiatric day-night units	14
Veterans Administration hospitals	140
Private office care	1,300
Total	3,921 [20]

1965; half were located in the northeastern section of the United States, while only 4 percent were in the rural areas.

In 1965, 14,200 psychiatrists were members of the American Psychiatric Association. Of this total, 600 were employed in an administrative capacity, some on a part-time basis. Twenty-one state hospitals were without a psychiatrist. To relieve this shortage, it was estimated that about 10,000 more psychiatrists are required to fill vacancies in state mental hospitals, clinics, community mental health centers, and general hospitals.[21]

Although treatment services have been steadily improving in the United States, the overall cost of mental illness is staggering. Mental illness costs the people of the United States over $5 billion annually.

Below are examples of annual expenditures for mental health care and facilities during the mid-1960s.[22]

Public mental hospitals (1965) $1,201,000,000

Private psychiatric care (1965)   100,000,000

Public assistance costs to mentally ill and retarded (1965)	66,000,000
Income loss to confined mental patients (1964)	1,700,000,000
Veterans Administration expenditures on hospitals and outpatient clinics (1965)	322,000,000
Federal support to mental health research (1965)	113,000,000
U.S. Public Health Service allocation to states (1966)	7,000,000
Construction of community health centers (1967)	50,000,000

There is little factual information available regarding the incidence of mental illness in most foreign countries of the world. But a recent article of December 8, 1968, in the Denver *Post* gives us a current picture of the situation in Britain. It states that in Britain, mental illness continues to be an "unresolved problem in spite of the tremendous advances in the care of mental patients." This article goes on to say that over 500,000 people are being treated for mental illnesses in Britain, and that almost one-half of all hospital patients are mentally ill. As in the United States during the past ten to twelve years, there has been a decrease in the number of patients in mental hospitals in Britain. In 1956, there were 150,000 patients in mental hospitals but by 1967, the total number was reduced to 121,000. But first hospital admissions during this period doubled. In Britain, twice as many of the mentally ill are now being cared for in the community. This trend is similar to that in the United States, where the community general hospital and community mental health centers are taking over part of the enormous burden of treating the mentally ill.

According to Maxwell Jones, the psychiatric hospitals run by the National Health Service in Britain generally afford better facilities for treatment than the state hospitals in the United

States.[23] The majority of British psychiatrists are employed by the National Health Service. Moreover, much closer cooperation exists between the hospital and the community in Great Britain than in, the United States. Careers in hospital psychiatry have been made more attractive by the British than by the Americans. The autocratic superintendent of the past has largely vanished and the consultant has complete freedom to treat his patients in whatever manner he sees fit. Characteristically, the consultant psychiatrist has his own beds in the hospital and, through out-patient departments and visits to the patients' homes, functions in the wider community.

David Vail was most impressed in the course of his study of the British mental hospital system with the variety of industrial therapy facilities available to patients. These included on-grounds hospital work; on-grounds nonhospital work; off-grounds work, and basic pension allowances for the nonworking patient. Hence, industrial therapy is at all points tooled to patients' needs. No British patient has to beg, steal, make objects for sale, or be subject to exploitation just for pocket money.

Aside from the development of patient work programs, Vail was impressed by the continuity of care that can be accomplished in Britain between pre-admission contacts with patients, their careers in the hospital, and aftercare services. Vail surmised that the level of care in Britain was generally superior to that in the United States, and that the poorest of British mental hospitals were superior to the most deprived in the United States.

In his review of the mental health systems in Scandinavia, Vail noted the role played by a long-range concept of social policy in contrast to the ex post facto social measures aimed at alleviating crises in national social life in the United States.[24] In Scandinavia, the welfare of the private citizen is the conscious aim of the state's social activity. The basic principle of "social help" (*sosialomsorg*) activates social policy: all persons in need of help ought to receive it. Closely related to the principle of social help is the strong emphasis in Scandinavia on intervention and protection. In Vail's view, Scandinavian socialized medicine is successfully providing high standards of health care, freedom of professional practice to physicians, free patient choice of physicians, and prestige and satisfactory income to physicians. In their treatment of mental illness, Scandinavian practice is dominated by the medical model of disease. The profession of psychiatry and the mental health services are primarily psychosis-oriented, although there are signs of a shift away from this point of view. The approach, however, is still more "organic" than "psychodynamic." In contrasting his findings with American practice, Vail was most impressed by the way the Scandinavians handle the financial status of mental hospital patients, the design of mental health facilities, and the problems of forensic psychiatry.

In the United States, the problem of payment of patients for work or provision of funds for patients without funds has not been adequately solved. In Scandinavia, patient labor is not necessary to keep the institution going. When patients are assigned jobs within the hospital, it is for their good and they are paid at going rates. A wide variety of sheltered workshops and similar industrial programs are possible in which contracts are let to local industries to provide remunerative and useful work to persons unable to leave the hospital. Moreover, pensions are provided through the national welfare system, so that the patient who is not working has a source of funds for pocket money for ordinary personal needs.

Particularly in their newer mental health facilities, Scandinavian design is inclined to emphasize small group-living units with homelike atmospheres designed to provide both efficiency and individual privacy. For children, small group-living units are designed for eight to ten children; for adults, large dwelling units with eighteen to twenty-five patients are preferred. The emphasis is on single and double rooms rather than on dormitories. Furnishings are tasteful and neat, and striking use is made of wood, glass, and metal.

Finally, Vail was impressed by the following trends in forensic psychiatry in Scandinavia: a rejection of the M'Naghten rule in favor of the product test of criminal responsibility (as in the Durham case); reliance on the expert medical witness as amicus curia; rejection of the adversary system; the wide use of mental hospitals as a disposition locus for persons exculpated from responsibility because of psychosis or mental deficiency; and the use of the indeterminate sentence in detention centers for sociopathic cases.[25]

NOTES

1. Thomas S. Szasz, *The Myth of Mental Illness: Foundations of a Theory of Personal Conduct,* p. 296.

2. Ibid., pp. 296–297.

3. Ibid., p. 296.

4. Jaroslav Hasek, *The Good Soldier: Schweik,* translated by Paul Selver, p. 58.

5. Szasz, *The Myth of Mental Illness,* pp. 301–302.

6. *Encyclopaedia Britannica* (Chicago: University of Chicago Press, 1947) XII: 383.

7. Marshall B. Clinard, *Sociology of Deviant Behavior,* p. 497.

8. George A. Jervis defines mental deficiency as "a condition of arrested or retarded mental development which occurs before adolescence and arises from genetic cause or is induced by disease or injury." George A. Jervis, "The Mental Deficiencies," in *American Handbook of Psychiatry,* ed. Silvano Arieti, II: 1289.

9. "Alcoholics are those whose frequent and repeated drinking of alcoholic beverages is in excess of the dietary and social usages of the community and is to such an extent that it interferes with health or social or economic functioning." Clinard, *Sociology of Deviant Behavior,* p. 414.

10. The federal statutes define a drug addict as any person who "habitually uses a habit-forming narcotic drug as defined—so as to endanger the public morals, health, safety, or welfare, or who is or has been so far addicted to the use of such habit-forming narcotic drugs as to have lost the power of self-control with reference to his addiction." *Code of Laws of the United States of America,* sec. 221, title 21.

11. For a detailed history, see Albert Deutsch, *The Mentally Ill in America: A History of Their Care and Treatment From Colonial Times.*

12. National Institute of Mental Health, *Mental Health Statistics,* January, 1968, Series MHB-J-2, pp. 1–2.

13. Ibid., p. 2.

14. Ibid., pp. 2–3.

15. National Institute of Mental Health, January 1968, Series MHB-H-12, p. 2.

16. Ibid.

17. National Institute of Mental Health, *Patients in Mental Institutions,* II, 1965, pp. 2–5.

18. Mike Gorman, Jane McDonough, Mrs. Albert Lasker, Florence Mahoney, and Alice Fordyce, National Committee Against Mental Illness, Inc., Washington, D.C.: 1966, pp. 35–36.

19. Ibid., pp. 36–37.

20. Ibid., p. 4.

21. Ibid., pp. 1ff.

22. Ibid., pp. 14, 17.

23. Maxwell Jones, Foreword to *The British Mental Hospital System,* by David J. Vail (Springfield, Ill.: Charles C. Thomas, 1965).

24. David J. Vail, *Mental Health Systems in Scandinavia.*

25. The problems of forensic psychiatry in the United States are discussed at length in chapter 2.

2

MENTAL ILLNESS
AND THE LAW

Inasmuch as his disorder seriously disrupts the social relations of the mentally ill person, he presents a problem to the community. He may threaten to kill himself or his neighbor. He may imagine that a gang of thieves or communists is plotting against him. He may be convinced that his apartment is bugged and that people are listening to his conversation via radio, telephone, and television. To prevent this, he may cut the telephone wires and smash the radio and television set. In a fit of anger, fear, and suspicion, he may attack a neighbor, friend, or relative. In one way or another, the mentally ill person tends to run afoul of the law. The following are examples of the way the mentally ill person may create legal problems.

After residing for two years in a nursing home, Mr. Jackson, a seventy-eight year old retired business man, suddenly became suspicious and antagonistic. He accused other residents of stealing his personal belongings, shouted obscenities, struck out at other bedridden residents, and went about the nursing home in a state of undress. His children were heartbroken at this turn of events but nonetheless took legal steps to secure treatment for Mr.

Jackson, who had also turned on them. And since he had a sizeable estate, a guardian had to be appointed to protect his interests.[1]

Miss Corrigan, a sixty-six year old spinster, had lived alone in the family home since the death of her father ten years earlier. As a young woman she had taught school, but gave this up when she developed arthritis at age fifty. Her father, a printer by trade, had wisely invested in some blue chip stocks and she lived on the dividends. Although limited in her activities to some extent, Miss Corrigan was able to manage by herself but the house was a shambles. No repairs had been made on the house for some years, there were vermin and filth, and newspapers were stacked five feet high. A pet dog and cat added to the debris. The Board of Health had tried repeatedly to get Miss Corrigan to clean up the place. The backyard was filled with junk and constituted a fire trap. The neighbors were complaining to the authorities. When the Board of Health arrested Miss Corrigan for violating the health ordinance, the judge decided to give Miss Corrigan another chance and asked the local welfare agency to help her clean up the place or find her another home. Miss Corrigan would not cooperate with the agency; in fact she would not let the social worker into her home.

A few years later, when the neighbors again became concerned about the fire hazard and also about Miss Corrigan herself, who was rather odd and unsociable, one neighbor signed a petition for commitment alleging that Miss Corrigan was mentally ill. Miss Corrigan engaged the services of an attorney who protested that her civil rights were being violated and there was not enough evidence to prove mental illness. The case was dismissed after the attorney agreed to hire the services of a man to clean up the yard, make the necessary repairs on the house, and arrange for a cleaning woman to come to the house once a week.

Although Mr. and Mrs. Gladstone and their three children had occupied their suburban split-level house for only three years, they were about to lose it due to failure to make the mortgage payments. Mr. Gladstone, age thirty-five, was subject to manic-depressive episodes. He was employed as a draftsman for a large corporation and in addition worked on his own inventions at home. He was a likeable, highly intelligent man with great powers of persuasion. His wife never knew where he was, for he stayed up nights calling people all over the country and often left town at whim. During his manic phases, he ran up debts, promoted new inventions, took airplane trips, and so on. In his depressive phases, he was unable to follow through on all his ventures and had severe spells of depression with some suicide attempts.

Mr. Gladstone's employer was about to fire him for failing to show up on his job, his creditors were hounding him and his wife for money, people who had invested money in his inventions were suing him, and his driver's license was revoked after he was arrested for driving while under the influence of liquor. The family lawyer advised psychiatric care for Mr. Gladstone in a private hospital, which he agreed to undergo rather than face the legal complications. While he was in the hospital, Mrs. Gladstone, with the help of the lawyer, managed to save their home and straighten out some of their problems.

Any number of legal problems may result when a person suffers a mental breakdown. His legal interests have to be protected. A guardian may have to be appointed to safeguard his finances and property. If he will not be hospitalized voluntarily, commitment proceedings involving lengthy and costly legal services may be necessary. After recovery, there is the problem of restoring him to capacity. At this stage, he may counterattack all those who had a hand in committing him.

There are occasions when accusations of mental illness can mask attempts at exploitation. Relatives will sometimes attempt to declare an aged parent, uncle, or grandparent incompetent in order, they say, to protect his savings or property or to prevent an ill-advised remarriage. In actuality, the incompetency hearing may be intended as a legal device to secure the estate for themselves. Laws must be enacted to protect the alleged mentally ill person in such cases, for there are times when relatives do succeed in this attempt.

Mental illness may overlap in complex ways with spheres of criminal behavior. It is difficult in some cases to determine whether an offender is mentally ill, a criminal, or both. This problem has long plagued the legal and medical professions, for while it is objectionable to prosecute mental illness, it is hardly sensible to encourage outright criminality to disguise itself as mental illness.

The trends in mental illness and its treatment which blur the formerly clear lines between the normal and insane make the legal problems associated with mental illness more complicated.

LEGISLATION TO
THE EIGHTEENTH CENTURY

As long as mental illness was thought to be a punishment for sins, or a product of consorting with Satan or practicing witchcraft, the legal problems it presented were relatively simple. Persecution of individuals suspected of engaging in witchcraft or other magical practices has been known since early times. It was believed that if these people entered into an agreement with the devil, they would be able to perform a variety of supernatural acts such as foretelling the future, riding broomsticks through the air, making themselves invisible, and changing themselves into animals. The fact that people who were often convinced that they possessed such talents were suffering from mental derangement was not recognized.

Legal methods of dealing with persons accused of witchcraft have been traced as far back as the Sumerian codes. The Sumerians employed the water ordeal as a method of detection and punishment. A suspected witch was bound and thrown into the water. If she floated she was a witch and to be put to death. If she drowned she was presumed innocent. In the time of the great Roman statesman Cicero (106–43 B.C.), anyone afflicted with madness was not allowed to be in control of his property and a guardian or relative was appointed to supervise his finances.

In Europe witch-hunts reached their height from the second half of the fifteenth century to the end of the seventeenth century; during this period about 100,000 persons were put to death by burning at the stake and other forms of torture. In the view of some scholars, witch-hunts are forms of collective mental illness, with the possible irony that only the few poor wretches accused of being witches were sane. Brian Inglis describes the mental disorder which we call "witch-hunting" as a form of hysteria that has reached epidemic proportions.[2]

Even at such times of collective madness, however, there were a few physicians of the opinion that witches were sick people and should be treated with kindness rather than torture. For example, the Dutchman Jonathon Weyer wrote a book called *De Praestigiis Daemonum* in 1564, in which he advocated sympathetic, humane treatment for those afflicted with mental derangement. Included in this category were witches who, in his opinion, were not at fault due to their insanity. Weyer criticized the lawyers of the period for their persecution of the mentally ill.

Another medical practitioner of this period who spoke out against the inhuman treatment of persons presumed possessed by the devil was Paracelsus (Theophrastus Bombastus von Hohenheim), the great Swiss physician and alchemist who lived from 1493–1541. In opposition to the popular belief of his time, Paracelsus felt that there was no relation between the devil, evil spirits, and mental illness, and that afflicted persons were in need of curative treatment for their insanity rather than incantations and other magical practices. Two of his treatises, *Fools* and *Afflictions Depriving Man of His Reason,* reveal an insight and knowledge of mental derangement unusual for a man of his time. Interested in the poorer classes, he lectured in German rather than Latin so they would better understand what he had to say. Paracelsus anticipated the time when the popular understanding of mental illness would approach that of the trained specialist.

At the same time that the modern drift toward a fuller understanding of mental illness got underway in the West, it also appeared in the Far East. More lenient measures were introduced in the punishment of offenders thought guilty of witchcraft and other crimes during the Ta Tsing dynasty in China,

as evidenced by the Chinese Code of 1647. Most of the formulations of this code go back to Chinese antiquity. Exile was prescribed for many crimes, affording the offender an opportunity
for repentance and the mending of his ways. Degrees of guilt in
homicide were recognized. The unintentional inflicting of a fatal
wound in play was punishable, but if death resulted from such
an accident, the offender was chiefly responsible for damages to
the family of the deceased. In such conditional estimates of
guilt, the principle of "guilty mind," or mens rea, was clearly
grasped.[3]

As long as men have been regulating social interaction, they
have been legislating on the special psychological conditions we
tend to associate with mental illness. Such legislation has always
reflected the prevailing conceptions of the time. Mental phenomena such as trances, hallucinations and catatonic states have
always been viewed as an abnormal state: sometimes as supernormal, giving the individual unusual powers such as foretelling
the future; sometimes as subnormal, representing a depression
by evil powers, negative spirits, or by Satan that inclines the individual toward evil. Where such experiences have been interpreted as supernormal, individuals possessing them have been
treated as seers, prophets, or wizards with unusual gifts of healing. In such cases, mental illness may be above the law or even
a source of new law. In Old Testament literature, for example,
there are evidences of such supernormal conceptions of various
special mental phenomena. Saul, in search of lost asses, consulted a seer; on his way in search of them, he met a group of
corybantic ecstatics with whom he danced and sang, joined in
their induced ecstasy, and prophesied among them.

Established governments, on the other hand, have usually
found the supernatural interpretation of the kinds of psychological phenomena associated with mental illness to be highly
disruptive to the routine functioning of power. With considerable frequency, legislation has been promulgated to curtail
sharply the operations of seers, prophets, dream interpreters,
shamans, ecstatics, and the like. It often suits the convenience of
routine power holders to press the negative interpretation of the

kinds of psychological phenomena we currently take as evidence of mental illness as evil magic, witchcraft, or demonic possession. Legislation based on this conception deals harshly with the mentally ill: depriving them of their property without recourse, expelling or banishing them, or putting them to tortured deaths.

Well into the eighteenth century, legislation on mental illness tended to reflect these super- or subnormal conceptions. Only rarely were there brief moments, as with the Hippocratic school of medicine in ancient Greece, where a quasi-modern conception of mental illness as an organic or functional disorder appeared. With the transition to contemporary concepts of mental illness, the tone of legislation also inevitably changed.

MODERN CONCEPTS OF MENTAL ILLNESS AND THEIR INFLUENCE ON LEGISLATION

The idea sporadically appeared over the long span of human history that the mentally ill were neither super- or subnormal, hence neither above the law nor below it. But not until the eighteenth century did the conception of mental illness as merely a variation of normality and a product of natural rather than supernatural circumstances become increasingly common in Western society. The social and intellectual milieu of the Enlightenment and the theories of the rationalistic philosophers of the period undoubtedly played a role in the changed conception of mental illness. An influential group of social philosophers of the time maintained that the essential property of man was his reason; that human nature was everywhere essentially the same; that human behavior was to be explained by natural causes; that when a given individual did not rely upon his natural endowment of good sense, it was probably because of various accidents of time, place, and circumstance and certainly no product of mysterious supernatural intervention. In such a milieu the mentally ill were to be pitied or treated as objects of humor and ridicule, not apotheosized or demonized. There was a strong inclination to extend protection to them, since they lacked the common sense to take care of themselves. There was also the inclination to inquire into the reasons for their lack of common sense and assist them to a return to their senses.

While this Enlightenment perspective was initially confined to an intellectual elite, persons sharing it held important positions in the various branches of government, educational institutions, and learned societies. They set a new style for dealing with social and psychological problems, a style which tended gradually to transform the outlook of the whole of society. And although the older attitudes toward mental illness persisted among the lower classes, they met with declining sympathy from members of the upper social strata and were no longer able to trigger witch-hunts of the earlier type.

New elements in legislation regarding the mentally ill from this time forward comprised: legal protection of the mentally ill person's rights; the provision for public facilities for his care; the attempt to separate the problems of the mentally ill from those of other types of public charges, such as paupers and criminals.

There were few legal provisions to ensure adequate care for the insane in America in the colonial period. Care, however inadequate, was a responsibility of the local communities. If a mentally ill individual was fortunate enough to be a member of a well-to-do family, he was ordinarily cared for at home. If his family could not care for him, he was subject to ridicule and abuse as he wandered from town to town begging for handouts.

But even in these colonies, remote from Europe, the new spirit was manifest. A number of the colonies set up legal provisions for protection of a person's estate if he were declared insane by one of the town officials. As towns increased in size, it was usually acknowledged to be necessary to provide community facilities to house the poor, criminals, and indigent insane.

With independence, one state after the other followed the Williamsburg example and began to construct hospitals for the treatment of those afflicted with mental diseases. But as the population increased, so, too, did the number of patients requiring care. It is possible that as the mentally ill became recognized as a public problem, the number that became visible suddenly increased. By 1890, the population of the United States had grown to 62,947,714. The estimated number of insane was listed as 106,485, with 74,028 of these in hospitals and asylums.[4]

Although recognized as a distinct problem by the second half of the nineteenth century, many of the insane were still being sent to almshouses, jails, and poorhouses. A survey of insanity and feeblemindedness commissioned by the Massachusetts legislature in 1854 was undertaken by a commission headed by Dr. Edward Jarvis. It was found that less than one-half of the known cases of insanity were receiving treatment in hospitals or public institutions.

In April 1865, the state of New York enacted the Willard Act, establishing a state hospital for the chronic insane. The act authorized the transfer of all chronic insane persons from county poorhouses to the Willard Asylum. This act was based on the findings of a state legislature survey the year before on the care of the mentally ill in poorhouses. The survey had revealed local conditions of neglect and inhumane treatment. It was felt that the chronic insane could only receive proper care in a state supervised hospital, and that the indigent insane should be supported by state funds. The Willard Act proposed the separation of the chronic and acute mentally ill. Other states soon followed this lead.

A new stage in the attempt to break the problems of the mentally ill into subunits was achieved when the Illinois state legislature in 1869 allocated funds for the construction of two state hospitals. As a result, the Illinois State Hospital at Kankakee was built in 1877; based on the "cottage plan," the hospital consisted of a group of smaller units or cottages housing 100 patients each, with a larger building in the center. This plan made it possible to isolate and group similar categories of mentally ill individuals together.

Massachusetts created a state board of charities in 1863, when its legislature acted on the recommendation of a joint committee set up to investigate their nine state-supported institutions, including three mental hospitals. The permanent board of charities supervised and coordinated all public charities in Massachusetts, permitting an overall attack on the various problems presented by the state's dependents. This system proved so effective that other states soon began to establish similar boards.

A state commissioner of lunacy was established by law in New York, in 1873, to report on existing conditions in the mental institutions of that state to the state board of charities. The state board was also given the authority to license public and private facilities for care of the insane.

The system of county care for the mentally ill was enacted into law in Wisconsin in 1881. The "Wisconsin Plan" provided for county care for the chronic insane and state care for the acutely insane with both the state and respective counties sharing in the maintenance cost of the patients. Patients admitted for the first time were to be sent to the state hospital for evaluation and treatment, with later transfer to one of the county hospitals when diagnosis revealed a chronic condition requiring long-term care. The state board was authorized to inspect and regulate conditions in the county institutions and to send patients to other county facilities if they were receiving inadequate care.

Provision for complete state care of the mentally ill was first enacted into law in New York in 1890, with the New York State Care Act. A system of hospital districts, with a state hospital in each to receive both chronic and acute cases of mental illness, was set up. The insane who were then in poorhouses were ordered transferred to state hospitals. All indigent insane were to be supported by state funds. Public institutions caring for the insane were required to change their name from "asylum" to "hospital." The legal distinction between chronic and acute cases of insanity was eliminated. This legislative landmark in mental health care in the United States was a virtual death blow to the custom of burying the insane poor in the poorhouses. Similar legislation was soon passed by other states, so that today most follow the state care plan for treatment of the mentally ill.

By the opening of the twentieth century, a surprising number of progressive developments in the identification and care of the mentally ill had been made. The problem was acknowledged to be a public responsibility. It was realized that it had to be tackled at a translocal level. The need to separate the problems of mental illness from those of other forms of dependency had been formulated.

During the first half of the twentieth century, American developments primarily consisted of a diffusion of the more progressive achievements of the nineteenth. Besides, a number of dramatic developments at the national and international levels shifted the problem of mental illness into the background. World War I involved the nation in international affairs. The Great Depression thrust general domestic crises into the foreground. World War II once more engaged the nation in international crises. Hence, only after World War II were the times ripe for the next major series of developments, centering on political concern at a national level with the problems of mental illness.

The National Mental Health Act, passed on March 15, 1946, authorized the creation of a National Mental Health Institute; its purpose was to conduct research and training in mental health, by means of grants to the states for developing mental health services and grants to individuals and groups for research and training. Also included in this act was a provision allocating $7.5 million for the construction of a building to house the Mental Health Institute, and grants to the states of up to $10 million a year for providing mental health services.[5]

To alleviate the shortage of psychiatrists throughout the country, Congress in 1958 authorized funds on a national basis to assist general practitioners in continuing their education and training in the field of psychiatry, and to make grants available to qualified institutions for setting up postgraduate courses in the field of mental health for the general practitioner. Physicians were granted stipends which sometimes made it possible for them to leave their already established practices and take up a three-year residency training. By 1966, 800 additional psychiatrists were giving service in mental health clinics, public and state hospitals, and in private practice; about 10,000 doctors had enrolled in these postgraduate courses.[6]

On July 28, 1955, Congress passed Public Law No. 182, the Mental Health Study Act, which provided for the conducting of a study of the nation's mental health resources and recommendations for their improvement. This five-year study, the first of its kind in the United States, was undertaken by the Joint Commission on Mental Illness and Health, representing thirty-six national health and welfare agencies. Recommendations for improving the mental health program in the country were set forth by the Joint Commission in ten monographs.[7]

The Joint Commission on Mental Illness and Health presented the results of its study on March 23, 1961, in its book *Action for Mental Health*. Their five-year study revealed that:

> state mental hospitals currently were not used as true hospitals, but as "dumping grounds for social rejects"; 80 percent of the nation's 277 state mental hospitals had not employed new techniques, which would have made them treatment centers rather than custodial institutions; state mental hospitals carried a daily load of 540,000 patients, and over half of these "receive no active treatment of any kind designed to improve their mental condition"; many patients should not have been committed to hospitals but should have received outpatient care at mental health clinics; and with modern techniques, the schizophrenic had at least a three-in-five chance for return to society as a useful citizen.

Some of the challenging and major recommendations of the Commission were:

> the setting of a national goal of one mental health clinic for every 50,000 persons; gradual conversion of all existing mental hospitals of over 1,000 beds into treatment centers for all chronic illness, including mental illness; conversion of mental hospitals with no more than 1,000 beds into intensive treatment centers for the mentally ill; more and better use of nonmedical mental health workers with proper consultation and supervision; expanded recruitment for mental health careers ("The state hospital must cease to be treated as a target for political exploitation" and

"patronage"; hospitals and clinics must be manned "by properly motivated career workers and not by hacks"); increased use of preventive counseling to moderate stress at early stages of disturbance; provision for immediate care of acutely disturbed persons at the onset of their illness; establishment of aftercare, intermediate care, and rehabilitation services to restore the mentally ill to useful lives as soon as possible.[8]

Other proposals included an expansion of the research grant program administered by the National Institute of Mental Health; the granting of state and federal loans, scholarships, and income tax relief to young people to enable them to pursue a career in medicine, nursing, and other professions related to health; and the allocation of funds for basic and long-term research projects. It was estimated that state, local, and federal funds allocated for mental health services would be doubled in the next ten years and tripled in the following ten. This would be implemented by a federal program of matching grants to states.

In his message to the Eighty-eighth Congress on February 5, 1963, President John F. Kennedy proposed a new and challenging approach to the nation's mental illness and mental retardation problems. This address was the first to be delivered by a President to Congress on these two major social dilemmas. In response to President Kennedy's message, Congress passed the pioneering Community Mental Health and Mental Retardation Centers bill the following October. Title II of the act authorized:

> $150 million over fiscal years 1965–1967 in grants to the states, which were to pay from one-third to two-thirds of the costs of constructing public and private nonprofit community health centers for the prevention, diagnosis, treatment, and rehabilitation of mentally ill patients in their own communities. (Such centers could be built in connection with existing community hospitals or clinics.) The grants would be allocated to the states according to population, need for centers and financial need.[9]

This legislation later proved to be instrumental in reducing considerably the number of patients in state mental hospitals. The bill required each state to present a construction plan in order to be eligible for these funds. By July 15, 1966, $60 million had been authorized for development of 128 new community mental health centers in forty-two states, the District of Columbia, and Puerto Rico. It was then estimated that by 1970 about one-third of the nation would be able to receive treatment at such community mental health centers. In 1965, an additional $224 million was authorized by Congress to provide federal matching grants over a seven-year period to community mental health centers for personnel and operating costs.

Treatment in the community for emotionally disturbed children was accelerated when Congress passed legislation in 1965, authorizing, over a four-year period, $120 million for the education of teachers dealing with the handicapped and especially disturbed children. An additional $41 million over a four-year period was allocated for research and related projects.[10] In 1966, federal funds were granted for a nongovernmental study of the problem of mental illness in children. To conduct this study, a joint commission on mental health of children was appointed.[11]

Dramatic recent developments in mental illness have carried the problem to national attention. The powerful resources of the federal government have been brought to bear on the problem. Funds have been poured into research and training. Higher standards have been set and assistance has been offered to state programs.

The legal and legislative problems raised by the mentally ill are by no means confined to the problem of identification and care. While one of the basic conditions for progress in the identification and treatment of the mentally ill is the separation of their problems from those of the criminal, a clear line between the two does not always exist. When two psychiatrists may disagree on the extent and form of mental illness in any given case, it is hardly to be expected that two professions with such different orientations as psychiatry and the law would always see eye to eye. Moreover, as understanding and treatment of the mentally ill advance, it becomes necessary to redraw the line between mental illness and criminality. For this reason the problem of the criminal insane has been set up for specialized examination, apart from the general legislation on the mentally ill.

THE CRIMINAL INSANE

The problem of insanity and the criminal law arises because of the many borderline cases in which criminality and mental illness become confused. It is possible that the criminal act may be caused by mental illness; it is equally possible that the claim of mental illness may be an attempt to avoid punishment for criminal action. A recent prominent example of this was the defense of Jack Ruby—who shot Lee Harvey Oswald, President John F. Kennedy's alleged assassin—on the plea of insanity. Another is the plea of Sirhan Sirhan, assassin of Senator Robert F. Kennedy, for mitigation of his sentence on the grounds of insanity.

Not only in cases of murder may mental illness be alleged. Persons sentenced to jail for a wide variety of illegal acts have been willing to submit to probate court hearings alleging mental illness, with the resulting commitment to the state mental hospital in order to avoid a prison sentence. The more completely mental illness loses its stigma, and the more fully the civil rights of the mentally ill are protected, the more attractive mental illness may appear as an alternative to criminal prosecution.

On the other hand, there have been real or allegedly mentally ill persons who have killed relatives or strangers while on provisional or complete discharge from mental institutions. The St. Paul *Dispatch* of December 20, 1968, gave an account of a thirty-seven-year-old veteran who, after being discharged from the mental hospital, stabbed his father to death. Was this veteran cured of his mental illness, making this a criminal act, or was he insane?

In most early legal systems, individuals guilty of committing criminal acts were punished by a variety of methods without consideration for their mental state. There were, however, exceptions to this. Under Roman law, possibly because of the influence of Greek schools of medicine, a person afflicted with mental disorder was considered to be incapable of making decisions.

The Moslems who invaded and conquered southern Europe borrowed much from the advanced schools of medicine left by the Hellenistic world at Alexandria. They recognized mental illness to be a disease rather than an invasion by demons. At Granada they developed an institution for the care and treatment of the mentally ill, and in a hospital at Baghdad they treated mentally ill persons in a separate ward. One of the earliest legal provisions for the acceptance of insanity as a defense is found in a Moslem law, which considers an unintentional killing or a murder by a minor or lunatic as involuntary homicide, subject only to compensation (for which there was a fixed tariff) and religious expiation.[12]

Throughout the world, children have often not been punished for their behavior, even when it involved arson, destruction of property, or murder. Because of their youth, it was felt that they were not responsible for their conduct. Under the English common law since the time of Edward I (1272–1307), "children under age seven could not commit felonies, because they were considered incapable of *mens rea;* that is, of the *guilty mind,* of knowing the difference between right and wrong but still 'choosing to do wrong.' "[13] The moment that mental illness was likened to the problems of the young, the way was open for extension to the mentally ill of similar legal immunities. Many types of mental illness are manifest in the afflicted as childlike qualities, encouraging such extensions.

During the thirteenth and fourteenth centuries in England, the courts began to show some consideration toward offenders who were afflicted with mental illness. During the reign of Henry III (1216–1272), there were pardons given to some insane persons guilty of homicides. By the reign of Edward I (1272–1307), offenders found to be insane routinely received a milder form of punishment than did persons of sound mind.

A legal definition of insanity was formulated by Henrici de Bracton, author of one of the first books summarizing English law, *De Legibus et Consuetudinibus Angliae* (ca. 1265). In his opinion, "an insane person is one who does not know what he is doing, is lacking in mind and reason and is not far removed from the brutes." [14] For several hundred years in English courts of criminal law, this interpretation was referred to as the "wild beast" test.

By the eighteenth and nineteenth centuries, recognition of the role of mental illness in criminal actions was acknowledged by most Western legal codes. That the insane offender was not responsible for his actions was stated in the Bavarian Code (1813) and the Saxe-Weimar Code (1838). Insane persons, idiots, children under eight, the ignorant, the senile, and those who were in a confused state when they committed criminal acts received special consideration.

For the past 125 years, the M'Naghten case has served as a base line for determining criminal responsibility of the insane. In 1843 Daniel M'Naghten, a Scotsman suffering from what today would be interpreted as paranoia, shot and killed Edward Drummond, secretary to the conservative English prime minister Sir Robert Peel, in the mistaken belief that Drummond was the prime minister. In the trial that followed, M'Naghten was acquitted on the grounds of insanity. There was so much criticism by the public of the acquittal that the House of Lords requested a clarification regarding the law of insanity by the crown judges. In the opinion of the judges represented by Lord Chief Justice Tindal:

> The jurors ought to be told in all cases that every man is to be presumed to be sane, and to possess a sufficient degree of reason to be responsible for his crimes, until the contrary be proved to their satisfaction; and that, to establish a defence on the ground of insanity, it must be clearly proved that, at the time of the committing of the act, the party accused was labouring under such a defect of reason, from disease of the mind, as not to know the nature and quality of the act he was doing; or, if he did know

it, that he did not know he was doing what was wrong. . . . The usual course therefore has been to leave the question to the jury whether the accused had a sufficient degree of reason to know he was doing an act that was wrong.[15]

Although members of the legal and medical profession have strongly criticized the rules laid down by the M'Naghten case, it still continues to serve as a guide in most of our states. Among those who strongly objected to the right–wrong principle contained in the M'Naghten ruling was Isaac Ray, who had argued against the principle in *Medical Jurisprudence of Insanity,* which he had published in 1838. (Ray's book, incidentally, had indirectly played a role in the M'Naghten trial. It was also a force for going beyond it.) Dr. Ray, one of the organizers of the American Psychiatric Association, advocated a closer relationship between psychiatry and the law. His writings on insanity as related to the law had a profound effect on the decision made by the Supreme Court of New Hampshire in the Jones case of 1871. This decision was a benchmark in judicial decisions on criminal insanity, presenting a broader interpretation of criminal responsibility of the mentally ill than the earlier M'Naghten decision. Whether an alleged criminal act was the result of insanity became a question not of law, but of fact for the jury to determine:

Whether the defendant had a mental disease . . . seems as much a question of fact as whether he had a bodily disease; and whether the killing of his wife was the product of that disease was also as clearly a matter of fact as whether thirst and a quickened pulse are the product of a fever. That it is a difficult question does not change the matter at all. The difficulty is intrinsic; [and] symptoms, phases, or manifestations of the disease as legal tests of capacity to entertain a criminal intent . . . are all clearly matters of evidence, to be weighed by the jury upon the question whether the act was the offspring of insanity; if it was, a criminal intent did not produce it; if it was not, a criminal intent did produce it, and it was a crime.[16]

In addition to using the Jones and M'Naghten rules, approximately seventeen states have recognized the factor of "irresistible impulse," which was first mentioned in 1934 in Ohio. This refers to the notion that a person committing a criminal act may be led to it impulsively, as by a force beyond his control. Temporary insanity was beginning to be employed as a defense by persons committing criminal acts.

Among recent judicial decisions, the Durham case has been significant in establishing a new guide for criminal courts in the United States, similar in some respects to the New Hampshire rule. (In the Jones case, Judge Charles Doe's charge to the jury was if "the killing was the offspring or product of mental disease, the defendant should be acquitted.") [17]

In 1954, the conviction of Monte Durham for the crime of housebreaking was reviewed by the United States Court of Appeals for the District of Columbia, with Judge David L. Bazelon presiding. This review by the higher court was requested because it was felt that the trial court did not accurately observe the rules with respect to "burden of proof." Durham had had a long history of arrests and mental hospital treatment. At the age of seventeen, he was discharged from the navy because of a "profound personality disorder." He attempted suicide in 1948, and, at a lunacy hearing the following year, he was judged to be mentally ill and was committed to St. Elizabeth's Hospital; there he was diagnosed as psychotic with a psychopathic personality. He was discharged as recovered after fifteen months of treatment. Following more trouble with the law, he was adjudged to be of unsound mind at a lunacy hearing and was readmitted to St. Elizabeth's Hospital. Diagnosis on admission to the hospital was "without mental disorder, psychopathic personality." He was discharged in May 1951 and arrested for housebreaking two months later.

At the trial, Durham was convicted. Although a psychiatrist testified that Durham was of unsound mind when the crime was committed, this was regarded as "no testimony" by the trial judge. The court of appeals reversed the conviction, following a thorough review of the testimony. In the opinion of the court, a new set of rules for determining responsibility was needed, since they were not satisfied with the criteria currently used. They stated their opinion as follows:

> We find that as an exclusive criterion the right-wrong test is inadequate in that (a) it does not take sufficient account of psychic realities and scientific knowledge, and (b) it is based upon one symptom and so cannot validly be applied in all circumstances. We find that the "irresistible impulse" test is also inadequate in that it gives no recognition to mental illness characterized by brooding and reflection and so relegates acts caused by such illness to the application of the inadequate right-wrong test. We conclude that a broader test should be adopted.[18]

The new rule laid down in the Durham decision was *that an accused is not criminally responsible if his unlawful act was the product of mental disease or mental defect.* This formulation was to be followed in the retrial of Durham, and in future court cases. The court stated:

> We use "disease" in the sense of a condition which is considered capable of either improving or deteriorating. We use "defect" in the sense of a condition which is not considered capable of either improving or deteriorating and which may be either congenital, or the result of injury, or the residual effect of a physical or mental disease. . . .
>
> If you the jury believe beyond a reasonable doubt that the accused was not suffering from a diseased or defective mental condition at the time he committed the criminal act charged, you may find him guilty. If you believe he was suffering from a diseased or defective mental condition when he committed the act, but believe beyond a reasonable doubt that the act was not the product of such mental abnormality, you may find him guilty. Unless you believe beyond a reasonable doubt either that he was not suffering from a diseased or defective mental condition, or that the act was not the product of such abnormality, you must find the accused not guilty by reason of insanity. Thus your task would not be completed upon finding, if you did find, that the accused suffered from a mental disease or defect. He would still be

responsible for his unlawful act if there was no causal connection between such mental abnormality and the act.

In the retrial, Durham was once more convicted of petty larceny and housebreaking, and given a sentence of one to four years, but the court of appeals again reversed the conviction.[19]

Shortly after the Durham rules were adopted, Congress provided for the mandatory commitment to St. Elizabeth's Hospital of persons found not guilty in the District of Columbia on grounds of insanity. Hospitalization for an indeterminate period was required until such time as it could be proved beyond any reasonable doubt that the patient was free of "any abnormal condition," and that he was not likely to repeat the act for which he was acquitted on the grounds of insanity.

In the opinion of many psychiatrists and a somewhat lesser number of jurists, the Durham rules represent the best solution so far to the relations between law and psychiatry. A large number of states, however, have failed to adopt them and, if anything, the trend has been away from them. Even the United States Circuit Court of Appeals for the District of Columbia has complained that the concept of disease is left ambiguous by the Durham rules.[20] Along the same lines it has been claimed that the Durham rules provide the jury with no clear standard of exculpatory insanity.[21] It has also been objected that the Durham rules tend to equate mental abnormality with criminal irresponsibility, an equation which could well lead to the nonpenal treatment of all criminals.[22] Finally, it has been maintained that the Durham rules make the psychiatrist's judgment preponderant in criminal actions.[23]

At the present time, relations between psychiatry and the law have been wandering somewhere between the principles contained in the M'Naghten and the Durham decisions. While under contemporary conditions the M'Naghten rules are retrogressive, at the time they were formulated they summed up a perception that from ancient times had gradually been established in many systems of law: that the state of mind of the criminal should be considered in adjudging his guilt for criminal acts. Widely established in various Western systems of law in the seventeenth and eighteenth centuries were various rationalistic principles. In the M'Naghten case, it was assumed that a man was to be presumed sane until proven otherwise. It was also assumed that, if the accused was conscious that the act was one which he ought not to do and was contrary to the law of the land, he was punishable. Finally, it was assumed that the accused could be under an insane delusion which would make the act appear to him neither wrong nor contrary to law, and hence lack the basis for blameworthiness. While from the standpoint of a rationalistic theory of human nature these formulations are progressive, the developments of contemporary psychiatry have called rationalistic theories of human nature into question.

Modern psychiatry has long since rejected the idea that good sense and rationality are universal. If anything is universal, it is man's ambiguous emotionality. Moreover, the contemporary psychiatrist is quite familiar with the fact that individuals may know what they are doing and be aware that they are wrong, but may nevertheless be quite psychotic.

> Except for the totally deteriorated, drooling, hopeless psychotics of long standing, and congenital idiots . . . the great majority and perhaps all murderers know what they are doing, the nature and quality of the act, and the consequences thereof, and they are therefore "legally sane" regardless of the opinions of any psychiatrist.[24]

From such perspectives, the M'Naghten rules are hopelessly dated. For this reason a large number of students are convinced that a precondition for a more adequate relation between psychiatry and the law is abolition of the insanity plea in criminal cases. In Lady Barbara Wootton's opinion, mens rea should be discarded as a definition of legal accountability, for it belongs to an outdated concept of punishment as retribution and ignores the fact that except in cases of total irresponsibility no clear line can be drawn between the wicked and the sick.[25] Chief Justice Weintraub of New Jersey observes that there is a basic conflict between the assumptions of the law and of psychiatry. The alternative between civil or criminal procedure for the restraint of mentally ill persons who have committed socially dangerous acts is made on the ground of blameworthiness. Blameworthiness assumes that the person can distinguish and choose between right and wrong. Psychiatry, however, is concerned with matters other than blame. Since definitions of insanity are notoriously vague, psychiatric testing tends to be inconsistent. The defense of insanity, under such circumstances, becomes a means of avoiding the death penalty.[26]

Dr. Seymour Halleck has raised the point that, even granting that a person's criminal behavior may be partly caused by mental illness, this would hardly seem to be a reason for justifying this behavior any more than criminal behavior engendered by poverty or persecution. Moreover, Halleck observed that psychiatrists on the witness stand are often compelled to assert that the accused was not responsible for his acts, while the same psychiatrist in his consulting room attempts to persuade the patient to accept responsibility for his aggressive or erotic tendencies. And finally, Halleck noted that the success of a plea of insanity often rests on the credentials of the psychiatrist, giving an advantage to those who can afford a good one.[27]

Thomas Szasz insists that all men, including the mentally ill, are responsible for their conduct. The psychiatrist's job is not to assign responsibility, but to make scientific judgments. Moreover, the involuntary commitment for indefinite duration which often follows a successful insanity defense is often more punishment than treatment.[28]

Norval Morris, professor of law and criminology, sums up many such notions in the following words:

> Historically the defense of insanity made good sense. The executioner infused it with meaning. And in a large sense, all criminal sanctions did so too, since they made no pretense of being rehabilitative. At present this defense is an anachronism in the context of the expressed purposes and developing realities of both the criminal justice system and the mental health system. In the future this defense would be not only anachronistic; it would

be manifestly inefficient as well. . . . The accused's mental condition should be relevant to the question of whether he did or did not, at the time of the act, have the prohibited *mens rea* of the crime of which he is charged. There should be no special rules like M'Naghten or Durham; the defense of insanity would be eliminated. Evidence of mental illness would be admissible as to the *mens rea* issue to the same limited extent that deafness, blindness, a heart condition, stomach cramps, illiteracy, stupidity, lack of education, "foreignness," drunkenness, and drug addiction are admissible. . . . If convicted, the accused's mental condition would, of course, be highly relevant to his sentence and to his correctional treatment.[29]

Professor Morris feels that psychiatry has made little progress in treating the disturbed criminal and in defining criminal insanity. Today, he believes, very few psychiatrists are engaged in this work, preferring instead to practice in large metropolitan centers, teaching hospitals, and diagnostic clinics. Many state hospitals with special facilities for the dangerous insane are located in the country, hundreds of miles away from large urban centers with all their social and cultural attractions. More emphasis is placed on diagnosing the dangerous criminal than in treating him. What is required is the mobilization of psychiatric and correctional resources as a means of treating the dangerous criminal and preventing crime.

As a model, Professor Morris proposes a security institution with one hundred beds, divided into twenty-bed wards or houses, located near a psychiatric hospital, with recreation and exercise facilities provided. Heading this institution would be a medical director associated with the psychiatric hospital, and as his assistant a member of the department of prisons, with experience in correctional work and training in the social sciences. Five half-time psychiatrists would be responsible for each of the five wards or houses, assisted by two or three social workers and other staff workers. The psychiatric hospital would provide psychological services. Prisoners would be given industrial work to keep them busy.

Those prisoners should be sent to the model institution whom nobody else wants; whom other institutions reject because they are too disruptive, too turbulent, too unpromising—but not those who are certifiably insane or retarded under the state's civil commitment process. . . . I would exclude no category of offender from this institution. . . . If I were in control, the principle of selection would be the seriousness of the threat that the offender poses to the community and the extent to which the treatment resources in the institution might reasonably be expected to bear upon his problems.[30]

One additional development should be taken into account. The American Law Institute, a group of scholars, judges, and lawyers who assemble from time to time to study various legal problems, began work in 1953 (one year before the Durham decision) on a model penal code which proposed a new test of insanity to overcome the shortcomings of the M'Naghten rule. It proposed that:

1. A person is not responsible for criminal conduct if at the time of such conduct as a result of mental disease or defect he lacks substantial capacity either to appreciate the criminality of his conduct or to conform his conduct to the requirements of the law.
2. The terms "mental disease or defect" do not include an abnormality manifested only by repeated criminal or otherwise antisocial conduct.[31]

In the opinion of some authorities these rules preserve the realistic approach to the psychiatry of criminal conduct of the Durham rule, while correcting some of the limitations of the Durham rule which juries find vague. The rule permits the entire mind, not simply cognition, to be considered. Modern psychiatry has demonstrated that an accused may in some sense know that an act is wrong while lacking substantial capacity to do otherwise. The M'Naghten rule, by contrast, gave almost exclusive importance to cognition.

The Second Circuit Court of Appeals for New York, Connecticut, and Vermont adopted this test in February 1966. It is, however, only the law in federal cases in those states. Some other circuit courts have adopted modifications of M'Naghten and one has adopted the Durham rule.[32] The situation, thus, is spotty.

It is hardly surprising that Sheldon Glueck should have subtitled his book, *Law and Psychiatry,* with the arresting phrase *Cold War or Entente Cordiale?* [33] Glueck believes that the present state of affairs between the disciplines is in fact one of cold war. He is, however, also convinced that, properly amended, the Durham rule could turn the state of affairs between psychiatry and the law into an entente cordiale, although he by no means wishes to stop developments at this point.

In any case, the contest between the two disciplines goes on, and, in the opinion of the present writers, can never end because of the character of the two disciplines. The law is a normative discipline whose task is to find workable compromises between a wide variety of conflicting social interests; psychiatry is a scientific discipline, whose task is to understand the causes and cures of mental illness. Too often the psychiatrist on the witness stand is asked not for judgments of fact but for normative evaluations, a task for which he is professionally unqualified. But the psychiatrist can contribute facts pertinent to the criminal act, the accused's personality, and the possible consequences of imprisonment or treatment.

In view of modern psychiatry's assertion that the criminally insane should be treated as responsible agents, the legal plea of insanity ought to be abandoned. Instead, the courts should regard mental illness as one special circumstance that bears upon both the degree of guilt and the most desirable manner of meting out sentence.

THE RIGHTS OF
THE MENTALLY ILL

In ancient times and in large parts of the primitive world, the mentally ill were either above or below the law: conceived as divinely inspired and hence a law unto themselves, or as demonically possessed and hence not deserving usual human consideration. It is characteristic of the modern mind that care is taken to preserve the rights of the mentally ill.

There are problems involved in the preservation of the rights of the mentally ill, for a precondition of the normal exercise of rights is responsibility in their use. Many forms of mental illness incline the individual to abuse his rights. This may be illustrated by a psychiatrist's study of young men on a college campus who rode motorcycles. He came to the unexpected conclusion that perhaps it would be wise to describe a new kind of mental illness, the "motorcycle syndrome." He concluded that a large number of the motorcycle buffs suffer from a strong sense of individual deficiency and impotence. The motorcycle and its attendant properties such as belts, helmets, and leather jackets were compensatory aggressive symbols. The exaggerated swaggering, reckless driving, and aggression of many young motorcyclists constituted an overt style intended to overcome inner feelings of incompetence. This seriously raises the question of whether the motorcycle, which may be driven up to speeds of 150 miles an hour—hence acquiring the properties of a deadly weapon—ought to be permitted in such hands. Similar reasoning could apply to automobiles or weapons. One can easily envision the possible consequences of permitting certain types of mentally ill persons to vote or hold public office.

On the other hand, the mentally ill person is already suffering because of his disease. To deprive him of his rights is to add to his problems. Negative consequences may follow as his spiral of alienation is deepened. The stigma of mental illness is worsened when it involves a loss of rights. The road back to sanity acquires new obstacles.

It is no great matter of wonder, under the circumstances, that the laws governing the rights of the mentally ill vary from one state to the next. Some of the statutes are precise in definition while others are vague, leaving it up to the judge in each jurisdiction to make the final decision.

Marriage

Laws relating to marriage of the mentally ill and retarded have at times been enacted not only for protection of the partners to the marriage, but of society as well. The responsibilities of marriage and parenthood are too great to be assumed by a mentally ill person, who may be able to function adequately at intervals but not under stress. Mentally ill and mentally retarded persons may pass on their defects to their children, thus increasing society's burden in the form of financial support, medical aid, special education, and rehabilitation. Many families with mentally ill members are unable to pay their medical and hospital bills, increasing the burden of the state or county.

Under the common law, a person lacking in mental capacity is prohibited from marrying. Restrictions vary among the states. Some states prohibit imbeciles, insane, and feeble-minded individuals from marrying. Other states allow this group to marry if the woman is over forty-five. Several states also prevent epileptics from obtaining marriage licenses. A few states require that an individual possess sufficient ability to make a contract before a marriage license can be issued. A few states prohibit marriage of a person under commitment to a mental hospital.

In spite of such statutory restrictions in some states, mentally ill persons often obtain marriage licenses from other states or by withholding information regarding their legal status and psychiatric treatment. When this occurs in some states, the marriage can be automatically declared invalid, while in others a guardian, parents, or even the mentally ill person himself can initiate annulment proceedings. But if the person, during a lucid interval, was married, the marriage is usually valid no matter how erratic his behavior before or after the marriage contract.

Divorce

As attitudes toward marriage and the family have changed over the past fifty years, the legal aspects of divorce have been made less difficult. Where one of the partners to a marriage is incurably insane, it is cruel to bind the normal partner to a union that offers no satisfaction for years to come. Prohibitions against divorce could increase the possibility of financial or mental breakdown of the normal spouse, with society having to support both partners. Their children could not only become state wards, but suffer serious psychological damage as well, which, in turn, could perpetuate itself in mental illness.

In the United States, laws providing for divorce of a mentally ill spouse are left up to each state. In some states, the law allows divorce on the grounds of mental illness if the individual has spent three to five years in a mental institution, and if the superintendent of that institution certifies that the individual is insane. A few states require that the mentally ill spouse have spent only two years in a mental hospital in order for a divorce to be granted. No mention of hospital care is made by statute in some jurisdictions; instead, the law provides for anywhere from two to five years of insanity as grounds for divorce. Proof of insanity is determined by two to three physicians in some states, or by a five-man commission in others. Approximately one-half of the states provide for divorce on the grounds of mental illness. At the present time, twenty-one states do not allow mental illness to be used specifically as grounds for divorce but allow other reasons such as cruel and inhuman treatment, which may result from the mental incapacity of one of the marriage partners.

Adoption

Relinquishing of parental rights, followed by adoption of the child or children, is sometimes necessary when all other methods of providing care for the children of a mentally ill person have been attempted. If the father is incapacitated, the mother is usually able to raise her children with assistance of relatives and/or state and county welfare agencies. On the other hand, if the mother has been committed to a state hospital or is unable to function adequately at home, adoption may be in the best interest of the children. In some cases, the father may be retarded, physically handicapped, or emotionally unstable, so that he cannot raise the children by himself. Or there may be no father in the household as a result of divorce, separation, or illegitimacy.

Adoption of such children is arranged by a professional staff in a state, county, or private welfare agency after a thorough investigation. These children may be difficult to place for adoption due to their background. Foster home placement is often necessary until adoption proceedings are completed.

Thirty-eight states do not require the consent of the mentally disabled parent or parents in order for their children to be adopted. Some states provide that the guardian of the parents may give consent for adoption; in others, if the parents are incompetent or insane for one year, no consent is necessary. There are various reasons given for this. One is that the mentally ill person is too sick to understand the nature of the proceeding. Or he may refuse to relinquish parental rights even though the children are being physically or emotionally neglected. However, care must be taken to protect the rights of the mentally ill in such cases, since the nature and extent of the illness varies with each person.

Incompetency

When a person is no longer able to manage his affairs due to physical or mental disability, he may be declared incompetent in a court of law and a guardian appointed over his person and estate. If the individual is spending his savings recklessly but is able to take care of his personal needs, the guardianship may be designated only to supervise his finances and property. Each year, the guardian in such cases must submit to the court an account of how the incompetent's money was spent.

Mental incapacity is one of the reasons for declaring a person incompetent. This proceeding is separate in some states from the judicial commitment to a state mental hospital as mentally ill. In other states, the declaration of incompetency and commitment as mentally ill are combined in one court hearing. Commitment as mentally ill, however, does not automatically render a person incompetent—he retains his civil rights, some of his legal rights, and the right to make decisions regarding his personal life. The laws vary by jurisdiction.

In order to declare a person incompetent, the family usually discusses the problem first with an attorney. Many states have recently provided legal aid services for those citizens who cannot afford to pay a lawyer's fee. The attorney counsels the family, schedules the case in court, and represents their interests in court. This same attorney may represent the alleged incompetent, or the alleged incompetent may engage his own attorney. A petition must be filed by a relative, friend, or interested person, depending on the requirements of the state. After the petition for incompetency is filed, the alleged incompetent is served with a notice required by law in most jurisdictions. Some states provide for notice to the subject, other states provide for notice to subject and relatives, and still other states provide for notice to the subject and relatives at the court's discretion. In a few states the subject is not given any notice.

The proceedings for incompetency are usually heard in probate court, superior court, county court or district court, depending on the state. In West Virginia, the Mental Health Commission makes the decision in these cases. In most states no jury trial is required. Presence of the subject, if he is able, at the court hearing is required in some states; other jurisdictions require his presence unless harmful; many states make no provision in the statutes. The alleged incompetent may have a guardian ad litem to represent him in some states; a few states allow him to bring witnesses to testify on his behalf. In some states previous hospitalization for a mental illness is sufficient evidence to declare him incompetent.

Contracts

"In terms of law, a contract is a mutual obligation between two people with a mutual right by either to demand its performance. The breach of this right, the failure to perform that promise, creates in the other person the right to relief and redress in a court of law." [34]

A person so devoid of mental capacity that he does not

understand the meaning of his actions does not have the ability to make a legal contract. If an individual makes a contract after he has been declared mentally ill at a court hearing, that contract is considered invalid and cannot be enforced. The following case serves as an example:

> Jane Brown was committed to the state mental hospital when she became extremely withdrawn, refused to leave her house, and suffered from delusions. After a course of treatment lasting about five months, she was provisionally discharged. Shortly after returning to the community she purchased a set of encyclopedias from a salesman who came to her home. When she failed to pay the $175.00 after receiving the books, the company threatened to take her to court. But when the company learned of her commitment on the grounds of mental illness, the contract was deemed to be void. Jane returned the books to the company and the court charges were dropped.

If an individual is suffering from a mild form of mental illness, but still understands the terms of the agreement, he is not necessarily considered incapable of making a contract. The extent and nature of illness must be considered.

In the United States, laws have been enacted which prevent the mentally ill from making contracts in twenty-one states. This is for the protection of both parties to the agreement. It prevents the mentally ill person from entering into agreements he does not comprehend and from exploitation; it protects the second party from unnecessary hardship when the terms of the contract are not satisfied. In some states, a mentally ill person cannot make a contract if guardianship proceedings have been started or if a guardian has been appointed. Other states specify that the mentally ill person cannot sign a contract if he is incompetent or of unsound mind. In a number of states, the mentally ill person is allowed to make a contract if his guardian is held responsible for carrying out the agreement. If the court decides it is in the best interest of the mentally ill person, some states specify that the contract can be made. One or both parties to the agreement can declare it void in some states.

Wills

The best reason for making a will is quite simple: it provides a way for the person making the will to dispose of his property after his death *as he wants it done*. If he doesn't make a will, his property may be disposed of in a way that he would not approve. For, if he dies without a will, his property is distributed according to the laws of the state in which he lived. And this may not be according to his wishes. So, the will gives him the privilege of deciding how his property is to be distributed among his heirs.[35]

In order to make a will, the individual must possess sufficient understanding about his personal possessions and property and have the ability to make his own decision regarding its disposition. If the individual is mentally ill or senile, he is allowed to make a will as long as he understands the nature of his actions. If his mental disability is chronic and severe but the will is made during a lucid interval, that will is held to be valid.

In most states a person has the right to make a will if he is "of sound mind." Even if he is declared incompetent or insane the laws in some states allow him to make a will. A few states prevent a person from making a will if he has been declared insane at a judicial hearing, but after his sanity is restored he may then make a will without being subjected to another hearing. Even in those cases where a legal guardian has been appointed to supervise the individual's person and finances, that individual has the privilege of making a will.

There are instances where the relatives will question the will in a court of law, alleging that the deceased was of unsound mind when he made the will. Such cases are difficult to prove, inasmuch as the testator is not available for questioning or examination by a psychiatrist.

Voting

The right to vote is granted to every American citizen over the age of eighteen, but each state sets its own requirements for voting. In regard to the mentally ill the laws vary in each state.

In Minnesota, under the Hospitalization and Commitment

Act effective January 1, 1968, the committed mentally ill patient retains his right to vote unless he is declared incompetent in a separate judicial hearing. Prior to January 1, 1968, a patient who was committed as mentally ill was denied the voting privilege in Minnesota; his commitment was reported to his registration board, at which time his registration card was removed from the files. In order to be eligible to vote a patient must have the capacity to understand the nature of the current election and differences between candidates, cannot be under guardianship or be declared incompetent, and cannot be diagnosed as psychopathic.

Through its local chapters, the League of Women Voters has been assisting patients in some of the Minnesota state mental hospitals with voting procedure and registration. They hold discussion groups on politics as well as on state and national election issues. This group as well as other volunteers arrange for transportation for local residents so that they may vote; they help other patients vote by absentee ballot. If the mentally ill patient expresses a desire to vote and meets the eligibility requirements, his participation in this civic activity can help bridge the gap between the hospital and community.

The majority of the states are more restrictive. Approximately forty states in the United States do not allow the mentally ill to vote. Some states specify that the mentally ill person may not vote if he has been declared of unsound mind in a court hearing. Other states do not allow a person to vote if he is under guardianship or insane. A few states use the term idiot. There are no restrictions to voting in a number of states. In Illinois, the mentally ill person has the privilege of voting even if he is a patient in a mental institution. New York has a few restrictions but grants the privilege of voting to the mentally ill.

Driver's License

In most instances, when a person becomes mentally ill his driver's license is revoked. This has created such a hardship for the patient as well as his family that the laws are gradually changing in this respect.

Under the State of Minnesota's Hospitalization and Commitment Act, persons committed as mentally ill in a judicial proceeding are allowed to retain their driver's licenses unless, in addition, they are declared legally incompetent in a separate court hearing.

In Minnesota, prior to this legislation, after judicial commitment as mentally ill a person's driver's license was revoked. This often made it difficult for the patient to get his license reinstated. A doctor's letter stating that the mentally ill person was capable of driving a car and a new driving test were often required. While on home visits, the patient was unable to drive. After release from the hospital, he had no way of resuming employment immediately, especially if his work consisted of driving a truck or salesmanship on an out-of-town or door-to-door basis. If his wife was unable to drive, the family had to rely on inconvenient public transportation. Anxious family members sought the reinstatement of his license from local government agencies. None of this contributed to the patient's recovery.

Holding Public Office

Holding public office carries with it great responsibilities. A public official represents the citizens in his community, and his decisions affect all their lives. Therefore, it was in the best interest of the office holder as well as his constituents that laws were enacted to prevent those of unsound mind from holding public office.

Approximately 50 percent of the states do not allow the mentally ill to hold public office. The laws vary in each jurisdiction. A number of states specify that persons holding office must be qualified electors. In other states, the law bars the insane or those under guardianship from holding public office. A few states prevent a person who has been declared incompetent from becoming a public official. In New Hampshire the public official who proves later to be mentally incapable of assuming the responsibilities of his role can be removed from office. In twenty-eight states there are no statutory provisions regarding the right of a mentally ill individual to hold public office.

NOTES

1. In these and later examples, significant details have been altered in a manner to make the persons described unrecognizable.

2. Brian Inglis, *A History of Medicine* (Cleveland: World Publishing Co., 1965), pp. 91–92.

3. John Biggs, Jr., *The Guilty Mind, Psychiatry and the Law of Homicide,* pp. 30–31.

4. Albert Deutsch, *The Mentally Ill in America,* p. 232.

5. *Congress and the Nation 1945–1964, A Review of Government and Politics in the Postwar Years* (Washington, D.C.: Congressional Quarterly Services, 1965), p. 1130.

6. Mike Gorman, Jane McDonough, Mrs. Albert Lasker, Florence Mahoney and Alice Fordyce, National Committee Against Mental Illness, Inc., pp. 37–38.

7. *Congress and the Nation,* p. 1136.

8. Ibid., p. 1144.

9. Ibid., p. 1147.

10. Mike Gorman, Jane McDonough, Mrs. Albert Lasker, Mrs. Florence Mahoney and Alice Fordyce, National Committee Against Mental Illness, Inc., p. 6.

11. Ibid., p. 7

12. Biggs, *The Guilty Mind,* p. 39.

13. George B. Vold, *Theoretical Criminology* (New York: Oxford University Press, 1958), p. 111.

14. Henrici de Bracton, *De Legibus et Consuetudinibus Angliae,* T. Twiss, ed. (London: Longman & Co., 1879), p. 153.

15. Daniel M'Naghten's Case, 10 C. & F. 200, 210 211, 8 Eng. Rep. 718, 722–723 (1843). Quoted by Sheldon Glueck, *Law and Psychiatry; Cold War or Entente Cordiale?* p. 20.

16. State v. Jones, 50 N.H. 369, 398–399 (1871). Quoted by Glueck, *Law and Psychiatry,* pp. 81–82.

17. Ibid., p. 81.

18. Durham v. United States, 214 F. 2nd 862 (1954).

19. See Durham v. United States, 237 F.2d 760 (D.C. Cir. 1956).

20. Blocker v. United States, 288 F.2d 853, 857–872 (D.C. Cir. 1961).

21. Commonwealth v. Chester, 337 Mass. 702, 713, 150 N.E. 2nd 914, 920 (1958).

22. Longoria v. State, 168 A.2d 695, 701 (Del. 1961).

23. State v. Andrews, 187 Kan. 458, 357 P.2d 739 (1960).

24. Gregory Zilboorg, *Mind, Medicine and Man,* p. 273.

25. Barbara Wootton, *Social Science and Social Pathology* (New York: Macmillan, 1957), chapter 7.

26. State v. Lucas, 30 N.J. 37, 82, 152 A.2d 50, 74 (1959). Justice Weintraub's notions were fully elaborated in his remarks before the Annual Judicial Conference of the Second Federal Circuit, 37 F.R.D. 365, 369 (1964).

27. Seymour Halleck, *Psychiatry and the Dilemmas of Crime* (New York: Harper & Row, 1967).

28. Thomas S. Szasz, *Law, Liberty, and Psychiatry* (New York: Macmillan, 1963).

29. Norval Morris, "Psychiatry and the Dangerous Criminal," 518–519.

30. Ibid., pp. 541–542.

31. The American Law Institute, *Model Penal Code* § 4.01.

32. Robert A. Farmer, *Crime, The Law and You,* pp. 90–91.

33. Glueck, *Law and Psychiatry.*

34. Martin J. Ross, *Handbook of Everyday Law,* p. 21.

35. Arthur Crabtree, *You and the Law,* pp. 125–126.

3

THE TRAUMA OF COMMITMENT TO THE PRIMARY GROUP

The wide variety of public agencies and officials who deal with the mentally ill are concerned, and quite legitimately so, only with the mentally ill individual per se, with his welfare, protection, and rights. But these professionals are often painfully conscious of the fact that most mentally ill persons come out of a context of immediate associations (family, friendship groups, and so on) that are affected by his condition. His mental illness, if necessitating commitment, involves considerable trauma to this social context. The trauma of commitment to the family and other primary groups is worthy of special review.

As general orientation to the effect of commitment on the primary group, it is helpful to explain the significant points of the Federal Draft Act and the Minnesota Hospitalization and Commitment Act. These will serve as an example of the application of federal statutes at the state level.

FEDERAL AND MINNESOTA LEGISLATION

The primary reference point for legislation by the separate states on commitment of the mentally disabled for treatment at various medical facilities is the Federal Draft Act.[1] The Draft Act defines the mentally ill individual as "having a psychiatric or other disease which substantially impairs his mental health." [2] In accordance with the Draft Act, involuntary hospitalization may be imposed upon an individual at a judicial hearing if

> the court finds that the proposed patient (1) is mentally ill, and (2) because of his illness is likely to injure himself or others if allowed to remain at liberty, or (3) is in need of custody, care, or treatment in a mental hospital and, because of his illness, lacks sufficient insight or capacity to make responsible decisions with respect to his hospitalization.[3]

The Draft Act outlines the various procedures covering the voluntary and involuntary hospitalization of mentally ill individuals and spells out in detail various postadmission proceedings.

The Draft Act was premised on the assumption that every mentally ill individual is entitled to humane care and treatment in accordance with the highest standards of acceptable practice and to the extent that facilities, equipment and personnel are available.[4] Strictures are imposed against the arbitrary imposition of mechanical restraints on a mentally ill patient, or interference with his rights to communicate, to receive visits, or exercise his civil rights. Any restriction of the individual's rights deemed necessary to his health by a responsible medical authority was to become part of the individual's clinical record. A detained individual was entitled to a writ of habeas corpus upon proper petition by himself or a friend to any empowered court in the county in which the individual was detained. The individual was to be safeguarded against disclosure of information to unauthorized persons and granted redress in the case of unwarranted hospitalization or denial of his rights.

While the Draft Act set up guidelines for the various forms of state legislation, it contained latitude for many variations. The Minnesota Act may serve as an illustration of the manner in which the federal statute is followed at the state level.

A detailed examination of all of the differences in the commitment act in all of the fifty states would be unnecessarily tedious. Hence, although some references will be made to variations, a single state commitment act may serve as a model.

In 1967 the Minnesota Legislature adopted a new Hospitalization and Commitment Act, effective January 1, 1968. This marked the first time in twenty years that the state's policies regarding commitment of mentally ill and inebriate individuals had been revised. For over three years the Forensics Committee of the Minnesota Mental Health Planning Council had worked on this legislation. Participating on this committee were representatives of the medical and legal professions, police and corrections divisions, county welfare boards, hospitals, and other public agencies.

In order to revise the procedures regarding commitment to the benefit of both the patient and society, the Forensics Committee reviewed the Federal Draft Act as well as a study prepared by an American Bar Foundation Committee. Recent legislation on mental health in a number of the states was also reviewed as well as legislation by some foreign countries, particularly England and the Scandinavian nations.

There are four ways a person can be hospitalized for treatment and care as set up by law in the Minnesota Hospitalization and Commitment Act.

1. Informal hospitalization by consent. In Minnesota any person over eighteen can enter the hospital as an *informal* patient, at his own choice, without written application, and with consent by head of the hospital. If the person is under eighteen, his parent, guardian, or custodian must give consent. Following admission to the hospital, the person is free to leave within twelve hours of his request, unless other legal steps are taken to keep him there—such as a court "hold" order under emergency hospitalization or a petition for court commitment.

Families usually prefer the informal method of hospitalization because it is less traumatic to the patient, as well as the primary group members. No stigma is attached and there is no court record on file. The patient does not have to undergo a court hearing. If the patient has enough insight into his own condition to consent to informal hospitalization, he has a better chance of recovering in a shorter period of time.

2. Voluntary hospitalization for inebriate persons. The Minnesota Act specified that an inebriate person eighteen years of age or over may be admitted as a *voluntary* patient to a public hospital for care and treatment upon his written application. A person under age eighteen must receive the consent of his parent, guardian, or custodian prior to admission. If the patient desires to leave the hospital a written request is addressed to the head of the hospital, after which the person may be detained for not more than three days exclusive of Sundays and legal holidays. The head of the hospital may petition for commitment of the person if he believes it in the best interest of the person, his family, or the community.

Voluntary admission for the inebriate person is a desirable method of hospitalization. Since the person is voluntarily asking for help with his drinking problem, he usually intends to cooperate in the treatment program. As a rule, the period of treatment is from thirty to sixty days.

When the patient is both mentally ill and inebriate, family members may look upon the alcoholism as the major problem and encourage the sick member to admit himself voluntarily to the state hospital for treatment. Once the patient is able to maintain a period of sobriety, his mental problems can be more easily dealt with by a private psychiatrist or the staff at the community mental health center.

3. Emergency hospitalization of mentally ill persons. A patient may be held at the hospital for *emergency* care and treatment upon the written statement of a licensed physician noting that after examination he has found the person to be mentally ill or inebriate and in imminent danger of causing injury to himself or others, and that an order of the court cannot be obtained in time to prevent such anticipated injury. The patient must be discharged in seventy-two hours after admission excluding Saturdays, Sundays, and legal holidays, unless a petition for commitment is filed in probate court. If discharge of the person is not in his best interest or that of his family or the community, the head of the hospital can file a petition for his commitment (prior to the expiration of the seventy-two hours). The court then can issue a hold order until the hearing. On written request and with consent of the medical director the patient can be transferred to informal status.

To the primary group members, emergency hospitalization of a mentally ill person is of much help in a crisis. When a person poses a danger to himself or others and must be removed from the home, the family can take him to the hospital for admission, treatment, and evaluation. After the patient is admitted by written statement of a licensed physician, he can be held for seventy-two hours. This allows the family a period of three days to decide what is best for the patient and themselves before they have to sign a petition for commitment in probate court. At such times a family council is often held, out-of-town members of the primary group are contacted by phone or telegram, the family doctor and lawyer may be consulted, and the minister and personal friends may be notified.

After admission, if the patient's condition improves and he is willing to remain in the hospital for evaluation and treatment, he can be transferred to informal status on written request and with the medical director's approval. This takes a heavy burden off the primary group members because they do not have to resort to legal procedures in probate court, with all the accompanying feelings of guilt, shame, betrayal and ambivalence.

4. Commitment. Hospitalization of a person for care and treatment by a petition for commitment in probate court is discussed in detail below.

The laws relating to hospitalization and commitment of the

mentally ill vary from state to state.⁵ In Minnesota, involuntary hospitalization consists of filing a petition, giving notice to the alleged mentally ill person and conducting a court hearing. In all states a petition has to be filed in court for involuntary commitment to be carried out. The petition can be filed in probate court, superior court, circuit court, or district court, depending on the statutes of the jurisdiction. Any person may file the petition in some states, while only a relative, friend, or interested party may file in other states. A number of states specify that family members, public officials, or family physicians may file petitions.

In approximately one-fourth of the states, no legal provision is made for notice of the hearing. Notice to subject and relatives is provided by law in one-half of the states; the guardian is notified in about one-third of the states; notice may be waived in one-fifth of the states, if it is likely to prove harmful to the mentally ill person. Presence of the mentally ill person at the court hearing is required by law in about one-fifth of the states; in about one-third of the states, the presiding official at the court hearing decides whether presence of the mentally ill person is in the best interest of the patient and his family. When presence of the patient is not required, it is sometimes easier for family members to file for commitment; facing the patient at a court hearing may be extremely traumatic for members of the primary group. On the other hand, the civil rights of the patient must be protected, and his presence in court may sometimes prevent their being brushed aside. In one-fourth of the states, the court may waive the presence of the mentally ill person if it is deemed harmful to him. In other states, the mentally ill person may demand to attend the court hearing.

A number of states require a trial by jury in order to hospitalize the mentally ill person involuntarily. Since this involves a public hearing, the family and patient are subjected to considerable publicity, making the entire proceeding more difficult to bear. In other states, the patient may request a trial by jury. Although this type of court hearing is seldom used, some states condone it despite its disruption of the privacy of the patient and members of his primary group. In approximately two-thirds of the states, the mentally ill person has the right to be represented by legal counsel. In the majority of these states an added stipulation provides for counsel appointed by the court if the person does not have his own. There is no provision for legal counsel in about one-third of the states, but the person in these states may still have the right to be represented in accordance with the United States Supreme Court's recent decisions.

Almost all of the states provide for and encourage voluntary hospitalization for treatment of mental illness. In the majority of the states, temporary and emergency commitment to the hospital is provided by statute. In one-third of the states, a board of doctors and attorneys may decide to admit a patient involuntarily. A medical certificate, usually signed by two doctors, serves as another method of involuntary hospitalization; one-third of the states have such provisions. Nonprotested admission is available in about one-fourth of the states. This procedure is used for those patients who, because of their mental condition, do not oppose the admission, yet will not go willingly for treatment.

THE ROLE OF THE PRIMARY GROUPS

Since our interest for the moment is centered on the problem of commitment for the family or other primary groups, it is useful to take as a reference point the statements of the typical commitment act.

The legislation on commitment of the mentally ill individual proposes to formulate the rights, responsibilities, and procedures of all parties involved: the patient, immediate family and friends, public officials, medical specialists, legal professionals, and hospital personnel.

When a family has to face commitment of a mentally ill member, it must radically reorient its social relations. A spouse formerly in a position of mutual exchange now has to take a different attitude. Children respectful of parents now have to "put them away." And although this is declining, commitment remains a stigma to the family. People may whisper about the family and the patient, and perhaps view them differently. After recovery, parents may refuse to forgive their children for committing them, or wives to forgive husbands. Their lives can never be the same.

The patient's mental illness affects the members of the primary group directly. Wives and husbands who share a mutual dependency and respect not infrequently look upon signing a petition for commitment as a betrayal of mutual trust. Their hesitation delays treatment and worsens the ill person's condition; delay in treatment is often accompanied by loss of job, withdrawal from reality, and a total disruption of family life. Inability of the healthy spouse to face up to the problem may lead to his or her own hospitalization.

A person may refuse to face up to his mental illness and represent it as marital conflict. To such a person, alcoholism seems the lesser of two evils. There are many sources of ambiguity. One of the big problems presented by mental illness from the beginning is that the persons immediately involved with the patient's commitment are not usually experts.

Filing of a petition for commitment of a mentally ill member has, at least in the past, usually been viewed by the family as a last resort. Typically, all previous attempts to provide treatment on a voluntary basis have failed. The sick member has consistently refused to consult his doctor, rejects his medication, will not attend the local community mental health center (if one exists within a reasonable distance), refuses to talk to his minister when the latter comes to the home at the frantic family's request, and so on. This state of affairs sometimes goes on for weeks or months until a crisis arises.

Such a crisis may take many forms. The sick member may attempt or threaten suicide or murder, may refuse to eat for days on end because he imagines the food is poisoned, or manifest other irrational behavior. The following case illustrates such a problem:

> Miss Fairfield, a single lady, age fifty-seven, had kept house for her parents on the family farm. After their death, she sold the

farm and moved to town to live with her niece. As a child, Miss Fairfield was afflicted with poliomyelitis; this had left her with one leg shorter than the other and she walked with a limp. The niece had no children and enjoyed her aunt's company. After Miss Fairfield's savings were depleted, the niece continued to support her. An attempt had been made through the local division of vocational rehabilitation to train Miss Fairfield for some kind of employment. But she had been so dependent on her parents and then on her niece for such a long time that she was unable to function at a job in the community.

Eventually Miss Fairfield developed asthma and became very depressed and withdrawn. She refused to eat, lost considerable weight, and had to be hospitalized. In the hospital she was given intravenous feedings. When alone, Miss Fairfield pulled the needle and tube out of her arm and tried to choke herself with the tube. Fortunately this was discovered in time. At this point, she was transferred to the psychiatric unit of the hospital, where she became confused and violent. She refused all medication, saying that God told her she did not have to take it.

Further treatment was recommended by the staff psychiatrist. Her niece was too overcome to sign a petition for commitment. Miss Fairfield's two brothers who lived out of town were notified; they immediately came to town to sign for commitment. At the probate court hearing, the court recommended that further treatment was necessary. Miss Fairfield was committed as mentally ill to the state hospital where she soon was making good progress.[6]

Many persons may undertake the responsibility for signing a petition for commitment: spouse, children over twenty-one, relatives, friends, neighbors, attorneys, clergymen, or institutional authorities. Often, everyone concerned recognizes the need for treatment, but no one wishes to sign the petition. As long as members of the immediate family are available, an institutional authority (such as the head of the local welfare board) may be reluctant to sign, lest the family or patient bring suit later. Sometimes the members of the immediate family are in agreement regarding the need for commitment but a friend or relative objects. All this is hard not only on the patient but on everyone else as well. Joint responsibility for signing a petition for commitment is sometimes taken when family members wish to support one another in the commitment proceedings. This precludes their being turned against one another later.

In a number of counties in Minnesota, the petition for commitment is drawn up at the county welfare department, then signed by the petitioner, notarized, and sent to probate court for processing. An interview with the petitioner is usually conducted by a social worker; if the petitioner is physically incapacitated, this may take place in the home. Before the petition for commitment is drawn up the social worker explains the implications of a commitment proceeding to the petitioner. Among other things, the petitioner is told that his presence is required at the probate court hearing and that his petition must be based on sincerity of purpose and freedom from malice. If the petitioner wishes to have the allegedly mentally ill person admitted to a private hospital, he must engage the services of a private psychiatrist to make the necessary arrangements. The petitioner is asked to cooperate with the psychiatric staff and superintendent of the holding hospital. Procedure regarding the apprehension and probate court hearing are also discussed. Frequently the implications of such legal procedure proves to be overwhelming for the primary group member; he may delay filing the petition for one or two weeks to think it over or seek out other members of the family for advice and moral support.

During the interview at the county welfare department, a detailed social history of the allegedly mentally ill person is obtained from the petitioner and any other members of the primary group present.

> The probate court shall direct the county welfare department to make an investigation into the financial circumstances, family relationships, residence, social history, and background of such patient and make a report thereof in writing to be filed with the court for the use and guidance of the head of the hospital to which such person may be committed. The court may require that such report be filed prior to the commitment hearing.[7]

This first step is an emotional one for the primary group member. His phone call or physical presence at the agency is typically precipitated by some crisis at home: a physical attack, a suicide attempt, an episode of hallucination. A careful screening is conducted to determine whether a petition is in order, or if other problems are the cause of the current crisis. Alternatives to petition for commitment and hospitalization are considered, taking into account the gravity of the present crisis and its best solution.

The potential petitioner sometimes stops with this first contact with the authorities. He may set up but never meet his appointment. The office interview with a professional person, moreover, often has a therapeutic effect on the petitioner; after he "gets it off his chest," he feels so good that he declines to complete the petition. Sometimes petitioners come in for several interviews, but cannot face up to the prospect of signing a petition for commitment. Delays as long as several months between the first contact with the welfare department and the actual petition are common; but if the sick member becomes worse, as is usually the case, there is no alternative. By this time the petitioner has discussed the problems with a variety of professional people in the community, understands himself and his problem better, and is able at least to assume the burden of signing a petition for commitment. Such prolonged periods of ambivalence testify to the complications that the mental illness of one individual causes to others.

Every available community resource is often explored as an alternative to commitment. But when all efforts fail and the mentally ill person continues to present a danger to himself and others, a petition for commitment is signed.

After the petition for commitment of an allegedly mentally ill person is completed at the county welfare department, it is taken to the probate court office to be filed and processed. At this time notice of the filing of the petition as well as order for examination is given to the patient and other interested parties. If notice of the petition might be injurious to the patient, and if a guardian *ad litem* has been appointed, it may be read or given to the guardian who represents the patient throughout the action.[8]

If the patient is already in the hospital at the time a petition for commitment is filed, it is unnecessary for the sheriff to pick him up. If, however, the patient is at large in the community, the court issues an apprehension order authorizing his removal to a hospital for evaluation and treatment. The sheriff's deputy or other peace officer executing the apprehension order must avoid all unnecessary force or restraint as well as visible symbols of authority such as uniforms and marked police vehicles.[9]

To members of the primary group, the apprehension of the mentally ill person is an additional source of extreme anxiety. Children at home may have to be taken to a neighbor or relative, for the witnessing of an encounter between a sick parent and the deputy sheriff or other public official would be traumatic. Although the family members have been told that in Minnesota the deputy sheriff is not in uniform and the automobile he drives is unmarked, the whole affair is still upsetting.

If the mentally ill individual is a woman, the apprehension is often done by a female deputy, usually accompanied by a male deputy in case the ill person becomes violent. If the allegedly mentally ill person is carrying a gun or other weapon, it may be necessary to enlist the aid of the local police to assist in apprehension. On some occasions members of the immediate family participate in the apprehension, if they so desire and if the situation permits it. It is preferable for a brother, child, spouse, or friend to be present when the sick person is removed from the home in order for reassurance. But at times the petitioner may prefer to wait nearby, rather than have the sick person hold him personally responsible for the incarceration.

A surprising number of employers who recognize that an employee is mentally ill continue for a time to allow him to work, even though he is functioning below capacity. If a mentally ill person has left home, refuses to divulge his current address, but does manage to show up on his job, he may have to be apprehended at his place of employment. The employer may be torn between his humanitarianism and the welfare of his business. Apprehension of a sick person at his place of employment may be embarrassing for the employer as well as for the family and the patient. Sometimes, however, it is unavoidable.

After a mentally ill person is taken to the hospital, a relative or friend can arrange for care of the children, if any, and for the disposition and protection of the mentally ill individual's personal possessions. Arrangements concerning rental payments or moving out may be made with the landlord. Newspaper and milk deliveries must be temporarily cancelled. A pet dog may be taken to the home of a friend or boarded at the kennel; a parakeet may be cared for by a neighbor. It is usually some member of the primary group who has to take the responsibility for taking care of the day-to-day affairs of the mentally ill individual. All the routine things associated with the mentally ill person's daily living are highly important to his sense of security, and the knowledge that someone is protecting his personal possessions and property helps to retain his ties with the community and thus hasten his recovery.

Once the mentally ill person is taken out of the home, the members of the primary group typically experience a new set of emotions varying from despair, guilt, and remorse to resignation, relief, and hope. When guilt and remorse are strong, the primary group members may withdraw the petition. On the other hand, for the first time in perhaps months or even years, their lives may assume an aspect of normality, accompanied by the prospect that the sick person, with treatment, may be cured of his mental disability.

The patient's resentment against the primary group members is often so intense, at this point in the proceedings, that he refuses to see the family when they come to the community hospital to visit him prior to the hearing. The patient may feel abandoned, incarcerated against his will; he may insist that everyone else is sick, but he is well. He may harass his spouse by phone. He may refuse to take his prescribed medication, refuse a physical examination, or refuse to submit to psychological tests. All his hatred is directed against the primary group members and the petitioner must bear the brunt of his accusations.

To further complicate matters, other family members may claim the petition for commitment was unwarranted and turn against the petitioner. The following illustrates such a situation:

Mrs. Lane, a schoolteacher of thirty-two, filed a petition for commitment of her husband, age thirty-eight, who had been recently admitted to the psychiatric ward of the community hospital. The couple had no children. Mr. Lane, a musician, had been suffering from a severe depression and paranoia. He imagined that cars followed him and thought the apartment was tapped. For the week previous to hospitalization, he had not eaten and had been unable to sleep. Commitment to the state hospital for treatment had been recommended by the staff psychiatrist of the city-county hospital. Insisting there was nothing wrong with him, Mr. Lane would not accept treatment on a voluntary basis. Reluctantly, Mrs. Lane filed a petition for commitment. A few days later, prior to the probate court hearing, Mr. Lane's father flew into town from Oregon and immediately went to the hospital to visit his son. The elder Mr. Lane was opposed to the petition, maintaining that all his son needed was a long vacation. At his request Mrs. Lane withdrew the petition and took her husband home from the hospital. That night, at 11:00 P.M., Mr. Lane suddenly became hysterical and irrational. He dashed about from one room to the other and pounded on the doors. It was necessary to readmit him to the hospital, and the following morning Mrs. Lane filed another petition for commitment. By this time the elder Mr. Lane realized the need for treatment, apologized to his daughter-in-law, and at once returned to his home.

Family quarrels arise when some of the relatives are in favor of and others are against a petition for commitment. Siblings of the mentally ill person who visit the sick person's home only once or twice a year are often the first to protest. Sometimes their inattention to the ill person, and subsequent interference when real problems arise, is not due to callousness; they may have sensed the onset of mental illness and hence absented them-

selves to retain an image of happier days. Such nostalgic relatives may accuse a husband of trying to get rid of his wife, or
harass a parent, all in an attempt to keep the situation unchanged.

The patient himself may persuade his family to withdraw the
petition and take him back home. Once a wife, for example, is
left alone at home with the children after filing a petition, she
has many doubts. For now the other phase of her ambivalence
can manifest itself unhindered. Did she do the right thing by
filing a petition for judicial commitment? Is he really that sick?
Will she be able to manage alone? What if treatment impairs
him? When she visits her tranquilized and well-cared-for husband at the hospital, he may suddenly appear much improved.
The doctor may tell her that the patient might be able to function at home if he takes his medication faithfully. The wife then
withdraws the petition and takes her husband home. Two weeks
later, the husband takes an overdose of sleeping pills and is
returned to the hospital by the police. The petition procedure
must be undertaken once more.

After a petition for commitment based on mental illness has
been filed in the probate court office, a date and place for the
probate court hearing is scheduled. To prevent prolonged detention, date for a hearing on a petition must be set within 14
days of the filing of a petition, except when good cause for
delay has been shown whereupon the court may extend the time
of the hearing another thirty days. The proposed patient or head
of the hospital or other institution may demand in writing that
the hearing be held immediately; the patient is then discharged
automatically if it is not held within five days.[10]

If at the time the petition is filed the patient is already in
the hospital, he will not know of his change of status until he
is informed about it. To be sure if he is picked up by the
sheriff he is notified of the filing of a petition at the time of
apprehension. But in either case, whether he is already in the
hospital or is taken there on an apprehension order he must be
notified of the hearing.

In the past there was some tendency to avoid as long as

possible the notification of a mentally ill person. With today's increased emphasis on civil rights, notice of filing of the petition has become scrupulously observed. This has proved to be the source of great distress to members of the primary group. A husband filing a petition on his sick wife, for example, may be reluctant to inform her that he is taking legal measures in order to keep her in the hospital against her will. He may dread the explosions that this information may bring. Notice of hearing to the alleged patient increases her hostility toward her husband, who by now may have endured months of conflict, tension, and family disruption at home. An adult son who must sign a petition to protect an aged father suffering from senile psychosis may react badly when he learns during the screening interview that notice of hearing must be served on his sick father; in a moment of lucidity the old fellow may run away from home like a child. In the metropolitan centers the mentally ill patient is often in the hospital, where he can be closely observed, when he is notified of the petition for commitment, but in spite of this a depressed patient may, after receiving his notice, attempt suicide. An agitated patient occasionally strikes out at the nurses or orderlies. A paranoid daughter may phone her parents to tell them she never wants to see them again since they are "plotting" against her in "collaboration" with the doctor. In short, the notice of commitment adds one more burden to the parents or other affected members of the primary group, who by this time may be so emotionally involved they can barely function at home or on the job.

This procedure, of course, prevents an allegedly mentally ill person from being "railroaded" into a state mental institution. The civil rights of the allegedly mentally ill individual must be protected; being alerted of the forthcoming court action gives him time to obtain legal counsel if he so desires. As the Commitment Act states, however, if such notice is likely to have a harmful effect on the patient, a guardian *ad litum* may be appointed to receive this notice; this guardian is empowered to represent the patient up to and through the probate court hearing.

In Minnesota, fourteen days plus a possible additional thirty days (on approval of the court) are provided for observation, evaluation, diagnosis, treatment, and recommendation regarding further care of the patient before the probate court hearing. This is a crucial period for both patient and family. If the patient's condition improves and he agrees to accept outpatient psychiatric care or treatment in a private hospital, the petition may be withdrawn, sometimes to the relief, sometimes to the apprehension of the primary group members. For the patient in a private hospital psychiatric unit, treatment for an additional period may improve his condition to such extent that he can return home and resume his employment. At this point, again, the petition is withdrawn.

Sometimes the patient demands an immediate hearing and the evaluation period is shortened. This may be beneficial, for it brings the crisis to a rapid conclusion and eliminates the long, agonizing period of waiting that precedes the probate court hearing.

Notice of hearing protects the rights not only of the patient, but of the members of the primary group as well. The petitioner and other family members and friends are given at least five days notice that a probate court hearing is to be conducted.[11] Such notice is usually sent by mail, inasmuch as interested parties may live out of town. This gives them an opportunity to consult with one another, to take sides in some instances, to arrange for transportation if they reside out of town, and to engage the services of a private attorney to represent them at the hearing if they deem it necessary.

Notice of a probate court hearing may come as a shock to some relatives. As an example:

An adult son, married and living thousands of miles away, suddenly learned that his sister had filed a petition alleging mental illness of their old father. Although the son had not seen his father in years, he was horrified. Among the questions he raised were: Why was his sister trying to put their father away? Did she have designs on the old man's savings or property? The son rushed to town in protest and berated his distraught sister for her actions. But when he visited his father at the community hospital he found the old man agitated, completely confused, and unable to recognize him. The doctor explained that state hospital care was recommended until the father improved sufficiently to be transferred to a nursing home.

At this point the son confessed to guilt feelings about his father. He was ashamed of not having visited more often while his father was alert and in better health. Although he rationalized that he would have done so if his wife had not objected and his job had not required that he reside at his present location, his feelings of guilt persisted.

This typifies the ambivalent complex of emotions that may plague a primary group member long after mental illness strikes a member of his family.

A variety of interested people may attend the probate court hearing, including friends, relatives, neighbors, employers, co-workers, the family clergyman, other physicians or psychiatrists, psychologists, social workers, and other public officials.[12]

In Minnesota the probate court hearing is usually conducted at the public or private hospital where the patient is being held for evaluation, diagnosis, and treatment. (If the patient is too sick to be moved, he may be examined by members of the court panel in his own home or a nursing home.) The hearing is conducted in a room set aside for this purpose in the hospital. Time is usually set for 9:00 A.M. Hearings last until the court calendar is covered, except in rare cases where lengthy proceedings drag the hearings out long after the noon hour or force adjournment for an additional session on the following day. Patients are brought to the hearing by the orderly, nurse's aid, or nurse. If the patient is too agitated to appear the members of the court panel examine the patient in his room and then conduct the hearing with the petitioner and family. The petitioner and other members of the primary group may have to wait several hours before their turn comes to appear in the court room. This is a tense period, filled with doubts and anxiety. There are times when the petitioner fails to appear because he is too overcome with emotion or fear of facing the patient.

The hearing shall be conducted in as informal a manner as may be consistent with orderly procedure and in a physical setting not likely to have a harmful effect on the mental health of the proposed patient. If the proposed patient is to be present, the hearing may be held at a hospital, a public health facility, the proposed patient's residence, or such other suitable and appropriate place as the court may determine. In all such proceedings the court shall keep accurate minutes containing, among other appropriate materials, notations of appearances at the hearing, including witnesses, of motions made and the disposition thereof, and of all waivers of rights made by the parties. In lieu of said minutes, the court may have taken and preserved an accurate stenographic record or tape recording of the proceedings. The court shall not be bound by the evidence presented by the examiners but shall make its determination upon the entire record. In all cases the court shall find the facts specifically, state separately its conclusions of law thereon, and direct the entry of an appropriate judgment.[13]

A typical court panel consists of two physicians, one a general practitioner, the other a psychiatrist, and two lawyers, one representing the patient, the other representing the petitioner. Presiding over the court panel is a probate judge, or a county commissioner acting on his behalf.

Members of the primary group who attend the probate court hearing with the petitioner experience this phase of the commitment proceeding as a highly emotional one. Now they are confronted not only with the patient, but also with his attorney, friends, and relatives who may protest the commitment. The petitioner is apprehensive about giving testimony when the patient sits next to him at the hearing. But it is important that the patient be present, not only to protect his civil rights, but to hear what the members of the primary group have to say about his behavior and their reasons for filing the petition for judicial commitment.

Marital conflict between a mentally ill individual and his or her spouse adds another dimension to the proceedings. In fact, the court may have to decide whether the basic problem is mental illness or marital conflict. For example:

> A wife, who had been separated from her husband for a year, filed a petition alleging her husband mentally ill on the grounds that he was harassing her and their children and threatening bodily harm. She was, however, understandably reluctant to confront her husband at a probate court hearing. The man's legal counsel cited the patient's excellent employment record, and the patient himself protested that his wife vindictively and unjustly wished to put him away. Although the husband was diagnosed as paranoid, he conducted himself so well in the probate court session that the petition itself was questioned. Shortly after the case was dismissed, the wife reported greater harassment than ever, now accentuated by the man's resentment of the commitment attempt.

All interested parties present at the probate court hearing are given the opportunity to testify. If the commitment is opposed by the patient and some of his relatives or friends, the court hearing may turn into a long heated debate. Such a debate may prove cathartic for the primary group members and even the patient. Marital conflict, family quarrels, hostile dependency, alcoholism, infidelity, drug addiction, or child neglect may be revealed for the first time. Things long unsaid are finally brought into the open. In this manner, the court panel sometimes functions as an impartial therapist.

> The court shall hear any relevant testimony and shall receive all relevant evidence which may be offered at the hearing.
>
> In all such proceedings the county attorney shall appear and represent the petitioner. The proposed patient shall be afforded an opportunity to be represented by counsel, and if neither the proposed patient nor others provide counsel, the court at the time the examiners or licensed physicians are appointed shall appoint counsel to represent the proposed patient. Counsel shall consult with the proposed patient prior to the hearing and shall be given adequate time to prepare therefor. Counsel shall have the full right of subpoena.[14]

If the patient's attorney requires additional time to prepare his defense, the probate court hearing may be continued for another week. During this time the patient may remain in the hospital for further evaluation and treatment, or he may be released until the hearing. This delay subjects the petitioner and other primary group members to still more tension.

At the hearing, the testimony of witnesses is augmented by other pertinent evidence regarding the patient's mental state. Placed in evidence are such materials as: the hospital record; a psychiatric summary and recommendation by the hospital staff; nurses' notes concerning the patient's behavior; a social summary covering the patient's background, work record, family relationships, and financial situation; and the findings of psychological tests.

As the testimony is heard, the patient may respond with resignation or anger. Bitter accusations may fill the courtroom. On rare occasions, the allegedly mentally ill person may turn on the panel.

> One such individual had long harassed his former family and had long refused to cooperate with welfare authorities of all types. He eventually faced court proceedings because of increased harassment of his ex-wife and children.
>
> During the court proceedings, he suddenly became icily calm. Taking a notebook and pencil out of his pocket, he proceeded to ask the name of each panel member and to carefully enter it into the notebook. He even demanded that each panel member spell out his name so that he could get it right.
>
> He was, of course, discharged.

A decision by the court to commit or discharge a patient is made after a careful review of all the facts, records, and testimony and with the welfare of the patient and the primary group members in mind. At all times, the civil rights of the patient and his family are protected.

Capable and conscientious public servants tend to be recruited for probate court service; less and less often does one hear of the abuse of mental illness proceedings. In general, the court prefers to err by failing to commit rather than by committing unjustifiably. If the court panel decides that the proposed patient is not mentally ill, the petition for commitment is denied and the patient is released from hospital custody.[15]

Discharge of the petition for commitment may be accompanied by a court recommendation that the patient seek some further psychiatric treatment.

Even if the patient is discharged, the probate court hearing is traumatic for the members of the primary group. A discharged wife may refuse to return home to live with her husband; a discharged husband may leave home or harass his family. Factions may develop within the family as a result of the commitment proceedings; family members may not speak with one another for long periods afterward.

When the court decides that a patient is in need of further treatment, he is committed to a state or private hospital.[16]

The patient is transported to the hospital under court order by a peace officer, a member of a county welfare department, or a member of a public health facility. The peace officer is not in uniform and drives an unmarked car. One or more interested persons may accompany the patient. The social service report, copy of the court order, and copy of the examiner's report accompany the patient; thus all pertinent information concerning his condition is available at admission. Hospital officials can then determine the degree to which the patient has to be watched, the sort of room to which he should be assigned, and the kind of medication and medical attention he needs.

Rights of the patient after commitment are set down by law and vary in each jurisdiction. More and more these rights are being liberalized in an attempt to keep intact the patient's contacts with his family and community and to treat him as an individual deserving of respect and dignity.

In Minnesota, the 1968 Hospitalization and Commitment Act formulated the rules for patient's rights during hospitalization. In general, they stipulate the following.

A patient committed by a court as mentally ill, inebriate, or dangerous to the public is committed for a sixty-day period to a hospital. After admission the patient must be examined by a doctor as soon as possible. Before the sixty-day period has ended the hospital is required to send a formal notice to the court, with a copy to the patient's attorney, stating the patient's diagnosis, his condition, his potential harmfulness, and whether further treatment and commitment are required, and if so, what facility is recommended. If the patient does not require further hospital care according to this report, the court proceedings are terminated and the patient is released from the hospital. But if he does require further treatment, hospitalization for an indefinite period may be ordered by the court.

Upon written application and approval by the medical director, within the sixty-day period, a patient committed as mentally ill or inebriate can be transferred to informal status. Every six months a review board comes to the hospital to reevaluate the patient's need for treatment and hospitalization. Any patient may request a hearing, which consists of an interview with the patient as well as a perusal of the medical records.

Although there has been increasing improvement in the lot of the patient after hospitalization, the ordeal of the family is not over. The attitude of society toward mental illness has changed for the better in recent years, but it is still not accepted. The social stigma remains strong. The family is afflicted with doubts. What will neighbors and friends think? Does mental illness have a physical base, and if so, will the children inherit it? Will commitment hurt the children's chances of marrying well? And so on. A multitude of problems remains for members of the primary group.

NOTES

1. Public Health Service, *A Draft Act Governing Hospitalization of the Mentally Ill* (Washington, D.C.: Government Printing Office, 1952), no. 51.

2. Ibid., section 1a.

3. Ibid., section 9g.

4. Ibid., section 19.

5. For a review of the variations as of 1967, see Robert A. Farmer, *The Rights of the Mentally Ill*. Since the laws are constantly changing, the picture at present may be quite different from Farmer's review.

6. In this and subsequent case materials, significant details have been altered to make personal identities unrecognizable.

7. Minnesota Hospitalization and Commitment Act, 1967, sec. 7, subd. 7.

8. Ibid., sec. 6, subd. 6.

9. Ibid., sec. 7, subd. 3.

10. Ibid., sec. 7, subd. 8.

11. Ibid., sec. 7, subd. 9.

12. Ibid., sec. 7, subds. 10, 11.

13. Ibid., sec. 7, subd. 13.

14. Ibid., sec. 7, subds. 14, 15.

15. Ibid., sec. 7, subd. 16.

16. Ibid., sec. 7, subd. 17a, b, c.

4

FORMAL
AND INFORMAL
ORGANIZATION OF THE
MENTAL HOSPITAL

Despite the radical critique of the whole notion of mental illness developed by Thomas Szasz and others, most persons would view the modern trend toward the separation of the problems of mental illness from criminality, on the one hand, and from magico-religious practice, on the other, as progressive. This, however, does not deny that some risk exists in identifying mental illness so closely with physiology that its peculiarities are missed. This, in fact, seems to be the major insight of Szasz's critique of current practice.

In forms of disease with a physiological basis, only special parts of the body are usually involved, and treatment is best left in the hands of specialists primarily skilled in the pathology of that body part. To be sure, if one shifts attention to the causes of the breakdown of some particular part of the body one may by degrees be led to a consideration of the patient's milieu, occupation, style of life, and so on. Furthermore, there are systemic upsets that involve the entire body system. As preventive medicine develops, the problem of man's physiological ailments will increasingly be seen as coextensive with his whole way of life.

Nevertheless, the critical difference between mental and physical illness at the present time lies in the role played by the mentally ill person's whole way of life. Moreover, when he enters the hospital there is increasing tendency to see the entire hospital, not simply some special wards and laboratories and operating rooms and specialists, as relevant to his career in the hospital and, eventually, to his prospects outside the hospital.

For this reason it is of value to review the various types of hospitals, their formal and informal organization, and the operations of the team of persons most directly involved with the patient—those in whose hands the decision lies to continue or change treatment and to eventually discharge the patient.

TYPES OF MENTAL HOSPITALS

Mental hospitals range from small private intensive treatment centers to large state and federal institutions. Treatment varies among these types. In small hospitals that receive wealthy patients the treatment program is intensive and tailored to individual needs. Because cost is usually not a major consideration in the veteran's administration hospitals, they also have fairly intensive treatment programs. City, county and state hospitals must often limp along on fewer facilities and funds. The majority of our mentally ill are cared for in four types of hospitals: state hospitals, U.S. veteran's hospitals, small private psychiatric hospitals, and psychiatric sections of general hospitals.

TABLE 2

NUMBER OF MENTAL HOSPITALS IN
UNITED STATES (1961)

TYPE	Number
State mental hospitals	270
Veterans Administration mental hospitals	41
Small private psychiatric hospitals	310
Psychiatric sections of general hospitals	789

In 1961, the Joint Commission on Mental Illness and Health surveyed the number of mental hospitals in the country; its findings are summarized in Table 2.[1]

The VA Hospital

The Veterans Administration hospitals treat the veteran who has a service-connected disability. Most of the patients on the mental ward have served in the armed forces. While most VA hospitals care for men, a few treat women veterans. Federal funds provide financial support that is about double the amount allocated for the state hospitals. The Veterans Administration hospitals' trained staffs tend to stay longer than those of state hospitals due to the incentive of better facilities and salaries. Other advantages of sufficient funds are reflected in the surroundings, treatment, facilities, and quality of the food.

Treatment in VA hospitals is intensive; recreational and occupational therapy programs are well-developed; and aftercare service was in effect long before the state hospitals were making use of it. The high staff–patient ratio promotes patient recovery.

All these advantages have created a favorable image of the Veterans Administration hospital. Most families do not experience as much anxiety when ill members are sent to VA hospitals for treatment as when they are sent to the state hospitals. When the veteran becomes ill his family seeks help earlier, assisting his recovery. In the community, too, treatment in a veteran's hospital carries less stigma than treatment in a state hospital.

The Private Mental Hospital

For care of mentally ill from the upper income strata the small private psychiatric hospital is available. It is often brilliantly staffed and equipped, for it services people who know and can afford the best. Physicians and psychiatrists who have been treating the patient in the community are often responsible for the referral and usually are kept informed of their patient's progress after admission; this procedure helps in continuity of relationship and care. The staff–patient ratio is high and specialized training is available in all areas. Intensive therapy is focused on individual needs and most patients are admitted on a voluntary basis. Psychotherapy is practiced to a great extent along with electroshock, drug therapy, and occupational therapy. Relatives often have a close relationship with the hospital staff; in fact, therapy may involve analysis of the family setting and contemplate altering the home unit.

The small psychiatric hospital provides the ideal care reserved for the privileged few. The stigma of mental illness is minimized for both the family and the patient. In fact, a curious kind of honorific status may attach to treatment by some private mental hospitals.

The Psychiatric Section of the General Hospital

The psychiatric sections of general hospitals treat mentally ill patients who live in nearby communities. These sections may consist of several wards segregated from the rest of the hospital by doors locked for protection of the patients as well as the public. With insurance programs expanding to cover mental illness, more people are being treated for emotional disturbances in psychiatric sections of general hospitals. City-county hospitals supported by taxes are able to treat the mentally ill patient who cannot afford private care. A general hospital which is associated with a medical school is able to make use of interns training on the psychiatric ward, as well as of residents and a director who are permanent staff members.

Treatment varies with the amount of money and facilities available. Rarely is it possible to match the all-out efforts of the small psychiatric hospital. Some psychiatric sections treat acute cases of mental illness until family resources are exhausted and then transfer patients to the state hospital for further treatment on either a commitment or voluntary basis.

Some psychiatric sections of general hospitals operate like small private psychiatric hospitals and are rather exclusive, accepting only patients in the higher income brackets or individuals who have extensive insurance coverage. The same psychiatrists who first treated the patient as an outpatient often continues to treat him as an inpatient. The psychiatric section is, in the long run, cheaper than a separate building or private hospital, inasmuch as such overall facilities of the general hospital as laboratories, X-rays, diet kitchen, surgery, pharmacy, and so on can be drawn upon. Patients may remain under this type of treatment in a general hospital for several months.

With the recent emphasis on retaining the mentally ill in the community, more general hospitals are establishing psychiatric sections. This delays or prevents commitment to the state mental hospital, with its subsequent trauma and stigma for both family and patient. Many families resort to extreme means to keep the patient in the community hospital; they may take out large loans or even mortgage their homes. Inasmuch as the majority of our hospitalized mentally ill are receiving treatment and care in state hospitals, a detailed account of them is presented in the following section.

The State Mental Hospital

By 1961, 80 percent of all mental patients in hospitals were cared for in state hospitals. The state mental hospital has been described as a large, isolated, impersonal, and self-contained institution with its own subculture. Together with prisons, homes for the aged or the blind, monasteries, orphanages, and prisoner-of-war camps, the mental hospital is viewed as a total institution. "A total institution may be defined as a place of residence and work where a large number of like-situated individuals, cut off from the wider society for an appreciable period of time, together lead an enclosed, formally administered round of life." [2]

Most state mental hospitals are located far from the metropolitan centers, often hundreds of miles away from the patient's home. Isolation serves a number of purposes: it removes the patient from the home environment where his illness was precipitated; it provides peaceful—usually rural—surroundings; it makes available cheap local labor supplies for hospital operation. Usually some wards are locked and in some hospitals a high wall surrounds the buildings to prevent the disturbed from wandering away to cause distress to members of the local community or harm to themselves.

Aftercare programs, the establishment of mental health centers made possible by passage of the 1963 Community Mental Health Act, the use of tranquilizers and anti-depressant drugs, and new hospital treatment programs have sharply reduced the patient population at the state hospitals. The size of the hospital staff, however, has remained about the same, resulting in a higher ratio of staff to patients. More intensive personal treatment rather than purely custodial care has become possible. The length of the average patient's hospital stay has been reduced. Nevertheless, the majority of the nation's mentally ill are still being cared for in the state and municipal hospitals.

With the ability to tranquilize over-excitement and overcome extreme depression with antidepressants, it is possible not only to shorten aberrant episodes, but to fit many patients (so long as they take their medicine) to less rigorous regimes than those of the mental hospitals. Hence, there is considerable pressure from state hospitals to place mentally ill individuals in nursing homes or halfway houses or even their own homes as soon as possible.

The arguments in favor of this are quite obvious. The facilities of the hospital are too valuable to be employed primarily for custodial problems. Furthermore, so long as the state hospital's staff–patient ratio is markedly out of line with that of the intensive treatment facility or veteran's hospital, one cannot hope for equivalent efficiency.

When mental patients are located in nursing homes, however, periodic complaints often arise. The charges made during the summer of 1969 against the nursing homes of Minneapolis and Saint Paul by members of the Minneapolis Age and Opportunity Center, Inc., illustrate this problem.

Members of the Minneapolis Age and Opportunity Center, Inc., contend that permitting a licensed practical nurse (LPN) to be in charge of the nursing service is ridiculous. They maintain that LPN's don't have enough training to handle many medical tasks themselves, to say nothing of supervising the rest of the nursing service staff.

LPN's and registered nurses are required to be on the premises of a nursing home only 56 hours a week. Any "responsible" person can legally be in charge at the home during the rest of the week. Nearly all of the homes are at least 90 percent full.

The kind of care patients get in nursing homes has been a controversial topic in Minneapolis during the last year with much of the criticism of nursing facilities being leveled by the Minneapolis Age and Opportunity Center, Inc. (MAO).

Among the charges made by leaders of MAO, which they say apply to St. Paul as well as Minneapolis, include [sic]:

—STAFFS at nursing homes are inadequate both in quality and quantity, and many nurses and aides don't have the competence or training to do what they're supposed to.

—FOOD is often cheap, poorly prepared, unappetizing and is frequently served cold.

—PATIENTS calling for help sometimes are ignored for hours.

— ACTIVITIES, entertainment, and individualized help for patients doesn't [sic] exist in a number of homes.

—PATIENTS unable to control their bowels often are left unchanged for hours.

— DISTURBED mental patients and the extremely senile often are placed in with normal patients.

Some of these conditions were found in most of 12 nursing homes in St. Paul which were selected at random and visited last week by a *Pioneer Press* reporter.[3]

It is notable that one of the major complaints was that in the nursing homes mentally ill persons were placed together with normal persons. But from the standpoint of psychiatry, this is a desirable practice, and one that facilitates the full return of the mentally ill person to the normal world.

Moreover, a nursing home by definition cannot have the facilities of a hospital with psychiatrists, medical doctors, nurses, and other trained personnel continuously on duty. Nor can the ordinary nursing home provide its patients with freedom to move about extensive grounds and participate in a wide variety of recreational and rehabilitative activities.

THE ORGANIZATIONAL
STRUCTURE OF THE HOSPITAL

It is conventional to describe the more or less permanent features of group activities as the group's organization. The flow of information, power and influence, responsibility, service, and material rewards are ordered; this order is the group's organization; and the single individual is a nucleus of this activity flow. The formal order of the group comprises those aspects of its organization that are officially defined in its rules and regulations. The informal order of the group comprises those aspects of information, power, responsibility, service, and material reward that structure the interpersonal relations of members of the group over and beyond the formal system. The informal organization may assist or contravene the formal organization.

The Formal Organization of
the Mental Hospital

The formal organization of the contemporary mental hospital is bureaucratic in the sense of Max Weber's famous description.[4] Its characteristics are: the establishment for individuals of fixed jurisdictional areas ordered by rules; the organization of a hierarchy of authority and service in a system of super- and subordination (a chain of service and command); and the management of the organization on the basis of documents.

The formal organizational structure of a state mental hospital may consist of a clinical and administrative staff headed by a superintendent and/or medical director. Usually the clinical staff includes doctors, psychiatrists, psychologists, social workers, nurses, attendants (ward aides), a pharmacist, a chaplain, laboratory and X-ray technicians, and occupational and recreational therapists; medical and psychiatric consultants also are on the staff. Many hospitals maintain diagnostic laboratories, and X-ray and dental facilities. The administrative staff includes a business manager who supervises the personnel section, an accountant, and those who take care of the food service, industries, agriculture, physical plant, supplies, and records. All the routine functioning of the hospital—paying the bills, feeding the patients, operating the laundry, maintaining the physical plant, ordering supplies, and keeping the grounds—is handled by the administrative staff.

Responsibility for the overall treatment program is in the hands of the physicians and psychiatrists; they make the decisions regarding type of psychiatric therapy for the individual patient, kind of drugs needed, treatment for physical ailments, surgery, and so on. Some mental hospitals are equipped for emergency and minor surgery, but usually when major surgery is necessary the patient is transferred to a nearby general hospital. The dental facilities of the mental hospital also may be adequate for emergencies, but the major work is done by the patient's private dentist either during or after his hospitalization.

The clinical psychologist has come to be a vital part of the treatment team in the mental hospital. He assists in determining diagnosis through psychological tests and personal interviews, and is often involved in teaching in staff training programs, in research, and in individual and group therapy sessions.

Serving to bridge the gap between the hospital and the community is the psychiatric social worker. In addition to receiving the information regarding the patient's social history that the county welfare social worker may send to the hospital, the state hospital social worker usually interviews the family at the time of the patient's admission or shortly afterward. He obtains information regarding family resources, which may be necessary in making discharge plans, as well as reasons for hospitalization. The strengths and weaknesses of the family members may later determine how soon the patient may visit his family, whether the family's visits to the hospital should be encouraged or discouraged, and whether the patient should return home or be placed in a halfway house after discharge from the hospital.

In the mental hospital the role of the nurse is different from the one she has traditionally assumed in the general hospital. Instead of spending a large part of her time with medications and treatments, she manages mental patients, supervises the aides, and creates a therapeutic environment. As an active member of the treatment team, she is not rigidly subordinate to the medical staff but is encouraged to voice her opinions at team meetings. She helps mental patients regain their self-confidence and their ability to get along with other people, to make decisions, and to cope with the problems of everyday living. The nurse encourages the patient to participate in activities and is watchful for any signs of regression or emotional excitement.

Many hospitals conduct inservice training programs for nurses and ward aides. Students from schools of nursing in the area may affiliate with the hospital for two or three months to learn the essentials of psychiatric nursing.

Adolescent mentally ill patients are set apart from the other patients in a ward of their own whenever possible. In a separate unit the adolescent can learn to socialize with his peer group under the supervision of a highly sensitive staff. Education is considered part of the therapy, and classes are held by teachers who work in the hospital on a part-time or full-time basis. Small-group therapy is often provided along with recreational and remedial programs. Since work with the adolescent mentally ill requires much personal contact and supervision, the number of adolescent patients that can be treated is limited; most hospitals do not have the finances to hire sufficient qualified staff members for this special treatment service.

Because of the large patient–staff ratio and the formal hierarchical structure of the state mental hospital, all phases of daily living (eating, washing, sleeping, recreation, treatment, dispensation of medication, job assignments, occupational therapy, etc.) are controlled by a set of regulations which apply to all patients regardless of diagnosis, degree of disturbance, or length of hospitalization.

Members of the clinical staff tend to change jobs more frequently than the housekeeping staff; the administrative workers often remain on their jobs ten to fifteen years or longer. Clinical staff members are hired at a fixed salary and status while administrative workers are hired through civil service examinations and start at the bottom level of the respective pay scales. Transfer from one department in the hospital to another is possible if the worker qualifies for the job. In any case, administrative workers can usually count on careers with regular increases of prestige and pay.

There is little social interaction between administrative workers and clinical staff due to differences in background, education, and interests; whereas administrative workers are career bureaucrats, the clinical staff has properties of the independent entrepreneur. Psychiatric aides who work with the patients on the wards often harbor a certain degree of hostility toward the doctors and registered nurses who give the orders and, at times, treat them as menials.

Although there has been a good deal of publicity, especially during political campaigns, highlighting the defects of state and municipal mental hospitals no radical changes have occurred. To palliate the negative press, the state mental hospital may receive a grant of money from the legislature for the construction of a new building. But after the political campaign with its promises is over, the plight of the mental hospital is forgotten until it becomes politically useful once more. Most mental hospitals continue to operate as they have in the past despite problems which include: ancient, fire-trap buildings, crowded wards, insufficient funds, understaffing, and inadequate treatment facilities.

The typical physician of the state mental hospital is in charge of several hundred patients. Because so few graduate nurses work in mental hospitals, the majority of the patients are cared for by attendants or ward aides ("technicians"). The educational backgrounds of ward aides are often four years of high school or less, their salaries are low, and their turnover is great. During the past decade, training courses to prepare ward aides for the civil service examination have been developed; the examination

qualifies them as psychiatric aides and provides them with honorific incentives and a wider range of skills in dealing with the
patients.

This basic organization varies, depending on hospital size,
funds allocated, and personnel recruitment possibilities. Psychiatrists are especially difficult to recruit since they not only
earn much more money in private practice, but often wish to be
associated with medical or teaching hospitals located in the
larger cities. As a result, a large number of foreign doctors are
recruited by the state mental hospitals, as well as doctors with
problems of their own who benefit by the atmosphere of the
state mental hospital.[5] Other professionals such as psychologists,
nurses and social workers also tend to accept jobs with higher
salaries and better opportunities for advancement than those
offered by the state mental hospitals.

The social structure of the state mental hospital has direct
relevance to patient treatment. With so many different professions and specialties involved there is bound to be a divergence
of opinion. Members of the medical hierarchy are concerned
with general professional needs and may experience multiple
lines of tension with the administration. The medical doctor may
be skeptical of psychiatrists and look upon them as faith
healers. Many psychiatrists view the medical doctor as a humble
little brother who never got beyond the material aspects of the
profession. The ward staff (nurses and aides) are responsible
to the doctors and hospital superintendent and are at times torn
between the two. Sometimes a considerable amount of knowledge is gained about the patient by one or more of the specialists
involved but because of staff conflict it is not brought effectively
to bear on therapeutic practice.

A dramatic example of the way structural weaknesses in a
mental hospital may affect its therapeutic program is reported
by Stotland and Kobler.[6]

A private mental hospital, the Crest Foundation Hospital, was
founded in the city of Columbia by two psychoanalysts who had
been stationed together during World War II. The plan worked

out in 1948 was put into practice in 1950 in a renovated rest home with a small staff and some part-time professionals. At its period of fullest development the hospital had a staff of eleven professionals and a staff–patient ratio of three to one. Its early days were attended by striking success and it served as a training center for a number of people in the area. From the beginning, however, there was a conflict of ideologies and a contest for power among various groups. Its first full-time medical director, Dr. Irving Davidson reported: "When I did come to Crest, a three-way controversy was raging; the conflict between the board of trustees and the consulting staff; the confusion of relationships between the board of directors and the professional staff at Crest; and the relationship of the professional staff of Crest and the consulting staff to each other." [7] The unresolved conflicts worsened until the once-high morale of the ward staff sagged, with evident effects on the patients. This culminated in a general disturbance among adolescent patients who "often maneuvered or induced others to violate some hospital edict. . . . The adolescent patients refused to retire in the evening, and often carried on their revels until three o'clock in the morning. They removed fixtures from the walls and ceilings. Some could pick any lock at the hospital and did so repeatedly, one taunting the staff by leaving on the lounge end table all new, recently installed, locks. One night a schizophrenic adolescent attacked an aide by hitting him over the head with a stocking containing a heavy object." [8] Finally a suicide epidemic broke out among the patients. Between December 23, 1959, and January 1960 there occurred one suicide attempt followed by three actual suicides. The hospital was closed in 1960.

This provisional sketch of the wide variety of skills required, the varied problems faced, and the potential tensions between various categories of hospital personnel is intended to highlight the importance of the formal organization of the mental hospital. The only purpose of the system of power, the set of institutional priorities, and the network of communications is to enable the mentally ill to be treated with the maximum efficiency that the resources (human and material) of the hospital permit. The collapse of Crest Foundation Hospital was directly traceable to its failure to establish such a clear uncontested formal organization.

But as one sets up a formal organization in any large-scale human enterprise, one introduces components of inflexibility. One or a few ways of doing things are given priority over alternatives. As new problems arise, the formal organization tends to be viewed by some as a network of obstacles. An informal organization inevitably makes its appearance.

Informal Structure

The informal structure of the mental hospital comprises the connections, cliques, and grapevines which bypass the formal organizational structure. The mental hospital tends to create a protective authoritarian environment whose formal structure is relatively inflexible. The more varied and rich the life of an institution is, the more certain it is to develop beyond the formal order. In the words of Stanton and Schwartz:

> Certain aspects of the institution are clear, explicit, subject to planning, and can be changed by order, whereas others are not immediately subject to order or even to clear statement. The former we have come to call "formal," "official," or "explicit" aspects of the institution; the latter we call "informal," "unofficial," or "implicit." This differentiation, while not always clear-cut, is nevertheless obviously of great operational importance to the administrator.[9]

Why are the formal and informal organizations of a mental hospital (or for that matter any large organization) so often in conflict?

Although the official and primary function of a mental hospital is treatment of the mentally ill, it has, like any large organization, many "secondary" values to persons involved in its existence. It provides jobs to a wide variety of persons ranging from the top administrative and clinical personnel to the housekeeping staff. It is a source of prestige to many of its employees.

It provides opportunities for a variety of social and romantic contacts between men and women. Through on-the-job friendships, professional and work relations come to bear some relation to leisure time pursuits.

The formal organization of the hospital normally originates from the top and not only implements the primary objective of the hospital—the treatment of the mentally ill—but also sets up a system of incentives. The philosophy or ideology of the enterprise's major powers is given precedence over alternatives. The hospital is organized primarily to facilitate the wishes of the hospital's authorities. The major rewards, both financial and honorific, go to them.

The informal organization of the mental hospital normally originates among the lower ranks of the organization. Ivan Belknap saw the informal structure of the mental hospital primarily as a phenomenon by which ward aides adjusted the formal requirements of the hospital to the day-to-day needs of patient management. In the hospital studied by Belknap, the informal social organization was sustained by a tradition he estimated to be at least seventy years old. The culture consisted of legends and rationalizations for practices incompletely defined by the formal hospital organization. The culture of the attendants primarily operated toward the patients on the wards as a set of behavior controls sustained by rewards and punishments. The culture of the attendants operated defensively toward the clinical staff: marking out lines of cooperation and defense. Toward each other the culture of the attendants operated both as a system of socialization, teaching newcomers the ropes, and as a system of social control, eliminating those who would not conform.[10]

It should be noted, however, that the informal organization of a mental hospital involves personnel other than ward aides and derives from motives other than mediation of the formal structure and patient requirements.

Those staff members who are at the lower end of the hierarchy may resort to unofficial methods of getting the work done; because of their eight-to-five type of job, position at the bottom of the pay scale, and minimum recognition, they may not feel a sense of loyalty to the hospital. On the other hand, the staff members toward the top of the hierarchy are career people with more pay, status and personal obligation to the hospital; they, therefore, are more likely to conform to the formal structure. For example, a psychologist who, because of a research project involving a group of hospital patients, works overtime, is likely to receive official commendation for his zeal.

On the other hand, professional staff members may resort to unauthorized methods to achieve personal ends: such practices as procurement of food supplies from the hospital store for home use; engagement of the free services of patients as maids or cooks; and use of the hospital garage and mechanic to repair their cars are not unknown.

Informal considerations may also include the attitudes, feelings and responses of staff to staff, of patients to patients, and of staff to patients. The longer the staff member works at the hospital, the more involved he becomes with the informal structure; his network of information extends as his range of acquaintance and his depth of involvement increase.

Dating may take place between the male and female staff members, during which time a confidential exchange of information about patients and the hospital staff occurs which may or may not be beneficial for the patients. A nurse on good terms with the psychiatrist in charge of her ward may try to obtain permission from him to let her boyfriend practice psychotherapy with a few select patients; or a secretary in the office may be able to provide her superior, the clinical director, with a current picture of the activities on the ward. An occupational therapist in need of more equipment for projects in her department may appeal to a patient who works as a part-time maid in the home of the business manager.

In the long run, as Stanton and Schwartz perceived, the informal organization of the mental hospital limits the operations of the top members of the hospital hierarchy. The administrators soon learn that policies which take no account of the informal organization have a way of failing.

According to Belknap the hospital administrator may initially have rather naive conceptions of the powers of his position, but he is not long in discovering that the hospital operates on an informal system that determines in advance how far he is able to go. Over and beyond the limitations set on decision making by the formal organization is the system of cliques, the antagonisms, the patterns of established practice which, if violated, will result in quiet sabotage which brings his hopes to nought.[11]

It goes without saying that the informal organization of the hospital may have a limiting or directing influence not only upon the hospital administrators but also on its clinical personnel.

The Staff or Team Session

In the general hospital, the decision to release the patient is purely a prerogative of the attending physician. In unusually difficult cases, however, other physicians may be called in for consultation. It is perhaps because mental cases fell by and large into the "difficult" category that the staff session developed into a routine feature of procedure. Moreover, as a wide variety of psychological and social elements were perceived as relevant, the staff session came to comprise all persons who had regular contact with the patient.

Meanwhile, theoretical developments were changing the conception of mental illness. The new conception was summarized by Esther Lucile Brown. The function of the mental hospital, according to Brown, is to exploit every form of treatment and to return the patient to normal life in the community as soon as possible. Its therapy, she urges, involves systematic use of the entire physical and social environment. Its research significance, she maintains, is found in the testing and utilization of the concepts and methods developed by the behavioral sciences.[12]

Although the change in the conception of the mental hospital from a primarily custodial to a therapeutic institution was traced in chapters 1 and 2 below, it is noteworthy that the rise of the staff session and the team meeting was part and parcel of this change. Furthermore, the staff session automatically provided a situation where both formal and informal organizations could be explored.

Staff or team sessions are important for the synthesis of the various operations of the formal organization; they bring together on a daily, biweekly, or weekly basis members of the therapeutic team who discuss the patient's progress, offer suggestions for treatment, appraise his ability to function in the hospital as well as in the community, decide when he is well enough for home visits or provisional discharge. At these sessions, the staff help one another to cope with the problems and frustrations that arise in working with patients and to improve their skills and knowledge through an exchange of ideas and information. Team members usually include a psychiatrist or physician who is the leader and final arbiter, a clinical psychologist, a social worker, an occupational and a recreational therapist, and a charge nurse or a ward aide; all have a specific relationship with the patient and may have a reinforcing effect upon one another.

Each member of the team is given an opportunity to relate his experiences with a patient, and his reactions and attitudes toward the patient's behavior. Other staff responses to the same patient are elicited and, after discussion, a decision regarding further treatment is reached by the psychiatrist or the group as a whole.

Staffing sessions can resemble elaborate primitive ceremonies in their reaffirmation of the prestige of the doctor, psychiatrist, or other staff members. In the course of such ceremonialism, the welfare of patients may be forgotten. Some members of the team may have to remain silent unless spoken to. Information can be lost as a result. A social worker could potentially have excellent ideas but the psychiatrist will be immune to them if he perceives them as a challenge to his authority. A social worker engaged in small group therapy meetings may not share her information with the psychiatrist because she fears his disapproval. A psychologist giving individual psychotherapy to a few select patients may be reluctant to share his special knowledge with the other members of the team, lest they then criticize his methods or feel he is encroaching on their territory.

Members of the professional staff may be highly competitive with and jealous of other staff members in their own discipline, or may disagree with their supervisors. Psychologists and social workers may be better informed about the patient's difficulties than a physician who may be learning about the social needs of the mental patient for the first time; this is especially true if the doctor specialized in internal medicine or is of foreign background. If the physician leader of the treatment team does not have a strong ego and is not relatively secure in his own personal life, he may not be able to accept suggestions from other team members without feeling threatened.

On the other hand, if the members of the therapeutic team are able to function harmoniously with each other and are willing to share the knowledge about the patient and their respective professions with other team members they can work together for a common goal—the patient. The group meeting then turns into a seminar which can be exciting and challenging for the staff; the insights gained in such sessions hasten the patient's recovery.

A harmonious staff session can be quite open, fluid, and democratic. One result of such meetings has been the recognition of the ward aide or attendant as a valuable member of the therapeutic team. Although the ward aide is at the bottom rung of the organizational ladder, he spends a great deal of time with the patient; increasing his skills and obtaining his support can markedly effect the patient's progress in the hospital.

It is largely the attendant–patient relationship that determines the amount and type of disturbed behavior of patients, the level of fear, the degree of arbitrary authoritarianism, and the point at which seclusion becomes the answer. The attendant can make or break the patient. He can arrange the situation so that a patient whom he fears, or against whom he harbors deep antagonism will eventually land in seclusion—and by the physician's order. . . . Bringing attendants into membership in this team implies, first, that they be accepted as individuals; that the fears, tensions, and frustrations facing them in the performance of their jobs be recognized and handled; that steps be taken to improve their skill in dealing with sick persons who present inexplicable behavior; and that they be given access to sources of information that help to guide the physician in his elaborate considerations of the welfare of the patient.[13]

Staff sessions have a direct effect on the patient in the mental hospital. Inasmuch as vital information is shared and decisions are reached by the group, delays in initiating treatment are avoided; fear of a patient's excitable behavior may be lessened by discussion and analysis of the patient's illness at the team meeting; patients' complaints may receive a more tolerant hearing; danger signs during crucial periods of treatment may be observed and reported immediately to the psychiatrist in charge.

Bizarre behavior is more readily tolerated if staff members understand why they react to the patient as they do. This can be openly discussed at staff sessions through members relating their experiences with and reactions to the patient. A revealing account of how staff sessions can benefit the patient is presented by Denis V. Martin, physician superintendent and consultant psychiatrist at Claybury Hospital, England:

> The regular opportunity for expressing disagreeable emotions in an atmosphere of mutual support and understanding helps us to avoid discharging it on to our patients in harmful ways. . . . An illustration of this function . . . is the recurring situation in which staff begin by suggesting that a certain patient should be discharged because he is not responding to treatment. Further discussion reveals that none of us like the patient and most of us feel angry with him. We may then discover together that it is the failure of this difficult patient to satisfy our need to make him better that has made us angry. As the discussion proceeds, one after another begins to say things which suggest the patient is in fact improving and ways may be suggested for helping him more. The initial request for his discharge is abandoned and it is agreed that he needs our continued help. . . . It is clear in such cases, which could be multiplied many times, that it was our feelings, aroused by the difficult patient, which were the real problem.

These were resolved through the medium of free expression and discussion and the patient ceased to be a serious problem.[14]

Some additional problems of the staff sessions will be discussed later when the transformation of the mental hospital from custodial institution to therapeutic community is reviewed. For the moment the staff session is of interest because of the frequency with which it blurs the lines between formal and informal organization; through it, the multiple tensions checked by the formal organization may be brought into the open.

NOTES

1. Joint Commission on Mental Illness and Health, *Action for Mental Health,* p. 173.

2. Erving Goffman, *Asylums, Essays on the Social Situation of Mental Patients and Other Inmates,* p. xiii.

3. Bob Goligoski, *Pioneer Press,* August 17, 1969, section 3, p. 1.

4. Max Weber, *From Max Weber,* ed. Hans Gerth and C. Wright Mills (New York: Oxford Press, 1946), pp. 196ff.

5. No study that we know of has been made on the phenomenon, but it is the frequent *informal* observation by students of the state mental hospital that their psychiatric staffs contain an unusually high proportion of foreign psychiatrists and psychologists with histories of mental problems of their own which would make it unusually difficult for them to survive in private practice.

6. Ezra Stotland and Arthur L. Kobler, *Life and Death of a Mental Hospital* (Seattle: University of Washington Press, 1965).

7. Ibid., p. 73.

8. Ibid., pp. 148–149.

9. Alfred H. Stanton and Morris S. Schwartz, *The Mental Hospital, A Study of Institutional Participation in Psychiatric Illness and Treatment,* p. 10.

10. See Ivan Belknap, *Human Problems of a State Mental Hospital,* pp. 151–152.

11. Stanton and Schwartz, *The Mental Hospital,* p. 111.

12. See Esther Lucile Brown, "Introduction" to Milton Greenblatt, *From Custodial to Therapeutic Patient Care in Mental Hospitals* (New York: Russell Sage Foundation, 1955), pp. 3, 18, 25.

13. Ibid., pp. 64–65.

14. Denis V. Martin, *Adventure in Psychiatry,* pp. 70–71.

5

THE CAREER
OF THE
MENTAL PATIENT

Apprehension by force is quite traumatic to the patient. Typically, his family has pleaded with him to consult a doctor or a psychiatrist and perhaps threatened to take legal steps, but the patient has irrationally refused to believe that any coercive methods would be employed. He may even have enjoyed the hold on the family his illness has given him. Secretly delighting in their concern over him, he may be playing games to perpetuate his sadistic domination. The wife of one mentally ill individual reported that once in desperation she said to her husband, "If you don't keep your appointment with the doctor and take your medication I'm going to have you committed to the state mental hospital." He retorted, "If you have me picked up by the sheriff I'll get a divorce" or "I'll kill myself."

When the deputy sheriff comes to the home with the "Order for Apprehension and Confinement" issued by the probate court, the mentally ill person is usually shocked. In the majority of cases the patient is so stunned that he submits to the law and accompanies the deputy sheriff without a struggle. But there are instances when he may become violent enough to require two or three policemen to restrain and control him. When a deputy sheriff, who for many years transported individuals on order from the probate court to the city-county hospital for evaluation and hearing, was queried as to his experiences, he asserted: "Most patients come along quietly, almost as if they expected it. However, some give one an argument and try to persuade you that the petitioner is insane. Over the years I've had my glasses knocked off a few times, my shirt torn off my back and I've been threatened with knives and guns. But these are the unusual cases."

Upon admission to the community or private hospital prior to the probate court hearing, the patient is placed in the psychiatric unit under detention. Only a key or an electronic buzzer may open and close the door. The patient is not allowed to leave the psychiatric unit and is closely watched by all staff members; the doctors, nurses, aides, orderlies, and ward clerks, as well as the cleaning women, kitchen help, and janitors quickly recognize the new patient and escort him back to his room should he manage to get away.

Except perhaps in the most extreme forms of disorganization, patients realize that their relations with the outside world have been dramatically broken. Although they were disrupting the lives of the primary group at home, many patients reported later that they had not anticipated this sudden and drastic break in family and community relations; to them, it seemed like the end of the world. However hard commitment is on the family, it is usually much harder on the patient. The relieved family can now resume, at least for a time, its normal activities. For the patient a series of additional traumatic events are set in motion.

Soon after admission to the hospital, the patient usually is informed about his legal rights. He may phone his family and plead to be released or immediately call his attorney. He is shortly served with a "Notice of Hearing" by the deputy sheriff. For the first time the patient may learn the names of the petitioner and other members of the primary group who are being notified of the hearing; his sick mind may consider them his "enemies," in collaboration against him. If he is released from the hospital on a writ of habeas corpus secured by his attorney, he may choose not to return home, but register at a motel or stay with sympathetic relatives or friends. However he still has to attend the probate court hearing and face the family.

In the event that he remains in the hospital, other patients who have undergone the commitment procedure may share their past experiences with him, further heightening his anxiety prior to the hearing. Like veterans everywhere, they tend to exaggerate their experiences to impress the newcomer. As a result the sick person, no matter what he thought before, is now determined to avoid being sent away to the mental hospital at all costs.

The patient is taken to the probate court hearing by an orderly or nurse. There he has to face a battery of people, and some whom he has never seen before will determine his fate. The examining board includes at minimum the probate judge or court commissioner, a psychiatrist, a doctor, two attorneys, his family and friends as well as other witnesses. Some of these present may testify against him.

If the probate court examiners decide that commitment is in the best interests of the patient and the community, the patient is transferred to the designated hospital that same afternoon or the following day. The patient often views this as a disaster. He feels that he has been reduced to a nonentity. His future is uncertain. His family has abandoned him. His job will be taken over by someone else.

THE ROLE OF THE MENTAL PATIENT IN THE HOSPITAL

When the mentally ill person is viewed as a lunatic separated by an unbridgeable gap from normal persons, his right to be treated as a person tends to be withdrawn. But when he is viewed as curable, his personal situation is handled as one perhaps only a few degrees removed from normal. Under such circumstances an informal organization develops, not only among members of the lower staff but also among the patients themselves. In many complex ways the informal systems of the staff and the patients may become interrelated.

On admission to the state hospital the patient is fearful of what the staff or the other patients may do to him. Science-fiction television series offer a large variety of tortures to incite the imagination of many of the mentally ill facing commitment to a mental institution. But it is not long after admission that the patient comes to realize that the hospital can be a haven, that the staff is often understanding, solicitous, and patient-oriented, that he is protected not only from himself but from other patients and from the family that he feels has abused and abandoned him.

Jaroslav Hasek described life in the asylum with the talents of the slapstick humorist:

> When Schweik later on described life in the lunatic asylum, he did so in terms of exceptional eulogy: "I'm blowed if I can make out why lunatics kick up such a fuss about being kept there. They can crawl about stark naked on the floor, or caterwaul like jackals, or rave and bite. If you was to do anything like that in the open street, it'd make people stare, but in the asylum it's just taken as a matter of course. Why, the amount of liberty there is something that even the socialists have never dreamed of. The inmates can pass themselves off as God Almighty or the Virgin Mary or the Pope or the King of England or our Emperor or St. Vaclav, although the one who did him was properly stripped and tied up in solitary confinement. There was a chap there who kept thinking that he was an archbishop, but he did nothing but guzzle. And then there was another who said he was St. Cyril and St. Methodus, just so that he could get double helpings of grub. One fellow was in the family way and invited everyone to the christening. There were lots of chess players, politicians, fishermen and scouts, stamp collectors and photographers and painters there. They used to keep one man always in a strait-waistcoat, to stop him from calculating when the end of the world was coming.

Everybody can say what he likes there, the first thing that comes into his head, just like in parliament. The noisiest of the lot was a chap who said he was the sixteenth volume of the encyclopaedia and asked everybody to open him and find an article on sewing machines or else he'd be done for. He wouldn't shut up until they shoved him into a strait-waistcoat. I tell you, the life there was a fair treat. You can bawl, or yelp, or sing, or blub, or moo, or boo, or jump, say your prayers or turn somersaults, or walk on all fours, or hop about on one foot, or run round in a circle, or dance, or skip, or squat on your haunches all day long, and climb up the walls. Nobody comes up to you and says: 'You musn't do this, you musn't do that, you ought to be ashamed of yourself, call yourself civilized?' I liked being in the asylum, I can tell you, and while I was there I had the time of my life." [1]

This, to be sure, is the account of a novelist inclined to exploit his subject matter humorously. But there is little doubt that Hasek had researched his subject well. He quite accurately characterized the mental hospital as a potential haven.

In the Mendota State Hospital of Madison, Wisconsin, Dr. Arnold M. Ludwig, director of a 30-bed special unit and an associate professor of psychiatry at the University of Wisconsin, and Dr. Arnold J. Marx, associate director of the treatment unit, ran a three-year experimental study of seemingly hopeless cases of chronic schizophrenics. In response to a reporter's inquiry as to why schizophrenia often becomes chronic Dr. Ludwig is reported to have replied as follows:

One reason . . . appears to be the reward of mental hospital life for certain patients. By remaining crazy, they escape responsibility and gain the security and privileges of the hospital indefinitely.

To a normal individual, life in a mental hospital might be regarded with dismay, but to the chronic schizophrenic, it represents safety and shelter from the threatening world outside.

A Mendota patient recently was asked, "What would you do if we decided to discharge you from the hospital tomorrow?"

The patient thought for a moment and replied, "I'd try to find out what I did wrong and try to correct it."

Another patient showed his attitude when several members of the staff were discussing plans for discharging him.

"You'll never railroad me out of here!" he declared.

Observing chronic schizophrenics . . . [we] began to notice that the patients had their own subculture, and that the subculture encouraged and reinforced crazy behavior . . . [we call] this the "code of chronicity."

Patients took no responsibility for each other. No one would intervene to save another from injury or assault. A patient often ate at the same table with another for years without knowing his name.[2]

The observations of Ludwig and Marx approach those of Hasek.

The contrary point of view, that the mental hospital is often a protected environment that the patient may in fact fight to leave, has been promoted with considerable skill by Erving Goffman in his essay "The Moral Career of the Mental Patient."[3] Goffman argues that the craziness claimed for the mental patient is largely a product of the observer's social distance from the situation of the patient rather than a product of mental illness.[4] The patient's perception that he is losing his mind rests largely on socially ingrained assessments of the significance of such symptoms as hearing voices, losing temporal and spatial orientation, and sensing that one is being followed.[5] According to Goffman, these symptoms may merely signify a temporary emotional upset.

In fact, Goffman believes the commitment of a person to an institution is often the result of offenses against some day-to-day arrangement—a domestic establishment, a work place, a semi-public organization such as a church or a store, or a public place such as a street or park.[6] Such action is often tolerated by the complainant until other personal pressures to commit the offender arise; a wife may find herself a boy friend or adult children may no longer have room in their apartment for the

parent they are trying to commit. Under such circumstances Goffman is convinced that there are probably as many or more
mentally ill outside the hospital as there are inside. "In the
degree that the 'mentally ill' outside hospitals numerically approach or surpass those inside hospitals, one could say that
mental patients distinctively suffer not from mental illness, but
from contingencies." [7]

Once the career contingency that may terminate with commitment to a mental hospital arises, in Goffman's view a whole
series of agents is prepared to speed the commitment of the
victim. In addition to the next-of-kin who now fails the patient
is the complainant who starts him on his way to the hospital.
The complainant is assisted by mediators (police, clergy, general
medical practitioners, office psychiatrists, personnel in public
clinics, lawyers, social service workers, school teachers and so
on) who reassure the relative and/or complainant and legitimize
the procedure. The commitment hearing at which witnesses
testify is interpreted by Goffman and Harold Garfinkel as a
degradation ceremony. [8] The prepatient, Goffman claims, starts
out with at least a portion of his rights, liberties, and satisfactions and ends up in a psychiatric ward stripped of almost everything by what Goffman describes as a *"betrayal funnel."* [9]

Goffman's interpretation of the inpatient phases of the mentally ill career is as bitter as his interpretation of the prepatient
phase. The individual has, in his view, not only been stripped
of his ordinary rights and satisfactions but "is subjected to a
rather full set of mortifying experiences: restriction of free
movement, communal living, diffuse authority of a whole eche-
lon of people and so on." [10] Most degrading of all is the "ward
system," which Goffman describes as a series of graded living
arrangements, stringent punishment for disobeying rules, and
minor satisfactions for obedience. In fact, the more the mental
hospital "attempts to be therapeutic . . . the more the patient
may be confronted by high-ranking staff arguing that his past
has been a failure." [11]

Among the endless ways in which the mental hospital de-
grades, in Goffman's view, is the development of a case history

which contains the sort of material a layman would consider scandalous, defamatory, or discrediting. "I think that most of the information gathered in case records is quite true, although it might seem also to be true that almost anyone's life course could yield up enough denigrating facts to provide grounds for the record's justification of commitment." [12]

Not only his case record but also what he does in the hospital place the patient under conditions of imminent exposure. This social milieu tends to engender a kind of cosmopolitan sophistication or civic apathy characterized by moral loosening and fatigue.[13] An example of such moral loosening is the free sexual license enjoyed by patients. "Some informal peer-group pressure may be brought against a patient who plays around with more than one hospital partner at a time, but little negative sanction seems to be attached to taking up, in a temporarily steady way, with a member of the opposite sex." [14]

As a second illustration of moral loosening, Goffman cites the ward system. Discreditings occur in part because of the lack of facilities and in part "through the mockery and sarcasm that seem to be the occupational norm of social control for the attendants and nurses who administer these places." [15] As a third instance, Goffman cites the conditions attendant on the release of a patient. Normally placed on provisional discharge and under supervision of his next-of-kin, he may be speedily returned to the hospital if he misbehaves. He therefore finds himself under the special power of ordinarily unimportant persons.[16] Goffman's conclusions are of particular interest.

> The moral career of the mental patient has unique interest . . .
> it can illustrate the possibility that in casting off the raiments of
> the old self—or in having this cover torn away—the person need
> not seek a new robe and a new audience before which to cower.
> Instead he can learn, at least for a time, to practice before all
> groups the amoral arts of shamelessness.[17]

One of the most telling formulations in Goffman's essay is the statement that the mental patient "in casting off the raiments of the old self—or in having this cover torn away" need not "seek a new robe and a new audience before which to cower," for this presumably reveals Goffman's view of the nature of the individual and of normal life. All morality is viewed as purely external, a robe behind which the real amoral individual hides. The most basic normal relation to others seems to be "cowering."

Since he conceives the normal person to be a frightened amoral animal cowering behind a mask of morality, Goffman's selectivity with regard to the career of the mental patient becomes clear. He suggests that the patient is virtually no different from anyone else even if he experiences himself as mentally ill. Commitment to a mental institution is largely a matter of accident. Everything in the hospital is degrading and apparently the more therapeutically oriented the greater the degradation. The only alleviating feature of the patient's condition is his privilege of practicing "before all groups the amoral arts of shamelessness." This, of course, is complete nonsense. There is no evidence that the mentally ill are more realistic than those who are not; the reverse is the case. Nor is there any evidence that the mentally ill act outside all culture, though long-time inmates develop a special patient culture. One must interpret Goffman's essay as a biased picture, a bitter indictment of ordinary life.

It is useful, however, to follow step by step the career of the patient in the mental hospital locating, among other things, those points where Goffman's indictment is appropriate.

WARD ASSIGNMENT OF THE PATIENT

Whether admission is temporary to a nearby hospital or whether admission is directly to the state hospital does not radically change the general admission procedure. The patient is registered and examined by the admitting doctor, and his valuables are placed in the hospital safe. A list of the patient's clothing is made. The patient is then assigned to a ward, a room with two to four other patients, or a solitary lock-up if he is violent. At the state hospital the patient is usually assigned to one of the staff physicians on a rotating basis and given a complete physical and psychiatric examination. Treatment begins almost at once by various members of the clinical team.

After admission in some hospitals, the patient is assigned for a few days or a week to the receiving section for observation before he is placed on one of the wards. In the receiving section the patient may have fairly good accommodations: a one- or two-bed room, some privacy, a day room well furnished with colorful drapes and easy chairs, small tables for games, a television set and radio, books, and magazines. The staff of registered nurses, student nurses, and male and female aides on the receiving section is usually excellent. The ratio of physicians to patients is fairly high. The considerable attention given to the patient helps to reassure him and quiet his fears.

After the patient's period of observation, he is transferred to the ward where he will remain until his discharge. The ward is the patient's "home" and the people who frequent it during most of the day constitute his temporary family. This family consists of other patients, ward aides, and nurses. It is with this group, if at all, that the patient establishes relations. Other staff members who visit the ward—psychiatrists, social workers, psychologists, and doctors—play an authoritarian role in relation to the passive role of the patient.

In most state hospitals the wards are large, with thirty to fifty beds placed close to one another. Some attempt has been made in recent years to replace white bedspreads with more colorful ones and window shades with flowered drapes. The day room adjacent to the ward usually has a large table in the center with straight chairs lined along the walls. A donated old upright piano, perhaps out of tune, may be against one wall and used for community sings during holidays. A television set is placed high up on the wall to prevent the patients from tinkering with the dials. There is little choice of programs. Lockers for each patient are supplied in some hospitals. A large bathroom with showers and toilets is located at one side of the ward. Off to the side are smaller rooms for storage of linens and clothing, the utility room, and a few single rooms with "peek holes" for noisy or violent patients. The windows of the entire ward are normally barred.

Located near the entrance to the ward is an office; there the ward aides and charge nurse keep the patients' records, and the medications are stored in a locked cabinet. Candy and fruit brought by relatives and friends are kept in a refrigerator here, and here also the mail is distributed. This office also serves as the focus of attention for the more rational patients who come to talk to the nurse and attendants, ask for a light and a cigarette (patients are not allowed to carry matches or cigarettes with them), watch the activities, listen to the gossip, harass the staff, beg to go home, ask to see the doctor, complain about the food, etc.

Some patients just sit around all day long, or stare out the window, or disrobe, or lie on their beds. A few pace back and forth or keep turning the locked door knobs. On the geriatric wards the problem of incontinence creates additional work for the aides and nurse. If bed patients are not changed often enough, bed sores develop. No matter how carefully the floors are scrubbed a smell of stale urine fills the air on a geriatric ward.

Those patients who are given work assignments leave the ward in the morning and return at night. Work assignments can be within the hospital or in a nearby city to which the patients are driven in a bus. But those patients who remain in the ward follow a routine schedule for eating, washing, recreation, occupational therapy, etc.

On the ward the aide is usually in charge of the patients. The better patients on the ward help each other and watch over the sicker patients, reporting anything unusual to the aide in charge. Some patients help with the bed making, wiping of chairs and windows, running errands, mopping floors. The majority of aides are women except on the male wards. If the aide in charge is understanding and sensitive to the patients' needs and abilities, he can manage his ward with patient help to the good of the hospital and the patients. While some people feel that patients are being exploited when they are given a work assignment on the ward or in the laundry or kitchen, this is actually one step in the socialization process which enables the patient to recover his self-esteem by performing a responsible, meaningful task.

Patients are usually assigned to wards on the basis of their behavior, that is, whether they have a good possibility of recovering within a reasonable time ("hopeful"), or whether they are not amenable to treatment and are likely to remain in the hospital for a long time ("chronic"), or whether they require special care because they are constantly going through periods of excitement ("agitated").[18]

A different atmosphere characterizes the hopeful patients from that found on the chronic wards. There is more interest in other patients on the hopeful ward because patients are coming and going from home visits with news of the community; more rational behavior meets with staff approval and leads to an earlier discharge from the hospital; patients are more apt to adhere to the ward regulations.

On the chronic wards a spirit of resignation is evident, for patients accept the fact that they probably will remain in the hospital for an indefinite period. Some patients are so accustomed to institutional life that they do not wish to leave and when discharge plans are made for them they suddenly regress. In the hospital these patients feel safe, realize that all their needs are provided, have come to accept the fact that they are mental patients, and are resigned to this role.

The ways patients react to life on the ward are broken down by Alfred H. Stanton and Morris S. Schwartz into three categories: withdrawn, intermediate, and active. When possible, these groups of patients are assigned to different wards; when facilities are insufficient, however, they may appear together on the same wards. Withdrawn patients talk little, often appear suspicious or fearful, and at times do not even acknowledge the presence of others. Some must be dressed, bathed, and fed by the ward personnel. Both staff members and other patients tend to reduce relations with them to a minimum. Patients designated as intermediate vary greatly, but generally evidence some degree of realism and display some capacity to enter into communication with others. But they often alternate unpredictably between meaningful-realistic and autistic behavior. The staff generally finds it easier to enter into and maintain social relations with them than with the withdrawn patients. Patients described as active are for the most part lucid, oriented to the realities of their situation, and sensible. They look and act "normal" in comparison with other patients on the ward, although there are marked differences between them and the ordinary man on the street. The staff prefers to deal with them and personnel tend to treat them as the core of the ward.[19]

LIFE ON THE PSYCHIATRIC WARDS

The quality of life of any human plurality is primarily determined by the character of its constituent members and the general properties of the milieu to which they respond.

The most immediate associates of the mental patient on the psychiatric wards are other patients and the various aides and nurses of the hospital. If one pauses to consider the influence on a "normal" social circle that may be wielded by even a single cynic, pessimist, chronic complainer, or other type of kill-joy, the possible difficulties of maintaining morale in a ward of mentally ill individuals immediately become apparent. The patient's associates are psychologically battered, profoundly distressed, tormented by irrational fears, bitterly suspicious, and responsive to voices or dreams or apparitions not heard and seen by others. The aides and nurses are separated from the patient by the authoritarian structure of the hospital and its assignment of status. They are the patient's keepers or policemen; their lives extend beyond the institution's confines.

The wider milieu of the mental patient is most immediately provided by the formal organization of the hospital. While in theory the patient and his problems are the mental hospital's raison d'être, in fact he is the lowest, last, and most passive recipient of its services, with less voice in its operations than anyone else involved. To facilitate the work of the professional and administrative staff, the hospital constrains the patient with a wide variety of rules and regulations. At the very time when the mental patient most requires individual treatment, the whole routinized structure of the hospital carries out an all-pervasive, continuous de-individualization. He is a bed, a number, a case.

Moreover, the still more remote outside world beyond the hospital tends—despite periodic public concern with the conditions of institutional life—to disregard the mental hospital, leaving it to its own devices. In times of public attention, institutional reforms are carried through and adequate budgets are voted. But after public attention has shifted elsewhere, subsequent budget allocations are not expanded in response to changing costs, and the operating personnel of the mental hospital gradually find themselves forced to get by on inadequate budgets. Eventually, a spirit of resignation characterizes the higher echelons of the institutional staff, and this attitude tends to permit the lower members of the hospital hierarchy to get by in any way they can.

Ironically, in the end, the patients and ward aides may come to "take over" the day-to-day life of the hospital, determining the quality of life on the psychiatric wards in ways that the higher echelons of the administrative staff find virtually impossible to change.

Furnishings in the psychiatric wards often meet only minimal standards of adequacy and neatness. There may not even be bedside tables for personal belongings; and even if there were, the fear of other disturbed patients rummaging through them would be constant. Some patients carry about with them a bundle of their most prized possessions for safekeeping.

In the spring of 1969, to check on numerous negative reports on conditions in Chicago's mental hospitals for the Better Government Association, reporter Kevin Mosley posed as a person suffering from suicidal tendencies and spent five days in the Chicago State mental hospital. He found fear of theft and violence among the inmates. On his first night he reported:

I knew the other inmates felt the same way. I could see pillows raised with their belongings pushed under them. I became aware of three young men laughing among themselves.

The leader was about twenty-three. He wore bright yellow bell bottom slacks with an orange sweater.

I remembered that I had not been searched after being admitted. No one looked in my pockets. My red canvas bag was never inspected.

The idea frightened me. If I wasn't searched neither were the other inmates. If I could conceal a knife or gun so could they.

Also I had not been asked to identify myself. They accepted the name I used. No fingerprints were taken.

What better place for a wanted man to hide than in a mental hospital?

I watched the three men as they laughed. I wondered if they would attack me.

The leader yelled to the old man, "Quit making so much noise, you drunk."

"Leave me alone, I don't want trouble. I'm trying to dry out. I don't have anything."

Ten minutes later I heard him being punched in the chest. It sounded like a wet paper bag being slapped against a wall.

The other inmates remained silent as the old man was beaten. The robber took a package of cigarets. That was all he had.

Suddenly the dormitory lights flashed. It was the attendant. "If you guys don't shut up now I'll give you all shots. Now shut up or you'll be tied to bed."

The ward became silent. I fell asleep.[20]

Later Mosley described direct violence attempted on him by a patient.

It was in A-2 that an inmate attempted to strong arm me three times. Once he tried to take the wrist watch. The other times he made a grab for my bag. I pushed him away.

Two hours later the same inmate was strapped to a bed in the dayroom in front of the nursing station. He attempted to beat up a patient about 60.

I never learned his name. But he was about 22. The staff kept him heavily drugged. He never spoke.[21]

The Chicago hospitals appear to have been in an especially poor state and not at all representative of all mental institutions. But in any case, such an atmosphere is particularly hard for middle-class patients. Some of Mosley's observations testify to his deep shock. When the ward was cleaned the inmates were removed to the dayroom. He reported:

The dayroom contained about 40 men. The only question asked was, "Do you have a cigaret?"

The older inmates borrowed cigarets from the new arrivals.

The windows looked onto a parking lot. Several of the windows were broken. A television rested on a table. The wires had been pulled out. A piano stood near the door. The keys had been damaged. Another table contained three magazines.

After everyone was in the dayroom the door was locked. This was done so the attendant could mop the floors

The room did not have a washroom An inmate needed to use the washroom. He pounded on the door. No one answered.

Another inmate yelled, "Use the floor. I do." [22]

The facilities were terribly overcrowded and one day at bedtime Mosley found that there were not enough beds.

I sensed a difference in the ward. The patients were restless. Later I began to feel the same restlessness.

Patients awoke at 6 A.M. and retired about 9:30 P.M. Between those hours they have nothing to do. The patients sat in the yellow arm chairs that encircled the dayroom.

Some watched television from morning to night. I could see them twisting in their chairs, hear their feet shuffling the floor.

During the day A-2 had acquired five new patients. However it wasn't until bedtime we learned that there weren't enough beds.

The five new patients were led to the women's dormitory. An attendant knocked on the door, "Cover up girls. I have some men with me."

When the door was opened I was stunned by the odor and heat. The room was like a steam bath. The smell of unwashed humans hung in the air like damp clothes.

"Each patient take an empty bed and push it into your dorm," the attendant ordered. I tried not to breathe as I pushed the steel bed.[23]

For the many patients who come from lower-class neighborhoods and poor families, the barren atmosphere of the hospital may be no different from their previous experience. In fact, it may be an improvement in many respects. For the patient who lived alone in a rooming house with only an electric hot plate for cooking and shared a bath along with six other tenants, the hospital may appear as a larger, cleaner, more sumptious home, even though he must share the bathroom with fifty other patients. Here meals are prepared for him three times a day (he may have eaten only once a day before) and the sheets on the bed are changed regularly (if he had had sheets, they were probably seldom clean). Previously lonely, in the hospital he may meet other patients in his age group with whom he can talk. He may even discover that some patients come from the same ethnic background and the same vicinity.

Nevertheless, as Stanton and Schwartz emphasize, adjusting to the hospital is a learning process for the patient. He must accept its peculiar pattern of rules, restrictions, and freedoms, accept removal from society, depend upon strangers, and respond to the staff's conception of what is therapeutic for him.[24]

Hospitalization has a depersonalizing effect on the patient. He moves into an authoritarian setting in which all decisions are made for him. All responsibility for himself and others is taken away so that he is left without incentive. The patient may lose weight even though he takes meals in the dining room or cafeteria three times a day and, in addition, has free access to the hospital canteen. Everything is routinized. He must follow the schedule that is ordered for him. He awakens at a certain time, washes in the same room with other patients, dresses and sleeps at a certain time in the same room. Medications, treatment, and recreation are all prescribed for him by the ward physician.

Throughout the twenty-four hour period the patient is under observation by members of the treatment team.

This depersonalizing effect simultaneously fosters in the patient a feeling of dependence. He becomes dependent on patients as well as staff members for gratification of all his needs. The longer he remains in the hospital the more dependent he grows.

Because of the large number of patients in relation to the staff, little attention is given to the patient's individual needs. This is contrary to the ideal of personal treatment stressed in the patient–psychiatrist relationship. Where one psychiatrist or physician is in charge of several hundred patients the possibility of the psychiatrist talking to the patient for more than fifteen to thirty minutes once or twice a week is not likely. In hospitals where a good proportion of the physicians are foreign born and can barely speak English the obstacles to communication with the patient in a meaningful fashion are almost insuperable. When a few staff members have to care for hundreds of patients a feeling of frustration and a "what's the use?" attitude often develop.

It is very easy under such circumstances for the atmosphere of the mental hospital to degenerate into the kind of concentration camp typified by the Chicago State mental hospital:

A pattern of violence at Chicago State hospital, including a torch murder, a scalding death under a bathroom shower, sexual attacks and aggravated assault, was charged in indictments returned today by the county grand jury.

Seven indictments naming 10 employees, former employees, or patients were returned before presiding Judge Joseph A. Power.

An official investigation was launched following disclosure of the violence in a series of articles in *Chicago Today*.

Murder indictments named Paul Aschfort, 26, and Ben Compton, 38, patients; and Larry Jackson, 22, a former patient. They are accused of setting fire to Anita Schectman, 46, another patient, last February 16, because she resisted their advances.

All the crimes alleged in the indictments were committed at the mental institution or at the Tinley Park mental health facility.

The other indictments and the accused persons are:

Dorothy Simmons, psychiatric aid, charged with involuntary manslaughter. She is accused of placing William Bauman, 78, a wheelchair patient, under a scalding shower August 18 and not removing him until an hour later. Bauman died the same day.

Allan Spenser, lieutenant of security guards at Tinley Park, and two fellow guards, Robert Craig and Norman Wiggins, charged with aggravated battery. They are accused of punching and kicking a patient, Carlton Edwards, 44, on June 17, 1968, as he awaited transfer to Elgin State hospital. Edwards died the following day.

Frank Marzec, 30, a patient also charged with aggravated battery. He is accused of beating a wheelchair patient, Sarah Bleeker, 85, last March 29 when she refused to give him a cigaret.

Taft Lewis, a patient, charged with attempted murder. He allegedly stole an auto on the Chicago State grounds and deliberately ran down another patient, Patricia Heth, 22, last May 23. She suffered leg injuries.

Tommy Coleman, 30, charged with rape. A former laundry worker at Chicago State, he is accused of raping a 23-year-old patient last April 6, and attempting to rape the same woman April 17.[25]

The conditions in the Chicago State mental hospital are extreme and, in the present authors' experience, in no way paralleled with the Minnesota state hospitals with which the authors are directly familiar. Minnesota is fortunate in having a fine scientist and humanist as Medical Director of the Department of Public Welfare. When David J. Vail read Goffman's study *Asylums* in 1961, he immediately undertook a review of the "dehumanizing" practices in the Minnesota state mental hospital system.[26] He and his colleagues (particularly Richard Ames) developed a check list to determine the extent of depersonalization in the mental institutions operated by the state. On September 9, 1963, Dr. Vail convoked Minnesota's first Institutional Assembly on the Problem of Dehumanization. Some 200 persons from the state's mental institutions attended. Later state meetings took place in 1963, 1964, and 1965. An attack on the problem of depersonalization in the state's mental institutions was initiated, and has vigilantly continued ever since. However, the estimate of Morris and Charlotte Schwartz still seems to be fair.

The Schwartzes are convinced that, under any circumstances, the patient's low status in the hospital and his immersion in a sick context with other patients have a negative effect on the individual. A caste-like line develops between patients and staff; the patient treated like an untouchable is more apt to worsen rather than improve as a result of the example of other patients.[27]

DEVELOPMENT OF A PATIENT CULTURE

Goffman was of the opinion that the mental patient had the opportunity, at least for the time, to practice before all groups "the amoral art of shamelessness." This, presumably, means that he is without culture—norms, standards, traditions, shared sentiments and the like. But students have discovered that a patient culture appears on every ward regardless of the classification of patients. As a matter of fact, in another essay in the same collection, "The Underlife of a Public Institution," Goffman documents the patient culture in institutions with which he was acquainted.

Among expedients (Goffman calls them "make-do's") that patients devise to make institutional life easier are such practices as laying out clothes to dry on radiators; sleeping on pillows made up of rolled newspapers, clothes, or shoes; using paper cups for ashtrays and spittoons; and substituting toilet paper for kleenex. The system was utilized by patients in a variety of ways. In order to call the ward doctor's attention to himself, a patient could feign illness or refuse to comply with the rules. In the cafeteria, food such as meat, cheese, bread, and fruit could be pocketed and later consumed as midnight snacks on the ward; milk was often carried off in empty bottles or cans. If free cigarettes were being distributed by a visiting volunteer group, some patients would stand in line over and over again. Other patients would poke through the garbage dump for usable items such as empty boxes, bottles or cans, old dishes, and magazines. Another means of "working" the system was to arrange transferral to another ward for whatever privileges were desired. In one case the patients on the desired ward were friendlier, and in another case the cloth on the pool table was in better condition.[28]

Every ward has its leader, bully, gossip, and helper, as well as its cliques, buddies, favorites, and outcasts. Patients compete with one another for attention or privileges from the staff. At the same time they tend to protect each other from outsiders, and also to help one another. For example, those able to go to the dining room bring back snacks for the bedridden patients; active patients roll cigarettes for their regressed fellows; and some patients share their gifts of candy and fruit with those who never have visitors.

Cliques form to play cards or to sit around and gossip about the staff and other patients. A favorite topic of conversation is the private lives of the staff, especially the doctors, social workers, psychologists, and the director.

Cliques devise means of systematically obtaining information of value to them. When new patients are admitted to a ward, a clique member usually interrogates him informally, and then passes on coveted information to his fellow clique members, leaving the rest of the ward in the dark. A given clique usually shares the same attitudes toward the staff and the rules of the hospital and are quick to raise complaints. Cliques help their members avoid discharge. Or if a member aspires to provisional discharge, they may, for example, tell him: "Don't tell the doctor that you're hearing voices."

THE OPEN-DOOR POLICY

In the 1950s, an open-door policy was initiated in many of our mental hospitals (except for geriatric and extremely disturbed wards). The objective was to remove as many of the restraints on the movement of mental patients as possible. This procedure has led to greater patient contact with the community and changed attitudes on the part of both patients and community. For the patient it has meant more freedom to come and go; it has given him a sense of responsibility for his actions and has tended to draw him out from the tight confines of the ward. All this has hastened socialization and his recovery. For the community, the image of the state hospital as a cold, impenetrable fortress has begun to fade. Family fears of permanent institutionalization have been allayed as patients are permitted earlier and more frequent home visits. Although some communities have viewed the open-door policy with alarm, their anxieties have been dispelled with the realization that the number of harmful incidents involving patients on home visits or provisional discharge has not considerably increased.

NOTES

1. Jaroslav Hasek, *The Good Soldier: Schweik,* trans. Paul Selver, pp. 29–30.

2. James Spaulding, "State Hospital's New Treatment Boosts Hope for Schizophrenics," *The Milwaukee Journal* (June 8, 1969).

3. Erving Goffman, *Asylums: Essays on the Social Situation of Mental Patients and Other Inmates,* pp. 127–169.

4. Ibid., p. 130.

5. Ibid., p. 132.

6. Ibid., pp. 133–134.

7. Ibid., p. 135.

8. Ibid., p. 139; see also, Harold Garfinkel, "Conditions of Successful Degradation Ceremonies," *American Journal of Sociology* 61 (1956), 420–424.

9. Goffman, *Asylums,* p. 140.

10. Ibid., p. 148.

11. Ibid., p. 150.

12. Ibid., p. 159.

13. Ibid., p. 165.

14. Ibid., pp. 165–166.

15. Ibid., p. 166.

16. Ibid., p. 167.

17. Ibid., p. 169.

18. Kirson Weinberg and H. Warren Dunham, *The Culture of the State Mental Hospital* (Detroit: Wayne State University Press, 1960).

19. Alfred H. Stanton and Morris S. Schwartz, *The Mental Hospital, A Study of Institutional Participation in Psychiatric Illness and Treatment,* pp. 170ff.

20. Kevin Mosley, "What It's Like Inside Mental Hospital Here," *Chicago Today,* May 4, 1969, p. 3.

21. Ibid., May 5, p. 20.

22. Ibid., p. 3.

23. Ibid., p. 20.

24. Stanton and Schwartz, *The Mental Hospital,* p. 170.

25. *Chicago Today,* June 19, 1969, pp. 1, 4.

26. David J. Vail, *Dehumanization and the Institutional Career* (Springfield, Illinois: Charles C. Thomas, 1966), pp. 74–77.

27. Morris S. Schwartz and Charlotte Green Schwartz, *Social Approaches to Mental Patient Care,* pp. 200–201.

28. Goffman, *Asylums,* pp. 208–214.

6

MENTAL DISORDERS, TREATMENT METHODS, AND THE THERAPEUTIC COMMUNITY

The type of treatment offered patients in a mental hospital depends in large measure on the size of the hospital in relation to the size of its staff. When one doctor is in charge of 400 to 500 patients, it is humanly impossible to conduct individual psychotherapy sessions except with a few select patients. In his account of the much overcrowded Chicago State mental hospital, Kevin Mosley described a group therapy session.

I was told to attend a group therapy meeting. There were seven patients and a special worker. The meeting lasted half an hour.

The main problem discussed was how to feed a dog belonging to a woman patient. The patient claimed she was concerned about the dog. He had been home alone for 5 days.

"I think he might of starved to death," she said, "I want to go home and see about him."

I watched the social worker. She was about 25. Her sandy colored hair was cut short.

She listened to the patients. She gave firm answers. She did not lie to them. She appeared sincere and dedicated.[1]

Shortage of ward staff also limits certain treatments. If only two ward aides and one nurse are responsible for one hundred patients, it may be impossible to give insulin shock therapy to more than a small percentage of the inmates.

Another factor that determines the type of treatment patients receive is finances. Unfortunately, state legislatures are reluctant to allocate funds for mental patient care, although they do a considerable amount of investigation into the deficiencies of mental hospitals during political campaigns. If greater funds were allocated for more staff and equipment, these deficiencies could be remedied; interesting and beneficial programs—in psychodrama, group therapy, and individual therapy—as well as the most modern concepts in care—could be implemented.

The following discussion covers the types and causes of mental illness and a variety of treatment given to mental patients in state and private psychiatric hospitals. The smaller the hospital, the more likely a patient will receive treatment involving a close relationship with a therapist. In large state hospitals, patients are more apt to be treated with drugs and electric shock and group therapy, since these treatments can be given to many patients by only a few staff members in a short time.

Determining the type of treatment for each patient is the patient's behavior. His ability to function adequately on the ward, in the cafeteria, on the hospital grounds, and at social functions all affect his treatment. As he begins to improve, his therapy is modified, with his release from the hospital as the ultimate aim.

THE CAUSES OF MENTAL ILLNESS

Mental illness is not one but a category of problems. The major distinctions usually drawn by psychiatry is that between neuroses and psychoses.

Neuroses are emotional disturbances which are generally less severe, though not always less crippling, than psychoses; neuroses involve neither major personality disorganization nor major distortion or misinterpretation of external reality. By major symptoms, neuroses are classified as: anxiety neurosis (excessive anxiety and panic, often associated with somatic symptoms); depersonalization (feelings of estrangement from the self, body, or surroundings); depressive neurosis (excessive depression); hypochondriachal neurosis (preoccupation with the body and fear of presumed disease); hysterical neurosis (psychogenic loss or disorder of function—blindness, deafness or impairment of bodily functions, or dissociative responses like amnesia, somnambulism, fugue, or multiple personality); neurasthenic neurosis (chronic weakness, exhaustion, and so on); compulsive neurosis (persistent unwanted ideas, urges, or emotions); and phobic neurosis (intense unrealistic fear of an object or situation).

Psychoses are major mental disorders of organic or emotional origin in which the individual's ability to respond, think, communicate, interpret reality, and behave is so impaired that he cannot cope with the ordinary demands of life. Among major types of psychoses are: schizophrenia (disturbances of thought, emotion, and behavior involving misinterpretations of reality, delusions, hallucinations, inappropriateness of emotional response, loss of empathy with others, etc.); manic-depressive illness (major affective disorders involving extreme alternations of mood, sometimes subdivided into depressed, circular, and manic types); reactive depression (morbid sadness, dejection, and melancholia involving loss of capacity to evaluate reality); organic brain syndrome (a disorder, caused by an impairment of brain tissue function, characterized by disorientation, loss of memory, and impairment of ability to learn, think, calculate, and adjudge).

These disorders overlap with one another to a great degree. When August B. Hollingshead and Fredrick C. Redlich studied the relations between social class and mental illness, they refused to define types of mental illness. They did find a statistically significant difference in the social class of people diagnosed as neurotic and those diagnosed as psychotic, but the possibility remained that this variation was an artifact of diagnosis rather than of disease.[2]

Three general types of causes underlie, either singly or conjointly, various forms of mental illness. They are: physiological, individual developmental (psychological), and social.

Physiolpgical Causes

Some forms of mental illness are traceable to brain damage incurred in birth accidents or later head injuries. Moreover, disease (syphilis is the most famous example) may result in brain damage. In the organic cycle, old age in some persons is accompanied by a hardening of the arteries of the brain, resulting in various forms of senile psychosis. Prolonged and excessive use of alcohol and drugs may also result in damage to the brain and nervous system.

In this connection, it should be noted that at present very little is known about the workings of the brain and the role of heredity in the incidence of mental illness. There have been some studies of identical twins who through some accident were raised apart in very different social and psychological environments. Such cases provide natural experiments in which heredity is held constant and psychological and social conditions are varied. Some of these studies have reported almost uncanny instances where identical twins raised in very different surroundings nevertheless have broken down with the same forms of mental illness at approximately the same times.

Individual Developmental (Psychological) Causes

Developmental theories of mental illness trace the disease to defects of personality or personal behavior. These, in turn, are traceable to individual failures of socialization. The Freudians have popularized a wide variety of individual developmental explanations. Freud himself assumed that the normal personality develops through a number of stages in which the pleasure drives (libido) of the individual are successively shifted to increasingly more comprehensive objects in the external world. He believed that the normal personality undergoes an oral phase, an anal phase, and, finally, a genital phase. During the course of this last phase, the individual's sexual impulses, which were first fixed on the parent of the opposite sex, are eventually transferred to an appropriate person in the world. For a variety of reasons, in the course of this successive development an individual may regress to some earlier stage of development and displace his drives onto all sorts of inappropriate objects.

No attempt will be made here to review all of the various developmental theories of mental illness, but it is worth noting that new theories are continually being introduced. One of the most recent is that of Thomas Szasz. He visualizes human social life as consisting of a series of "games" and argues that "the game model of human behavior appears well suited for unifying psychology, sociology and ethics." [3] In times of rapid change, from this point of view, new games constantly replace the old; the individual who cannot keep up tries to play the new games with old rules no longer appropriate.

> Loss of a sense of satisfying personal identity is linked to *modern man's inevitable loss of the "games" learned early in life.*
>
> *This fundamental game-conflict leads to various problems in living. It is these that the modern psychotherapist is usually called on to "treat."* [4]

There are, Szasz believes, three types of game conflict. One is typified by the individual's inability to forget old rules. Hence his refusal to play the new games is a "strike" against living. This produces disability attacks of malingering, hysteria, dependency reactions and so on. A second form of game conflict involves the imposition of old goals and rules on new games and is characterized by transference neurosis or neurotic character structure. The third form of game conflict derives from the realization that men can play no transcendentally valid game. This results in a general disappointment-reaction and the conviction that no game is worth playing.

Social Causes

It is possible that, over and beyond physiological and developmental factors in mental illness, social factors may be involved. One of the most common social situations which may place sufficient stress on individuals to cause mental breakdown is combat. Roy R. Grinker and John P. Spiegel have observed:

> The environment of combat produces an almost indescribable combination of physical and emotional stress on the soldier. It possesses an insane, nightmare quality, like a bad dream which keeps recurring. This is due not only to the senseless destruction and incredible waste of battle, but also to its interminable nature; it cannot be stopped or brought under control.[5]

Grinker and Spiegel also observed that the combat stress situations of ground troops and of fliers are quite different. Footsoldiers are often forced to make long marches with little sleep and must be prepared to go into battles lasting many days. Food and water are often inadequate. Bathing, shaving, and similar luxuries must be forgotten. Mud, rain and insects are a constant annoyance. Danger may be continuous and constant with no way, day or night, to escape the sounds of battle. Air combat crews, by contrast, alternate between periods of remarkably intense danger over the target and periods of relative peace far from immediate danger and the noise of battle. But they may have to endure long periods en route in uncomfortable positions with little to mitigate the build-up of tension. Somewhat different patterns of mental breakdown tend to characterize each type.

Hollingshead and Redlich set out to examine the relation between social class and mental illness in New Haven, Connecticut. They found that New Haven has a distinct class structure, that each class is characterized by definite types of mental illness, and that each reacts to it in different ways. Hence the treatment of mental illness varies by class.

They found five major classes in New Haven. When individuals were queried as to their class membership, they gave the following responses: upper-middle class, 4 percent; middle class, 18 percent; lower-middle class, 22 percent; working class, 53 percent, and lower class, 3 percent.[6] The major characteristics of the classes may be summarized as follows:

Class I. Community's business and professional leaders, college graduates, and high income-earners, viewed as "best" in community.

Class II. The community nouveau riche. Males in managerial positions and lower-ranking professions. High school graduates with some college.

Class III. Middle class status strivers pressing on class II. Males in salaried administrative and clerical pursuits. Some own small businesses. High school graduates. Desire to live in better neighborhoods.

Class IV. Skilled and semiskilled employees, sales workers. Some high school. Of partly assimilated ethnic stock.

Class V. Semiskilled and unskilled. Many first-generation immigrants. Tenement dwellers. Median years of school, six.[7]

Hollingshead found that the number of mentally ill persons classified as neurotic was highest for classes I and II and decreased systematically to class V; the number of mentally ill classed as psychotic was just the reverse, highest for class V and lowest for classes I and II.[8] For purposes of analysis mentally ill persons were classified by diagnostic category into affective psychotic (the highest percentage was found in classes I–II); psychotic as a result of alcoholism and drug addiction (the highest percentage was found in class II); and organic psychotic (the highest percentage was found in class V). Each class had approximately the same percentages of schizophrenia and senile psychosis.[9]

Hollingshead and Redlich concluded that every kind of mental and emotional disorder occurs in all classes but that they occur in different proportions, indicating that social and cultural influences do play a role in the various types of psychiatric disorder. They felt that some of the percentage variations might be due to the differences in the quality of hospitals catering to each class level. Cultural and social conditions may affect the content of mental illness; for example, some observers have noted that Japanese patients changed their paranoid delusion of being Emperor Hirohito to being General MacArthur after the fall of Japan in World War II. Finally, they found that perceptions of mental illness and conceptions of normal and abnormal vary from class to class. But while social class significantly affects the prevalence of treated disorders in the population, Hollingshead and Redlich conclude that evidence pointing to class status as an essential and necessary condition in the etiology of mental disorders is still insufficient.[10]

The report on the second part of the New Haven research study by Jerome K. Myers and Bertram H. Roberts complements the work of Hollingshead and Redlich.[11] Meyers and Roberts attempted to ascertain the influence of social and class-related factors and class mobility on the development of mental illness. They focused on white adult patients from classes III (middle class status-strivers) and V (semi- and unskilled workers) who fell into two diagnostic groups: schizophrenia and psychoneurosis. They sought to discover differences in the social, psychic, and mobility factors of the two groups, and differences in the experiences of the schizophrenic and neurotic patients at each class level and similarities in the socio-dynamic experiences of schizophrenic and neurotic patients that cut across class lines. The first hypothesis was supported; the second was partially supported. Between classes III and V differences were found in family roles, sex roles, developmental histories, external community pressures, and attitudes toward mental illness, therapy, and symptomology. It was found that mobility was associated with the development of psychiatric disorders in class III, but not in class V.

METHODS OF TREATMENT

Mental illness covers such a variety of conditions and degrees that it is difficult to set up some sort of simple, logical scheme for the review of the many utilized methods of treatment. Furthermore, methods of treatment vary according to type of illness.

Temporary Physical Means

When a mentally ill patient is in an extreme state of agitation, little can be done for him until he is calmed down.

Hydrotherapy uses water applications to subdue excited and apprehensive mental patients. One of the oldest methods of treatment, it is known to have been employed in some form by the ancient Greeks. In addition to its sedative effect on the patient, it can also be used as a stimulant. Hydrotherapy has long been employed in many state and county mental hospitals but its use is currently diminishing; in part this is due to the treatment's heavy demands on staff attention and to the introduction of the tranquilizing drugs, which have reduced the need for this type of therapy. But for those patients who are unable to take drugs, hydrotherapy can be beneficial.

Among the types of hydrotherapy currently in use are vapor and saline baths, sitz baths, douches, needle showers and sprays, wet packs, and continuous tubs. Most widely used are the wet pack and continuous tub. In the wet pack method, the patient is wrapped tightly in a wet sheet which has been wrung out in water, the temperature of which may vary from 48 degrees to 97 degrees. With this method, some patients grow calm within 10 minutes, although more excited patients take a longer time to be subdued. In the continuous tub method, the patient rests on a canvas hammock in a large, long tub filled with water (96 to 97 degrees) that is continuously circulated. The tub bath lasts about an hour and is repeated as often as necessary. It has proven very effective in reducing tension and great excitement, and its sedative effect lasts a long time afterward.

Drugs are increasingly being used in the temporary control of mental states. Drugs have always been used to treat the mentally ill, but in recent years some have proved particularly effective. These new drugs are the major tranquilizers and the anti-depressants.

The major tranquilizers—chlorpromazine (Thorazine), reserpine (Serpasil), meprobamate (Miltown, Equanil), promazine (Sparine), hydroxyzine (Atarax), azacyclonal (Frenquel)— are effective with such psychotic patients as schizophrenics, senile psychotics, and manic-depressive psychotics. These drugs tend to calm patients by decreasing anxiety, delusions, agitation, and hallucinations.

Anti-depressant drugs—methylphenidate (Ritalin), amitriptyline (Elavil), imipramine (Tofranil), tranylcypromine (Parnate), and isocarboxazid (Marplan)—are successful with patients suffering from involutional psychosis, senile psychosis, reactive depression, and the depressive periods of manic-depressive psychosis. These drugs help reduce depression, suicidal tendencies, withdrawal, and delusions.

For unknown reasons, some patients respond better to some drugs than to others. The duration of treatment and size of dosage will also vary with each individual. Some patients can get along without constant use of these drugs while others must take them continuously to avoid return of their symptoms. On occasion these drugs are administered alone, but they are most often used in conjunction with individual, group, or milieu therapy.

An exciting recent development is a drug still under study by the Food and Drug Administration, lithium carbonate. In the estimate of Surgeon General Dr. William H. Stewart, it has promise of being the best specific agent yet found for the treatment of any mental disease. Thousands of patients in Europe and Australia have been taking the drug for a decade without apparent negative results. And Professor Paul Blachly of the University of Oregon Medical School has estimated that, if available, it might have prevented as many as 24,000 suicides in the United States in recent years. Lithium seems to be particularly good at modifying states of depression and offers the possibility of milder and shorter attacks with prolonged use. In addition, lithium seems to be effective in the treatment of manic states, epileptic attacks, certain forms of schizophrenia, premenstrual tension in women, and some character disorders in teenagers. In Denmark, Doctors Mogens Schou and Poul Baastrup put eighty-eight Danish women who had suffered two or more manic-depressive episodes in the preceding twenty-four months under lithium therapy for twelve months and observed them for seven years following. After lithium therapy, their relapses occurred only every sixty to eighty-five months and were of shorter duration. Women not on lithium spent an average of thirteen weeks a year in a psychotic state, while those women under lithium treatment spent an average of less than two weeks a year in a psychotic state.

In some ways, drugs are more flexible than hydrotherapy techniques, for they can be used to excite patients as well as to calm them down. Moreover, they are far easier to administer. This, in fact, may be one of their drawbacks, for a harried hospital staff may try to ease its problems by the routine mass distribution of tranquilizers.

It goes almost without saying that some types of mental illness (such as senile dementia) may receive no treatment other than the routine administration of tranquilizers.

Permanent Physical Means

Hydrotherapy and drugs only induce temporary changes in mental states. More drastic physical modifications of the behavior of the mentally ill are induced by a variety of techniques ranging from shock treatment to lobotomy.

In the 1930s, the use of insulin to treat schizophrenic patients was successfully attempted by Manfred Joshua Sakel (1900–1957). Injections of insulin cause the blood sugar level to fall, producing a state of coma. About one-half hour later, glucose is given to awaken the patient. After arousal, many patients are more rational, suffer fewer delusions, and experience a diminished state of tension. This treatment results in shorter hospital stays. Sakel's method has been used by many hospitals and clinics. Today, however, it is not used as frequently because the procedure requires about five hours of close supervision by the hospital medical and nursing staff. It has been replaced to a great extent by electric shock therapy.

Electric shock therapy, developed by L. Bini and Ugo Cerletti in 1937–1938, involves a machine that can send a safe amount of current through a patient's brain. This method of treatment requires less preparation and supervision than insulin therapy. It is also easier to administer. The patient's anxiety about the oncoming seizure induced by the electric shock is lessened by the amnesia created by the electric shock shortly before the convulsion. Electric shock therapy has proved to be one of the most succesful methods of treating psychoses, and reduces significantly the acuteness of depression. For depressed, melancholic, and neurotic patients it has shortened duration of hospitalization.

At about the same time that electric shock therapy was being developed, lobotomy was first performed. In 1936 Dr. Antonio C. de Egas Moniz (1874–1955), a Portuguese neurologist, and Almeida Lima, a Portuguese surgeon, performed the operation known as leukotomy on a group of their chronic patients. The operation itself consists in cutting the fibers in the motor areas of the frontal lobes using a scalpel called a leukotome. It necessitates the cutting of a trephine opening near the vertex of the skull; another technique, developed later, makes an opening through the orbital bone plate above the eye (transorbital operation). This operation may result in some improvement.

Many psychiatrists have opposed this type of therapy because the lobotomy patient loses a depth of emotional experience and is a changed person following surgery, sometimes reduced to mere vegetative existence. In any case, rehabilitation is always a long, slow process. But many neurosurgeons and doctors in state institutions, especially those dealing with chronic mental patients, have favored it because it reduces anxiety to such a great extent. By 1951, 20,000 lobotomies had been performed in the United States. This number, however, has declined in the last decade, and this type of surgery continues to be the subject of much controversy.

Psychoanalysis

The development of psychoanalysis is familiar to all modern students. In the nineteenth century it was discovered that hypnosis could sometimes bring about positive, although seldom permanent changes in the behavior of schizophrenic and hysterical patients. Starting with these findings, Freud proceeded to isolate techniques that dispensed with hypnosis and apparently could sometimes secure more permanent and deep-seated behavioral changes.

Psychoanalysis, as developed by Freud, is a method for the exploration and synthesis of patterns in emotional thinking and development. Its main concern is the conflict between instinctive drives and parental demands and the effect of this conflict on emotional development. Painful repressed experiences driven into the subconscious can later in life emerge in the distorted form of mental disorders. Through the use of "free association" techniques, the psychoanalyst attempts to release repressed experiences into the conscious where the patient can more easily deal with them. "Free association" involves encouraging the patient to talk about anything that comes to mind, until he finally is able to freely relate repressed thoughts and feelings.

Dream analysis is another method used by psychoanalysts to uncover the patient's hidden emotions. Although dreams may sound distorted and fantastic, their content often reveals much that otherwise remains buried in the subconscious. Characters in the dreams, for example, may be disguised versions of the patient's parents, siblings, or himself; what these characters say or do reflect the patient's disguised attitudes toward them. The psychoanalyst, through his interpretation of dreams, helps the patient recognize the true nature of his feelings.

During psychotherapy the patient may repress anxiety-provoking or painful experiences. This "resistance," or blockage of thoughts, can be overcome with the aid of the psychoanalyst. As the course of treatment continues, the patient often comes to regard the therapist as though he were the father or mother of his childhood. This phenomenon is called "transference" and is a vital factor in psychoanalysis. Instead of being met with disapproval or rejection, however, the patient is treated with understanding and tolerance by his surrogate "parent." Because he can freely express his emotions of hostility and guilt in a therapeutic setting, his mental symptoms diminish. Once expressed and understood, the patient's feelings of guilt and fear can be replaced by healthy attitudes toward his therapist and people with whom he lives and works.

Psychoanalysis has proved most effective with patients suffering from hysteria, obsessional states, and phobias, as well as with some depressed patients. The psychoanalyst's training is lengthy and difficult; treatment is of long duration and costly. But the results of psychoanalysis are in many instances worth the time and expense involved.

Only a fraction of the nation's mentally ill are receiving intensive individual psychoanalytic help. In an article written for *Playboy,* published in October 1969, Morton Hunt estimates that only about 1,700 of the nation's physicians (10 percent of the members of the American Psychiatric Association) have undergone advanced training and become practicing analysts. In addition, about 700 psychologists, a few social workers, and others have undergone special psychoanalytic training. America's less than 3,000 well-trained psychoanalysts treat on the average only 8 patients at a time in individual analysis. Hence there are under 24,000 persons in the country currently undergoing psychoanalysis, or one-half of one percent of the total Americans currently receiving some form of psychological or psychiatric treatment. This, in turn, is about one-tenth of one percent of the Americans who suffer from any major or minor mental disorder. Moreover, when one takes into account the fact that therapy today takes four to five years and costs a total of about $20,000, it is evident that it is a form of treatment available only to the relatively well-to-do. Moreover, many practitioners maintain that psychoanalysis is likely to benefit only the relatively healthy, articulate, and fairly successful patient. The significance of psychoanalysis in the treatment of the mentally ill lies primarily in its role as pioneer of the modern forms of individual therapy.

From the earliest days of the development of psychoanalysis various other non-Freudian therapies have appeared, partly supplementing, partly opposing Freud's theories and techniques. The first variations appear in the works of Carl Jung, Otto Rank, and Alfred Adler. More recently, an array of therapies, described by their adherents as neo-Freudian, have won significant followings in America from traditional Freudians. It should be noted that Freudianism has had a profound influence on many other therapies which do not claim derivation from the orthodox position.

Hypnotherapy and Narcosynthesis

To many, the major difficulty with psychoanalysis is that it is only effective with neurotic, not psychotic, individuals. From this perspective, psychoanalysis is of no use to the very ill patient. This has led some to explore the possibility that hypnosis, which stimulated the development of psychoanalysis in the first place, might hold open wider potentials. The resistance of some patients to hypnosis, however, has led to the use of drugs known as "truth serums." These compounds lower the individual's inhibitions, enabling him to talk freely about matters he would resist if fully conscious.

The technique of narcosynthesis, a form of psychotherapy utilizing drugs, was perfected by Grinker and Spiegel; it was first used for the treatment of psychically disturbed individuals suffering from battle fatigue and breakdown under prolonged periods of stress during World War II. This type of therapy is used in cases where the patient has a mental block so that he is unable to talk about himself. Amytal sodium, the drug used by Grinker and Spiegel in their experiments, is administered intravenously to relax the patient to the point where he is able to discuss his problems freely. During the procedure it is essential that the patient be kept quiet and in a prone position on the bed. As the drug is slowly being injected into the vein, both patient and physician are talking to each other. The reason for the discussion with the patient during administration of the drug is to maintain contact and make sure that the drug does not operate like a sleeping pill. It is also essential to gauge the dosage sufficient to lower inhibitions without losing contact. The questions may then become more serious and repressed emotional material may burst passionately into expression. These sessions may be profoundly exhausting to the patient, but his range of self-expression is widened and deepened.

Although remarkably effective results were obtained by Grinker and Spiegel, this is obviously a highly expensive therapeutic procedure. Moreover, its most effective application apparently requires very special skill.

Behavior Therapy

Behavioristic psychology deals only with observable behavior. Developed by Ivan Pavlov, it became popular in America during the 1920s. The behaviorists, whose basic concept of learning is equated with conditioning, found that they could produce the equivalent of neurotic behavior by use of conflicting conditioning. If, for example, a dog is conditioned to expect food at the sound of a bell, but receives an electric shock instead, his resultant behavior will be confused. B. F. Skinner of Harvard has extended the behavioristic theory of learning with his concept of "operant conditioning," and behavior therapy has been elaborated into a general method of treatment by Joseph Wolpe, a formerly Freudian psychiatrist at Philadelphia's Temple University School of Medicine.

In behavioristic psychology, forms of mental illness are viewed as "bad habits." Wolpe's basic procedure is to permit the patient to perform undesirable activity, but to give it a negative value by, for example, administering an electric shock. He also utilizes a method described as "desensitizing"; in this procedure, intense anxiety is avoided by instructing the patient to think of pleasant images at the onset of the anxiety. Albert Bandura, a psychologist at Stanford University, has extended Wolpe's desensitization method by having neurotic patients imitate nonneurotic individuals.

Neo-Freudian Therapy

Freud assigned major importance to the instinctive drives (the id) of the individual. He believed that in the course of individual development, failures to channel these drives force them to seek expression in socially and individually unacceptable ways. When these unpleasant manifestations are repressed, the instinctual energies are expressed as various neurotic substitute behaviors. Freudian therapy concentrates on the drawing out of repressed material so that it can be consciously faced.

Toward the end of his life, however, Freud became increasingly preoccupied with the problems of the conscious self (the ego) rather than the unconscious self (the id and superego). Following this lead the so-called neo-Freudians have shifted ego analysis to the forefront of their therapy. Harry Stack Sullivan, Erich Fromm, and Clara Thompson broke with orthodox Freudians in their stress on interpersonal relations rather than biographical parent–child relations, and in 1943 they formed an institute of their own, the William Alanson White Institute. Another prominent neo-Freudian, Karen Horney, made so little use of unconscious conflicts in her analyses that in 1941 she was forced out of the American Psychoanalytic Association (whose members pride themselves on adherence to the classical Freudian tradition); she established her own institute soon thereafter.

Reality Therapy

The Los Angeles psychiatrist William Glasser has developed a therapeutic procedure which, in contrast to psychoanalysis, makes the therapist's role active rather than passive. Reality therapy requires that the therapist set up an intense personal relation with the patient, set aside all inquiries into his past, and seek to persuade him to confront the implications of his present behavior. In the course of the dialogue between patient and therapist, the patient is often persuaded to act with more responsibility in his problem situations.

Client-centered Therapy

Carl Rogers was chiefly responsible for the development of client-centered therapy. Rogers believed that, in the course of his experience, the individual comes to view himself as variously brave or cowardly, aggressive or submissive, friendly or unfriendly, and so on. If his self-image more or less accords with his behavior, the individual gets along reasonably well. If, however, major discrepancies appear between his self image and behavior, he develops problems. Rogers' therapeutic technique involves establishing a warm personal relation with the patient, seeking to increase his self-understanding, and assisting him in developing a flexible realistic self-image.

There have been many additional forms of individual therapy, but, like the one described above, they are primarily confined to the private hospitals serving upper and upper-middle class circles. In various ways, however, individual therapy has influenced the methods of treatment used in state mental hospitals.

Psychodrama

Psychodrama was invented by Dr. Jacob L. Moreno, who in 1921 organized the Vienna *Stegreiftheater* (Theater of Spontaneity) as a means of treating mental illness. In 1925 psychodrama was introduced in the United States. Since that time, such other modifications as sociodrama, role playing, and analytic psychodrama have been developed.

In psychodrama, situations that present a conflict for the patient are acted out before an audience of about twenty to twenty-five staff members and patients. This type of treatment is designed to teach the patient social skills to help him solve the problems of everyday life. The actors on stage are encouraged to be spontaneous and to say and do whatever comes to mind. The problem situation and the actors are chosen by the audience, which serves as both jury and discussion group. The leader of the group may comment upon and interpret the actions of the performers from time to time. After one performance, roles may be reversed, with the patient assuming the role of therapist and vice versa. Discussion by the actors is encouraged, with each one explaining why he performed in a certain way and his reaction to the other performers.

Psychodrama has proved effective in increasing the understanding between staff and patients. It has also been used to prepare the patient for his eventual return to the community.

Group Therapy

Group psychotherapy brings several patients together with one therapist. Through involvement in new experiences, members of the group learn to modify their emotional attitudes toward themselves and each other.

Some patients are actually more at ease in a group rather than in a patient–analyst relationship. In sharing others' problems and experiences, the patient often loses his sense of shame. He can discuss his fears, voice his approval, and vent his hostilities. Some transference takes place toward other members of the group or the therapist. Group discussions may be stimulating as well as supportive and encourage the shy patient to verbalize his problems more easily.

This method of treatment is sometimes used in conjunction with individual psychotherapy. Although it has not attained the latter's status, group psychotherapy is invaluable in the larger, understaffed mental hospitals. In outpatient psychiatric clinics and community mental health centers, group psychotherapy provides specialized treatment to a large segment of the mentally ill. Group psychotherapy is also being used with adults under treatment in family agencies and with children in institutional treatment settings.

Although some feel that group therapy is useful only in relatively superficial cases, it was successfully used to treat members of the armed forces afflicted with mental disorders during World War II. Grinker and Spiegel's estimate of group therapeutic techniques points out both their values and limitations.

> When the group psychotherapeutic techniques used in military hospitals are reviewed, we find that they have several real advantages. They reincorporate the individual into a group similar to the one in which he lived and worked and where he felt strong and secure. The whole group can be reassured and given rational explanations regarding symptoms that they learn are not their exclusive burden. Common group experiences are valuable in dealing with irrational guilty feelings. Everyone can be desensitized to dangerous stimuli of combat, to which all were originally exposed. However, extensive unburdening of personal problems or personal reactions cannot be accomplished. . . . We have found in our own work that, when the patient really has personal problems to expose or develops transference attitudes which stimulate anxiety, he spontaneously seeks out the therapist for an individual interview.
>
> If all that is desired is merely an outward appearance of

unstable normality, group therapy can achieve the goal. For patients who are mildly ill, group therapy suffices, proving care be taken to separate the severely disturbed from the group as their condition becomes apparent.[12]

Grinker and Spiegel note that, to some extent, alcohol may operate like a truth serum in lowering an individual's inhibitions. During World War II, disturbed soldiers drinking in bars sometimes suddenly exploded with murderous violence at those around them. A similar and potential risk in group therapy sessions where seriously disturbed patients are present is the unleashing of an individual's suppressed violence on the group.

Since World War II, despite the skepticism of practitioners of individual forms of psychotherapy, many new forms of group therapy have developed.

T Groups

In Connecticut in 1946, a conference on the training of community leaders was attended by a variety of prominent professionals and government officials. Kurt Lewin, the group dynamics specialist, brought along four members of his research staff to study the way those at the conference behaved and interacted. When the findings of the four researchers were presented, they initiated an intense interchange that galvanized the entire conference. The conference leaders set up an institute, the National Training Laboratories, to refine and promote the techniques of group self-study. The NTL conceives of itself as engaged in sensitivity training which utilizes the form of T groups. The typical T group consists of approximately a dozen private individuals who meet with professional leaders from NTL. For up to six hours a day over a five-day period, they learn about the forces that influence the behavior of individuals and groups. The ordinary rules of conduct are suspended, and there are no lines of authority in the T group sessions. The members are on their own. Extraordinarily frank discussions typically occur and individuals are amazed at the freedom and relief that result as they reveal their deepest problems and opinions to one another. T groups are being widely used today among businessmen and other community leaders.

Encounter Groups

Encounter groups are an offshoot of T groups. At Esalen and other centers, interested individuals are assembled under the direction of individual leaders. T group participants are usually of similar background (business men, professionals, and so on); those in encounter groups are usually drawn from all walks of life. Encounter group members are inclined to lower their reserves much more rapidly and to reveal their problems, desires, and hostilities to one another much more quickly and forcefully than are members of T groups.

The Western Behavior Science Institute gathered interviews from some thousand encounter group participants. Examination of these protocols led Richard Farsen to conclude that the encounter group is a form of therapy that can succeed without a professional leader. Farson and an associate have developed a do-it-yourself kit for nonprofessional use. The kit consists of a set of tape recordings, each running about an hour and a half, that are designed to be played by a group over eight meetings. The voice on the tape makes a variety of suggestions for activities or practices found helpful in other groups; after the tapes have been played, the members are free to unburden on one another their anxieties, hostilities, and suppressed desires. The encounter tapes are manufactured by the Human Development Institute of Atlanta, a subsidiary of Bell & Howell.

Like many of the newer forms of individual therapy, the various sensitivity and encounter group therapies still remain primarily practices of the upper-middle class; in fact, they are now assuming some of the properties of a fad. Ernest Havemann, in the November 1969 issue of *Playboy,* estimates that there are no fewer than 200 schools of thought on how to make Americans less neurotic and that they employ as many as 10,000 specific techniques. Although most will be wiped away by time, some of these developments are affecting the group therapeutic practices of the mental hospitals.

Occupational, Recreational, and Industrial Therapy

Long a part of the techniques of mental hospitals, occupational, recreational, and industrial therapies provide patients with constructive activities that compose mental life and supply skills to ease the transition back into normal society.

Occupational therapy has been used both as an economic necessity and as a method of treatment in America since 1752, when patients at the Pennsylvania Hospital were given wool and flax to spin. The Quakers responsible for the establishment of this hospital believed that working steadily each day at a constructive task helped build sound character and promote good health.

Occupational therapy is used with those convalescing from physical and mental disorders. It consists of some kind of light work or recreation, such as basketweaving, leather work, or carpentry, and is designed to take the mind of the patient off himself, aid in recovery, and serve as a form of vocational training. At first, activities such as arts and crafts, games, music, and light exercise were supervised by nurses, but a professional body of therapists gradually evolved; this development culminated in 1917 with the Society for the Promotion of Occupational Therapy and the establishment of training centers for occupational therapists.

In many state and county hospitals today, patients work in the laundry, kitchen, and garden, and in general maintenance work according to their ability and needs. The length of time spent on each task is determined by the patient's physician and he is closely supervised while at work. In this manner the patient develops good work habits, a sense of responsibility, a feeling of satisfaction in contributing to the welfare of the hospital, and a sense of pride in accomplishing a meaningful task.

Recreational therapy provides a variety of activities for the patient as he improves and is able to function more adequately. Entertainment includes Saturday night dances where staff and patients may socialize, weekly movies, supervised indoor sports in the gymnasium, and stage shows presented by various civic, student, or volunteer groups. Coffee hours, a daily occurrence on the ward, sometimes involve visiting between two wards. Baseball and volleyball are favorite outdoor sports and competing teams from other community clubs may come to play against the patients. Overnight camping trips during the summer months and year-round excursions to museums, zoos, or art galleries may be conducted for the better patients. Some hospitals have well-stocked libraries with books to satisfy a variety of tastes. Also, current event clubs may meet weekly to discuss recent developments on the local and national scene.

Religious services are held regularly in the hospital chapel. Clergymen also mingle freely with patients in the wards or visit at the request of an individual patient.

Industrial therapy serves two purposes for the patient. On the one hand, it provides him with a task he is capable of performing while in the hospital (therapeutic), and on the other hand, it prepares him for a job in the community after his release (employment). As the patient begins to improve, his progress is discussed by the industrial therapist at the team meeting. The industrial therapist must look into the patient's background for previous work history, discuss with the patient his preference for certain jobs, and determine, in consultation with his physician, the most suitable work assignment for the patient. If the patient's former job was a major factor in his breakdown, he is often assigned to a different type of work.

A recent survey of about 200 state mental hospitals, conducted by the President's Committee on Employment of the Handicapped, revealed that 86 percent of the hospitals have vocational rehabilitation counselors or employment service officers to help patients make plans for their future jobs in the community. Eighty-nine percent of the hospitals sponsor salaried work programs. Fifty-one percent of the hospitals offer sheltered workshops that train patients in work skills and good work habits under supervision. Some of these workshops subcontract jobs for local industries. In 12 percent of the hospitals, volunteer committees of employers assist patients in making future work plans.[13]

FROM CUSTODIAL CARE TO THE THERAPEUTIC COMMUNITY

One of the most notable general developments in the contemporary mental hospital is its change from a custodial to a curative institution. This has been concomitant with the decline in the conception of mental illness as an irreversible condition.

As long as the mental hospital was seen as an asylum whose task was custodial, this very definition sharpened the distinction between custodial staff and patients and placed an unbridgeable gulf of power between the two groups. In turn, the power differential hardened the staff into an authoritarian structure.

Many factors have combined to narrow the gap between hospital staff and patient. Perhaps the most important developments are the changed conception of mental illness and the increasingly prevalent view that psychic phenomena exist in infinitely varied degrees. It is a brave man who would attempt to fix for all time the precise point where normalcy ends and abnormalcy begins.

Important social factors, however, have also tended to blur the line between the normal and the mentally ill. In the last fifty years or so, the processes that have weakened the family's ability to care for deviants have accelerated. For this reason, more and more persons who in the past would have been viewed as merely a little odd have been experienced by society as insufferable burdens and pressed toward the mental hospitals. The mental hospitals, as a result, no longer receive only the most severely and permanently impaired, but also persons who once might never have entered at all. Out of sheer necessity, hospitals have had to reduce their patient loads in order to receive ever new contingents. Many hospitals have attempted to abrogate all custodial functions, because they conceive of themselves as therapeutic centers, too valuable to be wasted on custodial problems.

This shift in the view of hospital function is epitomized by the popular concept of the therapeutic community.

> In the therapeutic community the whole of the time which the patient spends in the hospital is thought of as treatment time, and everything that happens to the patient is part of the treatment program. Thus, the therapeutic community is to be found ultimately in a point of view which seeks to integrate every detail of mental-hospital life into a continuous program of treatment. Viewed in this way, the aesthetic qualities of the grounds and the interior appointments, the way the food is served, and the behavior of all personnel, without exception, are part of the program. All activities are organized with regard to maximal therapeutic effectiveness.[14]

No attempt can be made here to examine all the developments which have influenced the contemporary concept of the therapeutic community, but a few highlights are worth noting. Stanton and Schwartz believe that the origins of this concept can be traced to the work of Harry Stack Sullivan.[15] From 1929 to 1931, at Sheppard and Enoch Pratt Hospital in Towson, Maryland, Sullivan made a systematic study of schizophrenic patients in the context of institutional operations. His procedures achieved such remarkable success that he reformulated the whole study of psychiatry as an examination of interpersonal relations.[16]

By no means did Sullivan have a one-sided view of the mental hospital. He noted that the mental patient typically ends up in a hospital because he cannot manage in the outside world; and the longer he continues to struggle, the worse grows his degree of estrangement and disorder. The hospital eases his problem by removing him from these unworkable interpersonal relations. The individual finds some relief in the discipline and order of the ward, and in the comfort of being surrounded by others with similar problems. Sullivan opened the way for a reconceptualization of the hospital by gearing his therapy beyond these standby expediencies toward the eventual return of the patient to the wider world outside the hospital.

A second major boost toward the therapeutic community was contributed by Howard Rowland, who described the way that patients in mental hospitals informally organize themselves to obtain information and to deal with physicians. The informal organization of the hospital thus came to be seen as an important part of the therapeutic process.[17]

But an institutional milieu may fall short of everyday situations in facilitating the progress of disturbed individuals, as was unexpectedly dramatized in a wartime study by Anna Freud and Dorothy Burlingham. They were in charge of nurseries housing orphans from the Nazi blitzkrieg and V-2 attacks on London during World War II. These temporarily and permanently orphaned children had undergone the terrors of bombing, fire, and the death of loved ones. When such traumatized children were treated uniformly by the attendants, they showed retarded development and were far slower in overcoming their problems than children of normal families. When the innovation was introduced of dividing the children into artificial families (that is, assigning a group of them exclusively to the care of a single attendant), a remarkable transformation occurred. The children experienced new levels of joy and sorrow and a highly accelerated rate of progress.[18] Generalized, Freud's and Burlingham's findings unmistakably demonstrated the powerful role exerted by the organization of an institution on its clients.

Bruno Bettelheim and Emmy Sylvester were doubtless influenced by the Freud-Burlingham study in their elaboration of the concept of the therapeutic milieu.[19] Institutions, they theorized, tend to sustain a syndrome of emotional deficiency. The institutional setting, according to Bettelheim and Sylvester, fosters formal and impersonal relationships and behavior ordered by rules and regulations; it provides none of the personal identification necessary for internalization of standards and development of apparently spontaneous behavior resting on a set of inner controls. From this it follows that the therapeutic milieu is adequate only when it permits a high level of personalization.

Further insights into organization's role in the recovery, or lack of recovery, of mental patients were added by G. Devereux [20] and S. A. Szurek,[21] who traced the effects of staff interaction on patient recovery. Caudill, Redlich, and others studied the influence of hospital personnel's complicated interlocking expectations on patient recovery; their work stressed the significance of informal patient group life. [22] T. F. Main achieved a new level of integration of the various and complex factors bearing on the therapeutic process; his work led him to abandon his conception of the hospital as an essentially passive institution in favor of one which was active and therapeutic.[23]

With Maxwell Jones' study, *The Therapeutic Community,* one fully reaches the contemporary conception of the mental hospital.[24] The experiments he reports were designed to direct institutional resources to the particular problems of patients. The therapeutic effect, in this conception, was visualized as a product of the behavior of the entire group, psychotherapy, special group operations, and close integration with the neighboring community.

What does the conception of the mental hospital as therapeutic community add to the methods of treatment reviewed above? Experiments conducted at the Mendota State hospital in Madison, Wisconsin, by Doctors Arnold M. Ludwig and Arnold J. Marx provide some answer. Their three-year study of seemingly hopeless cases of chronic schizophrenia, led them to conclude that elements in the patient subculture—patients' failure to assume responsibility for each other's safety and their failure to socialize with one another—was a factor in chronicity.

Doctors Ludwig and Marx deliberately set out to transform this patient subculture. Accountability was to become the keystone of treatment.

Accountability meant that good behavior would be rewarded and bad behavior punished—a concept still regarded with horror in some psychiatric circles. But behavior, rather than attitudes and feelings, has been the main focus of the experimental program.

As part of this, the patients are rated weekly for a wide range of behavior. For instance, neatness, cleanliness, and shouting are rewarded or punished accordingly.

To break the code of chronicity, Ludwig and his staff decided to hold all 30 patients responsible and accountable for one another —particularly in what were looked upon as the three worst sins of behavior—fleeing, fornicating, and fighting.

This meant that the entire group lost privileges for the misbehavior of a single member. Ludwig said patients soon began helping the staff in trying to improve behavior.[25]

Accountability proved so successful that the experiments generated a program of emotional rallies, suggestion and inspiration periods, and re-education meetings. Also successful was the experimental pairing of comparatively poor with comparatively better-off patients, holding each member of a pair accountable for the behavior of the other. The guardian (as designated by the psychiatrists) of the pair rewarded his buddy with some favorite treat (ice cream or a cigarette) when he responded normally, and the guardian was rewarded with coupons redeemable at the canteen. Once a patient approached discharge potential, important social skills were programmed into the experiment. Of the fifty-two patients who had gone through the special program, thirty-one were discharged by the end of the study.

OBSTACLES AND LIMITS TO THE THERAPEUTIC COMMUNITY

The most powerful argument for the therapeutic community is that the system of care which now exists in most mental hospitals tends to promote some forms of mental illness and to interfere with various kinds of treatment. This effect, it is argued, is a product of the authoritarian structure of the traditional mental hospital: a structure which reserves prestige and power to the top staff; separates the upper from the lower levels of staff; and finally, establishes a caste-like division between the staff as a whole and the patients.

Inevitably, some argue that no true therapeutic community could exist within the despotic paternalism of the traditional hospital; authoritarianism would have to be replaced by a democratic structure in which patients are admitted, not as passive subjects, but as full participants. The term "milieu therapy" has come to signify the theory that patient-staff sessions (functioning, presumably, like a kind of town-meeting democracy) are the key to the full development of the therapeutic community.

In *The Sharing of Power in a Psychiatric Hospital,* Robert Rubenstein and Harold D. Lasswell combined the talents of clinical psychiatrist and political scientist to study attempts to introduce democratic patient-staff sessions into the authoritarian structure of mental hospitals.[26]

Rubenstein and Lasswell reasoned that the therapeutic community—a healing situation designed to return the mentally ill individual to society as soon as he can function adequately—poses a challenge for the traditional mental hospital. Conventional psychiatric institutions, they observed, tend to reinforce the patient's self-image of loser, sufferer, and victim whose proper role is passive subjection to the authoritarian healing process. As experts, doctors wield extraordinary authority over the lives of patients; in their professional role, they are exempt from the requirement to treat patients as democratic equals. But if the therapeutic community conception is correct, to view the mentally ill as fragile, child-like, irresponsible, and dangerous to themselves and others is to define them in a manner that hinders therapy.[27]

At the Yale Psychiatric Institute, group therapy was introduced in 1953. Physicians led groups, comprised of seven or eight patients and a nurse and social worker, that met at first weekly and, later twice each week. Patient-staff meetings proper began in 1956, at first on a weekly, then twice-weekly, and by 1960, on a thrice-weekly basis. The meetings were attended by about sixty people, including all patients, physicians, social workers, nurses and aides, higher administrative staff, and students in the hospital.

Rubenstein and Lasswell hold a theoretical position best described as social behavioristic—that is, they view any given social process as a strategy by a plurality to achieve a variety of ends. Their position bears many similarities to that of W. I. Thomas, who visualized two basic terms to any social process: the "definition of the situation" by social agents; and four wishes he thought were shared by all men (desire for new experience, cognition, mastery, and security).[28] Rubenstein and Lasswell believe men pursue eight types of values: affection, respect, rectitude, power, enlightenment, skill, wealth, and well-being.[29] They hold that the decision process consists of such activities as promoting, prescribing, invoking, applying, appraising, and terminating.

Rubenstein and Lasswell analyzed the patient-staff sessions at Yale in terms of these values and techniques. They aimed to determine the extent to which a genuine sharing of power by patients and staff, hence a true democratic therapeutic community, had been achieved. They concluded that patients participate actively in the flow of talk in the meetings and discussion is relatively rational and realistic. The principle question is to what extent power is genuinely shared by patients and staff. Their analysis revealed that the functions of intelligence and appraisal are conspicuous in patient-staff meetings; promotion plays a modest role; the other phases of the decision process, invocation and application, and especially prescription and termination, are much less visible. Despite the informality which characterized patient-staff meetings, the ascendency of the director was maintained. Comments and interpretations emphasized the effective control of the director and senior staff over policy toward individual patients and hospital issues.[30]

The patient was given a measure of freedom that often terrified him. But despite the innovations, fundamental decisions regarding the patients continued to be made by others, leaving the authoritarian character of the hospital unchanged.[31] The doctors constituted a power elite in the hospital whose basic ideology identified the mentally ill as dangerous to themselves and to society. According to Rubenstein and Lasswell, the doctors were reluctant to give up their power because: (1) it was necessary for the expiation of their own "original guilt"; (2) it enabled them to meet their obligations to their superiors; and (3) it gratified their inner strivings for power.[32]

Yale's failure to achieve a full-fledged therapeutic community is of special interest, because one would have assumed in advance that its comparatively small size and high-quality, research-oriented staff should have provided it with more than usual prospects of success. The incomplete realization of a therapeutic community under such ideal circumstances points to the strength of the forces operating against the complete transformation of mental hospital into therapeutic community.

Another experiment in developing a therapeutic community was undertaken by Denis V. Martin, psychiatrist and superintendent at the Claybury Hospital in England.[33] In 1955, Claybury Hospital contained 2,200 beds and admitted some 1,300 patients annually; of the total number, 750 patients were over age sixty-five. Martin first transformed only one ward into a community unit; gradually, other units changed over too, so that, by the time the author wrote his book, all admission units had become community units except for those of the senile patients. Sixteen wards in all were acting on the community principle.

Community meetings were held several times a week with all members of the ward staff and patients sitting together and discussing problems in a spirit of mutual exchange. Proposed changes in hospital routine or activities were discussed with the patients first; patients were encouraged to help one another; and the staff tried to use restraint in directing or interrupting during the discussions.

After six years of experimentation, the study revealed that changes were still taking place. Conflict remained between the traditional and new systems; resistance to change was marked in understaffed wards. New changes were being generally accepted only during the last two years under study.

More positively, the hospital atmosphere had become more

cheerful, and staff and patients were friendlier. Patients enjoyed greater freedom and responsibility, were more tolerant of each other's disturbed behavior, and had even learned to interpret one another's emotional responses. Fewer patients were being transferred to the chronic wards; and on two chronic wards, physical treatment and sedatives were practically eliminated. Disturbed behavior was dealt with by the ward staff, and fewer formalities were used among the staff as a whole—respect for each other was increasingly based on personality rather than on status and rank.

But after six years of community therapy, Martin remained unsure that there had been an improvement in the effectiveness of treatment. He suggested that a few years' additional experience was desirable before the results could be appraised.

There is a tendency in the field of mental health to welcome each new drug, therapeutic technique, or concept as the miracle solution to all problems. The reception of the therapeutic community was no exception to this essentially magico-religious way of thinking. However, common sense suggests that this eagerness is quite unrealistic.

For the mentally ill do not present a single problem but a variety of problems. Some, such as those suffering from senile dementia, are basically a custodial problem, and the resources of a therapeutic community operation will not essentially change their condition.

In addition, some mentally ill individuals do not appear to respond to group or community therapy, but do respond to various types of individual therapy. A realistic solution would separate those categories of patients with differential treatment requirements by either specialized hospitals or wards. Therapeutic community techniques will have to be confined to special hospitals or special wards.

The Rubenstein-Lasswell study raises the question of whether the therapeutic community necessarily requires a democratic sharing of power by patients and staff. It is possible that a democratic sharing of power may not always be desirable.

As reported by Ludwig and Marx, the culture of the Mendota

State schizophrenic ward prior to study seems to have been quite anarchistic with no patient ever interfering with another. Ludwig and Marx clearly set out to change this with, by their own description, a kind of paternalistic despotism. They held the ward collectively responsible for the violations of individuals; they rewarded individuals for acts of responsibility on behalf of others; and they created and rewarded a guardianship system. In short, they set out not to create a democracy of power between patients and the staff, but to transform the culture of the ward. They seem to have enjoyed some success.

But if the therapeutic community is oriented to persons generally responsive to the various forms of group, occupational, and industrial therapy, a democratic milieu may be more desirable. The more completely the patient shares power, the more quickly will he be prepared for life on the outside.

NOTES

1. Kevin Mosley, "Inside View of Mental Hospital," *Chicago Today,* May 5, 1969, p. 20.

2. August B. Hollingshead and Frederick C. Redlich, *Social Class and Mental Illness,* p. 223.

3. Thomas Szasz, *The Myth of Mental Illness,* p. 307.

4. Ibid., p. 308.

5. Roy R. Grinker and John P. Spiegel, *Men Under Stress* (Philadelphia: Blakiston, 1945), p. 28.

6. Hollingshead and Redlich, *Social Class and Mental Illness,* p. 104.

7. Ibid. Summarized from chapter 4, pp. 66ff.

8. Ibid., p. 223.

9. Ibid., p. 228.

10. See ibid., pp. 359–360.

11. Jerome K. Myers and Bertram H. Roberts, *Family and Class Dynamics in Mental Illness.*

12. Grinker and Spiegel, *Men Under Stress,* pp. 387–388.

13. Chicago *Tribune,* November 14, 1968.

14. Louis Linn, "Hospital Psychiatry" in Silvano Arieti, ed., *American Handbook of Psychiatry* (New York: Basic Books, Inc., 1959), II, p. 1831.

15. Stanton and Schwartz, *The Mental Hospital,* pp. 13ff.

16. Harry Stack Sullivan, "Socio-psychiatric Research: Its Implications

for the Schizophrenia Problem and for Mental Hygiene," *American Journal of Psychiatry* 10 (1931): 977–991.

17. Howard Rowland, "Interaction Processes in the State Mental Hospital." *Psychiatry* 1 (1938): 323–337; and "Friendship Patterns in the State Mental Hospital," *Psychiatry* 2 (1939): 363–373.

18. Anna Freud and Dorothy Burlingham, *War and Children* (New York: International Universities Press, 1943), pp. 156–161.

19. Bruno Bettelheim and Emmy Sylvester, "A Therapeutic Milieu," *American Journal of Orthopsychiatry* 18 (1948): 191–206.

20. G. Devereux, "The Social Structure of a Schizophrenic Ward and Its Therapeutic Fitness," *Journal of Clinical Psychopathology* 6 (1944): 231–265; "The Social Structure of the Hospital as a Factor in Total Therapy," *American Journal of Orthopsychiatry* 19 (1949): 492–500.

21. S. A. Szurek, "Dynamics of Staff Interaction in Hospital Psychiatric Treatment of Children," *American Journal of Orthopsychiatry* 17 (1947): 652–664. S. L. Sheimo, J. Paynter, and S. A. Szurek, "Problems of Staff Interaction with Spontaneous Group Formations on a Children's Psychiatric Ward," *American Journal of Orthopsychiatry* 9 (1949): 599–611.

22. William Caudill, Frederick C. Redlich, Helen R. Gilmore, and E. B. Brody, "Social Structure and Interaction Processes on a Psychiatric Ward," *American Journal of Orthopsychiatry* 22 (1952): 314–334.

23. T. F. Main, "The Hospital as a Therapeutic Institution," *Bulletin Menninger Clinic* 10 (1946): 66–70.

24. Maxwell Jones, *The Therapeutic Community* (New York: Basic Books, 1953).

25. James Spaulding, "State Hospital's New Treatment Boosts Hope for Schizophrenics," *The Milwaukee Journal,* June 8, 1969, Section 2.

26. Robert Rubenstein and Harold D. Lasswell, *The Sharing of Power in a Psychiatric Hospital.*

27. Ibid., p. 5.

28. See Don Martindale, *The Nature and Types of Sociological Theory* (Boston: Houghton Mifflin, 1960).

29. Rubenstein and Lasswell, *The Sharing of Power,* pp. 16–17.

30. Ibid., pp. 200–201.

31. Ibid., p. 257.

32. Ibid., p. 261.

33. Denis V. Martin, *Adventure in Psychiatry: Social Change in a Mental Hospital.*

7

RETURN TO
THE COMMUNITY

Despite attempts to transform the ward into a community, the hospital remains a specialized social situation differentiated by many properties from the world outside. The hospital exists for the patient, while the world outside does not. The hospital operates on an organized schedule that affects everybody, while the world outside operates on a multiplicity of time schedules. In the hospital, the key functions are under expert control; the affairs of the outside world are not conducted by interrelated series of experts. When the patient leaves the hospital he must enter a variable, amorphous world. Therefore, the hospital may, even as part of its therapeutic program, undertake to resocialize the patient for the outside world.

RESOCIALIZATION

Patients who have grown dependent on the institutional setting may be afraid to leave the protection of the hospital. Often, after a social worker has interviewed a mental patient regarding possible living arrangements after discharge, he is informed by the hospital that all plans for discharge have been abandoned because the patient has suddenly become severely disturbed. This type of experience, familiar to every social worker responsible, for resettling mental patients in the community, points up the necessity for resocialization of patients preparatory to their return to the community.

In some respects, resocialization begins almost from the time a patient enters the hospital. Earlier and more frequent home visits coupled with more liberal visiting hours have tended to speed up the resocialization. The patient may be discharged from the hospital after only a few months of treatment. No longer isolated from their spouses and children for years, as was the pattern in the past, patients are less susceptible to subsequent withdrawal. Frequent contacts encourage them to continue their ties with the outside world.

All forms of therapy are directed at preparing the patient for normal interaction with others. Moreover, discharge plans are usually started from the first interview between hospital social worker and family. The social history seeks to answer such questions as: what resources are available for the patient on his release to the community? can he return to his job? and with whom should discharge plans be made?

The hospital tries to make available to the patient all the activities he would ordinarily encounter in his daily life at home. He is encouraged to participate in co-ed activities, attend social functions such as movies and ball games, take an interest in current events, speak up at ward meetings with the staff, and help perform hospital chores. In addition, the hospital staff tries to create a more home-like atmosphere on the ward; they may even provide a beauty parlor and barber shop to improve patient morale. By reducing the difference between the hospital and the outside world, the treatment staff hopes to resocialize the patient and help him cope with the multitude of problems he must face after discharge.

Dr. Milton Greenblatt has described the way behavior of male and female patients—formerly completely segregated for thirty years—began to improve when they attended common occupational therapy sessions. After this innovation was instituted at the Boston Psychopathic Hospital,

> All the uncouth practices of men without women vanished. The men tucked in their shirt tails, buttoned their trousers, combed their hair, and their language became acceptable. The women took more pride in their personal appearance; they, too, combed their hair, and used lipstick. Interest in personal appearance was later furthered by special beauty culture and postural exercises through courses given by the physiotherapist to the women and the opening of a beauty parlour on the women's convalescent ward. Friendships between men and women developed which added meaning to life. Aggressive or crude sexual behavior diminished sharply as sexual interest was directed into more wholesome channels of socialization.[1]

Initiating changes for patient resocialization requires the cooperation of the professional and ward staffs and the integration of treatment services. Otto Von Mering, an anthropologist, and Stanley H. King, a social psychologist, studied thirty mental hospitals, including twenty large state hospitals, to ascertain the affect of improved environmental conditions on patient progress.[2] The authors found that in spite of such major obstacles as inadequate staff and overcrowded wards, changes in the physical and social environments of mental patients are somewhat successful. The removal of restraints and more optimistic staff attitudes toward mental patients and existing conditions also made a difference. It was found beneficial to include members of both the professional and ward staffs in the treatment team and to foster mutual assistance among the patients.

The Use of Community Resources

Professionals generally have an inborn suspicion of laymen who presume to assist them in their official work. But experience has demonstrated that volunteers can be of considerable value, not only in speeding the resocialization of the patient, but in creating good will for the hospital.

Many hospitals now maintain a volunteer coordinator to plan for volunteer services and recruit women and men from the community to provide a variety of programs. These programs may include coffee hours, group or individual shopping trips, visits with disturbed patients, and voting during election campaigns. Volunteers may serve as tour guides in the hospital, act as informal public relations speakers, and encourage church and civic groups to take on projects or donate contributions for the hospital's benefit.

Enthusiastic participation in a local hospital volunteer program indicates a degree of acceptance by the community—an acceptance that is revealed to the patient in a number of subtle ways.[3] Volunteers help a patient feel that he is being accepted by the outside world, and this, in turn, affects his degree of willingness to return to it. Volunteers can be instrumental in locating places for patients to live. Most importantly, volunteers often take considerable personal responsibility for patients with whom they have established a personal bond. One retired schoolteacher volunteer of the authors' acquaintance became so interested in the plight of certain patients after discharge that she eventually took three chronic geriatric patients home to live with her.

Group counseling for patients and their relatives is another important step in the preparation of the patient for discharge. By involving the family in patient treatment and reestablishing family concern, group counseling speeds the resocialization process.[4]

In group counseling, parents, spouses, and other interested relatives participate in evening meetings at the hospital. The hospital social worker in charge tries to learn the relatives' needs, encourages the group members to support one another, and answers all questions about treatment, hospital programs, discharge plans, and aftercare. Apprehensive relatives can learn how to handle a patient during visits with him in the hospital and in the home. These meetings also help conserve the valuable time of social workers and doctors by enabling all such questions to be answered in a group setting. A number of hospitals also ask the community social worker involved in aftercare to participate in these meetings; his presence reassures both patient and family that a professional will be in charge of follow-up work. Relatives find these group meetings support-ive and informative and enjoy sharing their mutual problems with others in a sympathetic atmosphere.

Resocialization through Industrial Therapy

Industrial therapy programs, together with sheltered workshops and rehabilitation counseling, are of value in the resocialization process. Especially beneficial in some cases is a job assignment similar to the one held by the patient prior to his illness. Reas-sured that he has not lost his touch, the patient faces discharge with less anxiety.

Many hospital work programs provide full work schedules on a daily basis with salaries for services performed. Volunteer committees of employers sometimes discuss plans for future jobs with interested and qualified patients. Many employers have discovered that, apart from considerations of public rela-tions, former mental patients sometimes make unusually de-pendable workers, for they cling to their jobs as if their lives depended on them. They have come to terms with life and have developed a strong sense of the relation of a job to a stable existence. The job belongs to the objective world and in per-forming it well the individual receives external confirmation of his worth. At the same time its tasks permit the sublimation of emotional energies (uncertainty, insecurity, and so on) in the form of objective achievement. The job may thus be both an intensely personal form of self-expression and a transpersonal confirmation of the self.

PROBLEMS OF EX-PATIENTS

As mentioned earlier, a small proportion of patients have en-joyed the resources of highly specialized treatment in private sanitoriums or hospitals. The Menninger Clinic is an example of a nationally known psychiatric center for intensive therapy. Through intensive work with families of their patients, these places usually persuade families to welcome their patients home again. The patient's return to his own family is inevitable. The personal and intensive therapy provided patients in costly private facilities dramatizes the problem for those patients who have little or no resources to pay for care.

It is a matter of record that the wealthy can afford highly expensive facilities and private psychologists and psychiatrists; the non-wealthy must depend on public facilities which are often inferior. The wealthy can afford earlier consultation with the best available specialists; the non-wealthy must often postpone the problems of a mentally ill member until it has become so serious that they are forced to seek public aid. The families of the wealthy can often keep the problem off the public records; the families of the non-wealthy have to face the stigma of becoming a case in the files of various public agencies. The families of the wealthy can absorb the costs and strains of a mentally ill member more easily thàn the family of a non-wealthy patient. Our concern is primarily with the kinds of patients who must have access to public mental health facilities, but our picture would be incomplete if we did not take account of the situation of the well-to-do.

A number of obstacles face the less well-to-do patient as he attempts to return to the community. Family members may resent the patient's discharge and return home. Having developed a new life style which excluded the patient, they may not wish to contemplate another round of crisis, anxiety, frustration, and despair. Community social workers know how extremely difficult it is to counsel a family which is not ready to accept their patient. It may require months of intensive case work before the fear and hostility is resolved and placement plans can be completed.

The same considerations may apply to other former ties. For example, a patient's fiancée may decide to abandon wedding arrangements rather than bind herself to a sick husband for the remainder of her life. Or close friends may suddenly assume a distant and cold attitude toward the ex-patient.

Career plans may have to be changed, especially if the patient's job precipitated the crisis. The patient's career ambitions may have been unrealistic, or his employer may not want to rehire him. Time lost in the hospital may have seriously hampered professional objectives. If his former prospects are now closed, he will have to develop a new set of objectives.

In addition, the ex-patient must bear the social stigma of mental illness just at a time when he most needs special understanding. Government and industry may be unwilling to hire him. And there is always the danger that unscrupulous people might take advantage of an ex-patient's many weaknesses to secure their own ends. Although some professionals feel that all negative judgments based on a man's commitment are just pure prejudice, there are jobs in government and industry for which a history of mental illness is hardly a good recommendation. It is one thing, however, to be rejected for certain, specialized jobs in government and industry and quite another to face difficulties in obtaining any job at all.

The stigma of mental illness may extend into an ex-patient's social life. A male patient may find not only that his fiancée has broken their engagement, but that he is defined as a poor marriage risk by other women. Or a mentally ill girl may find her marriage opportunities diminished at the same time she finds unusual erotic pressure placed on her, for now she is defined as an easy mark. The former mental patient is well aware of the scars he bears because of commitment.

The Schwartzes have observed that, once they have been released from the hospital, many ex-patients tend to precipitously break off aftercare. The Schwartzes believe that these ex-patients may be partially motivated by desires to reintegrate into society as quickly as possible and to avoid being identified as former mental patients by those responsible for their aftercare.[5]

Erving Goffman has been intensely concerned with the problems of stigmatization and the manner in which the affected individuals seek to deal with their "spoiled identity." He believes that attempts at "passing"—most commonly referred to as a process in which black persons seek to pass for white—also characterize the behavior of ex-mental patients. Goffman found that, in one mental institution, patients reentering the community consciously set out to pass for normal. But they were forced to rely on rehabilitation officers, social workers, or employment agencies for assistance in getting jobs, and their first employer unavoidably had to know about their mental illness. Nevertheless, lower levels of the organization and workmates could often be kept in ignorance of it. There always remained, however, the danger of this information leaking out from the employer and personnel office. For this reason, Goffman claims, patients planned to remain on the job only long enough to save some money, get out from under the influence of hospital and social work agencies, and establish a work record. By successive job changes the history of one's mental illness could be quietly lost from view.[6]

In the social phenomenon of "passing," there usually remain a few persons aware of the deception. Among blacks who have passed for white, it has been observed that, in the contingency of meeting a former black friend when in the company of whites with whom the passing was successful, no sign of mutual recognition was admitted. Goffman claims that this process also appears among ex-patients of mental hospitals who decline to acknowledge acquaintanceship when meeting in the company of a normal friend.[7]

As time goes by, increasing attempts will probably be made at preventive measures intended to avoid the stigma of commitment by keeping patients out of the hospital. The city of Philadelphia, with assistance from the National Institute of Mental Health, is already trying to set up a city-wide system of detection and treatment to this end.

> Despite the differences, all of the centers are committed to the philosophy that it is better to head off serious mental illness by detecting it early and treating the patient in the community than to compound the problem by adding the stigma of sending the patient away to a distant mental hospital.
>
> The main impetus for the program comes from the 1963 Federal Community Mental Health Center Act, which calls for the

establishment of centers throughout the country under a program that this year cost $89.8 million.

Since Philadelphia, with only 1-100th of the Nation's population, received $4.5 million or more than 5 percent of the funds, it's apparent that the city is far ahead in implementing the program.

In fact, the National Institute of Mental Health, which oversees the work, said Philadelphia was the first city in the country to settle on catchment areas for the entire municipality.[8]

COMMUNITY RESOURCES
AVAILABLE TO THE EX-PATIENT

Community Mental Health Centers

The multitude of problems facing the ex-patient upon discharge has generated a rapid development of facilities to help him. A comprehensive array of services is provided by the community mental health centers established by law on October 31, 1963, when the Eighty-eighth Congress passed Public Law 88–164, known as the "Mental Retardation Facilities and Community Mental Health Centers Construction Act of 1963." This legislation authorized, over a three-year period, federal matching funds to the states of $150 million, to be used for constructing community mental health centers.

In May 1964, the criteria by which a state could receive federal funds were set down. To be eligible, the community mental health center had to offer five *essential elements* of comprehensive mental health service: inpatient services; outpatient services; partial hospitalization services, including, at minimum, day care; around-the-clock emergency services for at least one of the first three services; and educational and consultive services available to professional personnel and community agencies. The regulations defined "adequate services" as including the first five services plus: diagnostic services; rehabilitative, vocational, and educational programs; community precare and aftercare services, such as home visiting, halfway houses, and foster home placement; training; and research and evaluation.

Since the passage of this legislation, mental health centers have been constructed and staffed throughout the nation. Some centers are associated with a general hospital, an outpatient clinic, or a private hospital. Their purpose is to serve all the people, and to coordinate and improve existing facilities, not to replace them. For the ex-patient, the community mental health centers have much to offer. Rehabilitation services and help with placement in foster homes and halfway houses is available as well as drug therapy and consultation with a professional staff of psychiatrists and social workers. Professional advice is available to the families of ex-patients. And if a center is connected with a hospital psychiatric unit, ex-patient admission for brief observation and treatment is provided as well.

Day Hospitals

Another resource available to the ex-patient is the day hospital, an innovation of the last decade. Day hospitals are usually located in community, private, or Veterans Administration hospitals and are often associated with a community mental health center. Their purpose is to provide support and treatment for emotionally disturbed individuals who would otherwise have to be committed to state or private mental hospitals.

At a day hospital, the ill person receives care and treatment during the day and returns to his home and family at night. In some day hospitals, staff members dress in street clothes to provide a more informal atmosphere; staff and patients discuss problems together in group therapy; individual psychotherapy, drug therapy, vocational training and psychological testing are provided; various kinds of recreational and occupational therapy are supplied to groups of about twenty to twenty-five patients; and staff and patients eat lunch together.

Day hospital care is intensive. Treatment extends from a few weeks to a few months. A critical feature of day hospital care is that the patient's family life and ties with the community are maintained.

Some state mental hospitals have recently set aside several wards to serve as day and night hospitals for members of the nearby community. In the night hospital, individuals who need treatment but are able to function on a job work all day and come to the hospital in the evening. A program of treatment similar to that of the day hospital is offered. The ill person sleeps at the hospital and returns to his job every morning.

Day Treatment Centers

Similar in some respects to day hospitals are day treatment centers, another fairly recent addition to the list of resources available to ex-patients and other mentally ill persons. As the name implies, their activities are conducted during the daytime. These centers are usually located in a community center or church. The local community mental health center usually supplies the staff and supervises and plans all activities; The staff may consist of a psychologist, an occupational therapist, a social worker, and a psychiatrist who comes to the center a few days a week to supervise and regulate patient medication. Some state mental hospitals have recently created day treatment centers to service the mentally ill within their receiving areas.

The primary purpose of the day treatment center is socialization: education toward relationship with others and teaching the social skills essential to living in the community. Stress is placed on group interaction and the constructive use of leisure time. Patients are involved in a variety of activities: exercises in the gymnasium and swimming pool; such arts and crafts as woodworking, sewing, weaving, and jewelry making; and voluntary tours of museums, arts institutes, industries, and parks.

A considerable proportion of the persons who attend day treatment centers are ex-patients on either provisional or final discharge. The center may provide them with enough support for their emotional problems to keep them out of the hospital.

Mental Health Rehabilitation Workers

A new addition to the psychiatric team in mental health clinics and community hospitals are mental health rehabilitation workers.[9] These workers, drawn from the lay people in the community, are usually stable, mature women in their forties or fifties who, after a period of intensive training (usually about one year), are qualified to assist the psychiatric team. A good part of their training is theoretical, but experience in clinics with emotionally disturbed persons provides a practical knowledge of the mental health field. These workers help emotionally disturbed individuals to meet everyday crises by consulting with them and their families in the home; when necessary, they will refer problems to appropriate agencies.

Where understaffing is a major problem, especially in the clinics and hospitals of large metropolitan centers, the mental health rehabilitation worker is a great help in alleviating the problems presented by the mentally ill. For the ex-patient, the services of the rehabilitation worker can often prevent his return to a mental hospital.

Volunteer Programs

The participation of volunteers in hospital resocialization programs has already been mentioned. As more and more community facilities have been expanded and developed to meet the needs of the mentally ill, the perceived value of volunteers outside the hospital has increased. Both private and public organizations now promote volunteer programs. Sometimes an active, though small, volunteer group becomes so vital to the mental health program of a community that it is taken over by the community as a whole and supported by the taxpayers.

County welfare departments and private agencies that are active in providing follow-up services for the discharged mentally ill often make use of volunteers. In these cases the volunteer works closely with the social work staff. If there is considerable demand for volunteer services, the county welfare department appoints a volunteer coordinator to supervise activities and conduct recruitment drives and orientation sessions. Volunteers, both men and women, perform diversified services, such as helping families use other resources; giving advice to patients on grooming, shopping and budgeting; taking ex-patients to ball games and the theater and driving them to clinics; visiting at halfway houses or at home; arranging parties for patients during the holidays or on a periodic basis; and taking patients into their (the volunteers') homes for a day—in short, treating them as normal members of society.

The successful use of mental health volunteers in the outpatient clinic of a general hospital is described by Dr. Jacob Christ.[10] In his estimation, the two main ingredients for a successful volunteer program are (1) making the volunteer a general part of the team, and (2) providing opportunities for the volunteer to obtain practical experience, usually in a group setting with other volunteers and a skilled professional in attendance.

Private Psychiatric Clinics

The private psychiatric clinic provides outpatient psychiatric treatment for those individuals who do not have the financial means to cover private psychiatric care. Some clinics are supported by private funds alone, while others receive additional county, state, or federal funds. Such treatments as individual psychotherapy, husband-wife therapy, family therapy, and group therapy may be offered.

Treatment is voluntary. For this reason, the individual referred for care may be required to call and make his own appointment to indicate his willingness to cooperate in treatment procedures. An evaluation interview, psychological testing, and diagnostic decision are undertaken before the individual is determined amenable to treatment in the clinic. Fees are based on the individual's financial resources and vary in each case. In some clinics, fees may range from nothing to $15.00 per interview. Individuals may be seen on the average of once a week for a period of four to six months; this also varies, depending on the need for intensive therapy. While under treatment, the individual is able to continue on his job and see his family doctor.

The staff here usually consists of a psychiatrist, a clinical psychologist, two or three psychiatric social workers, and several psychiatric consultants. Individuals who request help from a private psychiatric clinic are usually in the early stages of illness, have enough insight to cooperate with the staff in working through their emotional problems, are articulate, and are therefore able to avoid long-term inpatient care at a private or state mental hospital.

Suicide Prevention Services

Crisis intervention and suicide prevention services are offered in some cities to provide immediate and long-term assistance for area residents. On a 24-hour basis, trained counselors are on call at either their offices or their homes. Immediate help is extended to the troubled individual or family through a home call, an emergency hospital visit, or a referral to a specific community resource.

Educational Programs in Mental Health Needs

Educational training programs that acquaint social workers, public health nurses, and other professionals with the needs of the mentally ill are being conducted in some states. These programs are usually divided into three phases: the pre-hospital, the hospital treatment, and the post-hospital periods. The first phase involves meetings and lectures presented by psychiatrists, psychologists, social workers, and attorneys on various aspects of mental illness, including diagnosis, drug and other therapies, and legal aspects. In the hospital treatment phase, the meetings are conducted at the state mental hospital; members of the training group participate in a three-day session, sleep in the hospital or in town, eat in the hospital cafeteria, tour the wards and grounds, and even observe electro-shock therapy. In the third phase, meetings are conducted in the city with emphasis on community resources; again, a battery of experts from the community mental health program lectures to the group and answers questions.

This type of training program is especially valuable to those involved in continuous aftercare.

Social Clubs for Ex-Patients

Social clubs for ex-patients, which have become popular all over the United States, serve as a recreational and social outlet for the individual. Friendships formed at the mental hospital are renewed and new attachments are made. While no pressure to attend is placed on the ex-patient, he is encouraged to participate if he is able and willing. These clubs may be sponsored by church groups and conducted in an informal manner, or initiated by a community mental health center with some of the professional staff participating in more structured programs. Group methods are employed to activate the individual. Graduate students in nearby university schools of social work may work with the ex-patients in this setting as part of their field placement curriculum.

A nationally known group which seeks to help ex-patients adjust to community life is Recovery, Incorporated, founded by Dr. A. A. Low, a psychiatrist, in Chicago in 1937. From thirty ex-patient members at its start, the organization grew to 12,000 American members by 1967. Six hundred groups in forty states are active. Individuals with emotional problems but no record of hospital treatment are invited to participate in the meetings. In group sessions held several times a week, problems are dealt with in a realistic manner (perfection as a value is played down and conflicting situations dealt with openly). The group leader, a former mental patient, receives his training from the national organization. Members help each other with their problems and go to sick members at home on call. Recovery operates, in short, much like Alcoholics Anonymous.

Vocational Rehabilitation Programs

Divisions of vocational rehabilitation offer a variety of employment opportunities for the ex-patient unable to secure employment alone. Also valuable in this regard are sheltered workshops, which accept clients on the basis of their potential to learn skills; they conduct training programs adjusted to individual patients' progress.

In 1943, Congress enacted the Barden-LaFollette Act, which provided for vocational rehabilitation for both mental and physical disabilities. Social Security amendments passed in 1960 and 1962 made funds available to persons while in mental hospitals and after their discharges home. The 1965 Vocational

Rehabilitation Act Amendments provided services in vocational rehabilitation to cover a greater segment of the population by broadening the definition of what constitutes disabilities in need of public aid; it included mental illness as well as cerebral palsy, orthopedic disabilities, speech and hearing impairments, tuberculosis, heart and cardiovascular ailments, and mental retardation. Federal grants to the states provide 75 percent of the financial help necessary to establish sheltered workshops, rehabilitation centers, and hospital programs.

Referrals to divisions of vocational rehabilitation come from private and public welfare agencies, state hospitals, private doctors and psychiatrists, professionals in the community, and so on. Services include interviews to determine mental and physical limitations and strengths, psychological testing, assignment to a sheltered workshop program, and ultimately placement in a permanent job.

To study vocational rehabilitation requirements, Simon Olshansky divided ex-patients into those invisible and those visible to professionals. Some ex-patients leave the hospital and go to work with little or no help from others. They shed their identity as ex-patients and avoid post-hospital help. Others, however, remain unemployed or are employed only intermittently. Some wish to work but lack the capacity for its routines, while others have the capacity but lack the will to work. They constitute a hard core of unemployables.[11]

In Olshansky's view, there are a number of reasons why ex-patients prefer to work rather than receive welfare assistance. He argues that because self-support is esteemed and dependency is not, work tends to bolster the self-esteem of the ex-patient. Moreover, work is an effective way to shed the stigma of commitment. Even if the person is not completely well, so long as he is able to maintain the visible symbol of normality, work, he can usually avoid recommitment. Finally, work gives him something to do other than worry about himself. This is of special value for individuals with limited personal resources.[12] In general, ex-patients are good subjects for vocational rehabilitation programs.

Follow-up Service by Welfare Agencies

Follow-up service, or aftercare as some call it, is provided in many communities by social workers affiliated with state hospitals, VA hospitals, and community mental health centers; public health nurses also assist the ex-patient in his adjustment. Follow-up is a major factor in reintegration of the person and avoidance of re-hospitalization. Social workers play a major role in the aftercare program.

AFTERCARE AND THE ROLE OF SOCIAL WORKERS

The practice of placing discharged mental patients in family homes was first attempted in 1885 when a Massachusetts law making it possible was passed. Recommended for such placement were those patients who had improved sufficiently to be able to function moderately well under supervision and were not considered dangerous.

Earlier, family care of the mentally ill had been tried successfully in Belgium, Germany, the Scandinavian countries, and France. The methods used varied, with some countries preferring to place a few patients in one family home and others placing a larger number of patients in a series of closely grouped homes. Either way, the principle remained the same: care on a private basis for patients who did not require the special treatment of the hospital and who could function adequately enough under supervision on the outside.

Following the example set by Massachusetts, Rhode Island and Minnesota passed legislation providing for this type of patient care. By the 1930s, New York, Pennsylvania, and Nebraska had also set up similar programs. Ten years later other states, including Ohio, Maryland, Michigan, and California, did the same. The Veterans Administration undertook a family care program in 1949 and today has a well-established and comprehensive family care system for its ex-patients.

By the 1950s, a change in public attitude toward the mental

patient was becoming apparent. With the open-door policy that resulted from the introduction of the therapeutic community and the extensive use of tranquilizing drugs, people came to look upon the mentally ill as individuals who were "different" but who could be cared for in facilities outside of hospitals.

Many professionals had long felt that the ex-patient would integrate more quickly into society if he received aftercare by medical and social agencies in his home area. This would focus all activity toward normal living in the outside world, rather than in an institution.

Aftercare of the ex-patient by hospital staff was the usual method employed until the 1950s. The Veterans Administration still maintains today a comprehensive aftercare program for its discharged patients. When the community was hostile toward the mentally ill and afraid of his erratic, unpredictable behavior, few other community agencies were able or willing to take on such a burden. Aftercare services such as home-finding and home calls on the expatient were performed by the same social worker who saw the patient in the hospital. The same doctor who knew the patient in the hospital was consulted when problems in drug supervision or behavior arose after discharge. Most aftercare programs in the United States in the latter part of the nineteenth century and first half of the twentieth century were patterned after this method.

Aftercare as part of the treatment process for mental hospital patients has been developing steadily for the past two decades. It is by now considered to be an accepted part of the social service program of county welfare departments.

Some ex-patients object to aftercare as an invasion of their privacy, a reminder of their unpleasant experiences at the state hospital, and a part of the stigma attached to being mentally ill. But many ex-patients welcome the aftercare services of community agencies, especially those of the county welfare department whose social workers remain responsible for follow-up service on a continuous basis.

The patient who has no family of his own and lives in a halfway house or family care home suddenly finds himself surrounded by a foster family. Members of this "family" include: other patients or members of the household; the supervisor in charge; the social worker; the public health nurse; and other professionals from the community, community mental health center, or hospital outpatient department.

In accord with the 1968 Hospitalization and Commitment Act, Minnesota state hospitals notify the local county welfare department when a patient is about to be discharged, released, or placed on partial hospitalization status. Whatever public assistance the patient needs is provided by the county welfare department. The individual aftercare plan is set up by the county welfare department in consultation with the hospital, local community mental health center and, if notified, the patient's physician. Other health and social agencies in the community may also be contacted. It is the duty of the welfare department to supervise and assist the patient in locating employment, a suitable place to live, and adequate medical and psychiatric treatment—in general, to help him in adjusting to the community.

If an ex-patient has no financial resources of his own, his county of legal settlement is responsible for his support. When an ex-patient is sent to live in a halfway house in another county, his social worker notifies the county of legal settlement of their financial obligation. With the current liberalization of legal settlement laws as a result of a recent Supreme Court ruling, this sometimes aggravating process may be eliminated; each county simply assumes financial support for whoever is living within its boundaries.

The social worker at the county welfare department maintains a continuous, supportive relationship with the ex-patient. This relationship and service are continued until the ex-patient receives his final discharge from the state hospital. For when he is first released, the patient is placed on provisional discharge for about one year, sometimes longer; during this time the patient may return to the hospital if his condition worsens without being re-subjected to the commitment process.

Prior to the patient's discharge, his assigned social worker at the county welfare department begins to make the necessary plans for the patient's return to the community. A request is sent by the state hospital staff advising the county welfare department that the patient is ready for release. Accompanying this letter is a discharge summary of the patient's diagnosis, progress, and treatment at the hospital, recommendations for future living arrangements, and plans for vocational or recreational activities.

After receiving notice of the patient's pending discharge, the social worker contacts the patient's family or an interested friend; he alerts them to the coming plans and enlists their help in formulating discharge plans. The social worker is often met with hostility and anger by the family. They may resent the services of an outside agency, they may be unprepared for the patient's return, or they may view his discharge as a disruption of their peaceful living arrangements. Some families go to considerable lengths to conceal having a member of their family in a mental hospital, and they fear his return will reveal this fact to their neighbors or friends. The social worker's job is a difficult one, one that requires great patience and understanding; for he must often reeducate the family as well as rehabilitate the patient.

To allay the patient's apprehension of leaving the hosiptal and to secure his confidence, the social worker visits the hospital to interview the patient, his doctor, and the hospital social worker and to attend staff discharge conferences. He watches the way the patient interacts with other patients and staff on his own ward; he discusses possible living arrangements and post-discharge plans with him. He lets the patient know that he has visited with his family and may discuss the patient's home and neighborhood. He may accept an application for financial assistance which is later processed at the county welfare department. In short, the social worker conveys to the patient his interest in him as a person and assures him that he will be seeing him upon his return home.

At this point, too, the social worker has to face fear and hostility from the patient, He may be more reluctant to leave the hospital than he was to enter. He has come to like this institution where all his wants are met, where he need make no decisions, and where he feels safe.

If the patient is willing to cooperate in discharge plans—and some are—the next step in the discharge process begins. But if the patient is so upset by the thought of leaving the hospital that he regresses, discharge plans have to be postponed. In their effort to send the patients back to the community, hospitals often refer the patients before they are ready to leave. Such experiences have forced the hospitals to undertake resocialization programs.

Home-finding is the next step in the discharge process. Some county welfare departments have a register of homes willing to accept ex-patients for aftercare. But if the program of aftercare is fairly new, the job of finding a home suitable for the patient is not easy. Most people are still reluctant to take a former mental patient into their homes, especially if they have small children. Often the social worker must work almost as hard with the family that is being asked to accept the ex-patient as with the patient. If the social worker's judgment of both is accurate, and if he is ready to step in the moment misunderstanding arises on either side, the project may be a success. The boarding family in time may develop a sympathetic understanding of the mentally ill and be willing to accept increasingly more difficult cases. Some examples of boarding homes developed by the authors are described below.

In the 1950s in St. Paul, Minnesota, at a time when the therapeutic community concept was in an early stage at the state hospitals, a serious aftercare problem arose. There were suddenly ex-patients to place and virtually no halfway houses or boarding homes available in which to place them. Most boarding homes in the community had had no experience with ex-patients from mental institutions and were understandably uneasy about accepting them.

Mrs. Blair, a divorcee, was supporting herself in a residential neighborhood by taking in and caring for a few elderly women. It was felt that her home would be an ideal place for Jane, an attractive, mild seventeen-year-old ex-patient—who, incidentally, was six months pregnant as a result of events in the mental hospital. The whole problem was tactfully broached and an interview was arranged. Mrs. Blair took a protective interest in the girl from the start.

The arrangement worked out so well that Mrs. Blair was soon prepared to take on other ex-patients. Gradually, she developed considerable skill in handling their varied problems. At the present time Mrs. Blair owns three comfortable and cheery homes that house a total of some fifty ex-patients from both the state mental hospital and the state hospital for the retarded.

In another case, a Mr. and Mrs. Turner were running a small boarding house, which seemed to be an ideal placement for a middle-aged former carpenter. Mrs. Turner was asked to take him on a trial basis and promised that he would be removed instantly if problems arose. The ex-patient's praise of Mrs. Turner's home cooking got them off to a good start. The placement soon became permanent and Mrs. Turner proved exceptionally good with other ex-patients placed with her. She is today in charge of a large halfway house for some one hundred patients. They like it there so much that about the only time they leave is in the case of recurring illness.

When a suitable home is located and financial arrangements are completed, a date on which the patient can be transferred to his new home is set. If returning home is not desirable for the ex-patient, the case worker explains to the family why a halfway house or family care home is recommended and tries to enlist its help in making this type of a placement.

Leaving the hospital can be a sad occasion for the patient. He is leaving the only home he may have known for years. Although the patient is informed of his new location and the type of home he will be living in, he has not seen it and many doubts and anxieties are to be expected.

The patient returning to his own family may be picked up from the state hospital by his wife, children, or relatives. A hospital aide or nurse will accompany the patient without a family to the halfway house or family care home. Sometimes the hospital social worker joins the group to acquaint herself with the ex-patient's foster family and new home. The transfer of a patient to the community is usually easier if someone from the hospital staff accompanies him to his new home, stays to visit a while over a cup of coffee, and reassures the patient that he will receive good care. The ex-patient is then introduced to his new roommate or other people in the home and taken on a tour of the house and grounds.

When the hospital aide and social worker prepare to leave it is not unusual for the ex-patient to suddenly lapse into tears and beg to return to the hospital, or to become excited and create a disturbance. After the ex-patient has finally accepted the fact that the community is to be his new home, the next step in the aftercare process begins.

Shortly after the ex-patient arrives at his new home, the social worker from the county welfare department makes a home call. This first visit is crucial because it often sets the tone for much of the later interaction between the ex-patient and the public agencies. It is important for the social worker not to arouse the ex-patient's anxieties and to proceed only so far, if possible, as to establish confidence with the ex-patient. However, sometimes the following type of thing may happen:

When the first call on the ex-patient in the rooming house was made, I was told that she was upstairs ironing. The landlady who gave this information raised one eyebrow as if in warning. When I knocked lightly on the open door the ex-patient looked up with the query:
"Who the hell are you?"
"I am your worker from the welfare board. I just dropped by to say hello."
"Well, hello."
"How are you getting along?"
"Who wants to know?"
"Are you taking your medication?"
"None of your damn business."

"Is there anything we can do for you?"
The ex-patient raised her iron menacingly and said:
"Out!"
That ended the interview.

It is generally wise for the social worker to note signs of stress and not press an interview with an ex-patient at an unpropitious time. One worker learned this the hard way:

> When ordinary warning signs were ignored and one worker pressed an interview on an ex-patient, the patient locked the apartment door after letting her in. She then proceeded to threaten her with a pair of scissors for several hours, subjecting her to a tirade all the while.
>
> The cat-and-mouse game was played with the ex-patient reveling in the worker's terror. Before the ex-patient released the worker she cut off her hair with the scissors.

These, of course, are unusual cases. If such onerousness persists and is directed generally at the people around him, the patient's tour of duty in the community will ordinarily be quite short and he will soon be on his way back to the hospital. If he concentrates his hostility on the social worker, the worker will probably reduce her visits to a minimum and try to close the case as soon as possible.

Most interviews with patients are more satisfactory than the above examples; most patients come to enjoy them and will even call the worker. At the interviews, the ex-patient and social worker make future plans regarding the patient's adjustment in the community, job placement, recreational outlets, renewal of relationships with friends and relatives, and so forth. During the home visits, the social worker may talk to the housemother alone and then together with the ex-patient, thereby helping the housemother understand what is expected of the patient in the home. If the ex-patient is dissatisfied with the location of his room or with his roommate, this problem can often be resolved in such a three-way discussion.

In most cases, the hospital prescribes medication with the

recommendation for its continued use after discharge from the hospital. The supervisor or housemother is responsible for seeing to it that the ex-patient takes his medication daily and attends the outpatient clinic or the community mental health center for drug adjustment. If the ex-patient is active and alert he can make the visits to the clinic on his own; he may enjoy traveling on the bus with other patients and visiting with the clinic staff. Or the supervisor in the home may delegate a house staff member to accompany a group of ex-patients to the clinic. This phase of aftercare services is very important; one reason a patient may have to return to the state hospital is failure to continue with medication.

As the ex-patient becomes acquainted with his new surroundings he usually becomes involved in the activities in his new home. The support of other members of the halfway house or private house, in the experience of the authors, may have quite different results. The halfway house may continue various elements of patient culture developed in the hospital. The total result bears some resemblance to the TV series, "The Addams Family." The ex-patients manage well in their own private world, but outsiders coming into contact with the house for the first time get goose pimples.

If, however, the ex-patient is placed in a family home, either alone or with a very few other ex-patients, he participates in a more "normal" culture. In the authors' experience, ex-patients in placements like this often become virtual family members. They accompany the housewife on shopping expeditions, help with household chores, enjoy leisure time activities with the family, and even participate in family gatherings.

When the ex-patient lives in a halfway house and his family lives in the same city, visits between them are encouraged to slowly involve the ex-patient in the activities of his family. This may counteract exclusive involvement in the culture of the halfway house. Also, when the doctor feels that the ex-patient can return to his own home, the adjustment is easier. Relatives are also encouraged to phone the ex-patient and take him on family outings or visits to his home. During this time, the case worker is busy developing viable arrangements between the ex-patient, his halfway house staff, and his family.

Referral to other facilities in the community is a major device by which the social worker can meet the individual needs of the ex-patient. These referrals may be for vocational rehabilitation, day treatment centers, volunteer programs, evening social clubs, community mental health centers, outpatient clinics, and so on. A withdrawn ex-patient may greatly benefit from attendance at a social club or day treatment center, but he may be too shy to take such a step without encouragement by the social worker. If an ex-patient living alone in an apartment does not wish to be with other ex-patients, he often improves most rapidly if encouraged to develop his own friendships; but he still needs assistance in locating employment. The richer the social worker's knowledge of referral facilities, and the better her public relations with their professional staff, the more effectively she can tailor a program to a particular ex-patient's needs.

Aftercare service by the county welfare department social worker calls for frequent contacts with the ex-patient. It involves daily, weekly, or monthly interviews, depending on his individual needs. These interviews may take place at the halfway house, the boarding home, the ex-patient's home, or the county welfare department, where more privacy is available.

For the withdrawn ex-patient, traveling to the local welfare department can be a way of getting him out of the house and of renewing his acquaintance with his home town. Also helpful and enjoyable are shopping expeditions or lunch in town with friends or, on occasion, the social worker. The social worker sometimes personally assists the ex-patient in locating employment. Ex-patients who are incapable of following through with job placement have been able to work in small nursing or boarding homes by assisting with the kitchen chores or cleaning. This type of employment is usually secured through the personal efforts of the social worker; she may interview the prospective employer frequently on behalf of the ex-patient, eliciting personal interest in his rehabilitation of the mentally ill.

It may be necessary for the social worker to make frequent

visits to the halfway house to talk to the staff, or visits to the ex-patient's family or friends for the resolution of urgent problems. When a crisis arises, the social worker may be contacted by phone at any hour of the day or night by the ex-patient himself, the caretaker of his living facility, or his family.

Continuous aftercare service for the ex-patient is provided until he receives a final discharge from the state hospital. At the close of one year a letter is sent to the state hospital that reports on the progress of the ex-patient's adjustment in the community and recommends either final discharge or continuation of provisional discharge for another year. This report is based on the ex-patient's ability to relate to others, degree of independence, ability to hold down a job, mental stability, socialization, and, if he lives with his own family, the family's opinion regarding need for further aftercare.

In the experience of the authors, an enormous variability exists among social workers working with ex-mental patients. Professional responsibility, knowledge of community facilities, good relations with their staffs, and the capacity to appraise accurately the needs of the particular ex-patient all seem to be important. The super-dedicated, missionary complex of some social workers does not seem to work well with the ex-patient. Too often, it tends to minimize relations with ex-patients who appear taciturn, sullen, or hostile; and a poor relationship with the social worker gets them off provisional discharge—hence out of the case load—too soon. At the same time, such a social worker is inclined to spend excessive amounts of time with some ex-patients and become personally involved.

Very often the resistant patient strongly desires autonomy and self-reliance, and if the social worker is able to perceive and tap this, she can be a most constructive help to him. On the other hand, the excessively compliant patient is often only substituting one form of dependence—this time on the social worker—for others; all his constructive plans dissolve the moment personal support is withdrawn.

Genuine professionalism on the part of the social worker is of utmost value in dealing with ex-mental patients.

LIVING ARRANGEMENTS
FOR THE EX-PATIENT

Return to the Family

If the patient is fortunate enough to have a wife and children waiting for him, or parents ready to accept him back home, release from the mental hospital may be possible sooner than for less fortunate patients. But a host of problems still remain. Wives who have assumed the role of head of the household do not easily retreat to their more passive former role; a younger sibling who has assumed a more active role in family decisions is unlikely to abrogate his new responsibility. The ex-patient, moreover, is usually humbled by his experience in the hospital. If the ex-patient is unable to resume his employment immediately, he may have to apply for public assistance, and this can further damage his morale. Low morale is reflected in his attitudes toward family members and their attitudes toward him.

In addition, the ex-patient may never get over his resentment of the rest of the family for sending him to the state hospital. He may constantly remind them, for example, that he might still have his old job had they not send him away, or that he was never mentally ill, or that he will never be able work with his record of mental illness. His revenge may include fantastic plans to file for their commitment.

In one of the most extreme of such cases in the authors' experience, a woman who had been committed several times without improvement was eventually divorced by her husband. The court awarded her the house, and for a glorious year and a half, in between brief tours of the hospital, she squandered the money from its sale in improbable and unrealistic ways. By this time she was thoroughly acquainted with the system and with her rights, and was filled with resentment of her ex-husband. A week rarely passed in which she did not try, out of revenge, to file commitment papers on him.

In a few instances in the authors' experience, both members of the marriage team have turned up simultaneously to file on each other. And in some cases, a third party (a son or daughter or other close relative) has brought commitment proceedings against both.

Although the ex-patient is back home again, his release is usually only a provisional one. He may still possess many of the symptoms that first led to his hospitalization, although in milder degree. His family may harbor many anxious doubts: will he have another episode? how soon? what will happen if he doesn't take his medication as prescribed? how will he behave with friends and other relatives?

And the family must face the shame of commitment. To avoid stigma, family members may have gone to great lengths to conceal the fact that a relative was in a mental hospital. Concealment requires many difficult changes in daily routine, as for the housewife described below:

> Thus, to keep the neighbors from knowing the husband's hospital (having reported that he was in a hospital because of suspicion of cancer), Mrs. G. must rush to her apartment to get the mail before her neighbors pick it up for her as they used to do. She has had to abandon second breakfasts at the drugstore with the women in the neighboring apartments to avoid their questions. Before she can allow visitors in her apartment, she must pick up any material identifying the hospital, and so on [13]

By maintaining social distance, some wives are able to withhold information about their mentally ill husbands. One reported:

> I haven't gotten too friendly with anyone at the office because I don't want people to know where my husband is. I figure that if I got too friendly with them, then they would start asking questions, and I might start talking, and I just think it's better if as few people as possible know about Joe.[14]

After the patient returns home, his family's concealment and withholding of information continues. This is reflected in their resistance to follow-up services that reveal the identity of the ex-patient and expose the family to stigma once more. By treating the ex-patient as a normal member and refusing after-care services, both the family and the ex-patient attempt to take up life as before. If it works, this is the best solution; if not, the family must face the irony that aftercare service might have prevented a new breakdown.

The Halfway House

The halfway house is designed, according to most official views, to be an intermediate stage between the mental hospital and the community. The purpose of the halfway house is to provide an environment for the ex-patient that is not too different from that of the hospital; he continues to receive some supervision, his meals are prepared for him, his activities are planned, medical and drug supervision is provided, and he can renew his acquaintanceship with the community by degrees.

The halfway house arose as a double response to the rise of the therapeutic community concept. The idea of the mental hospital as a therapeutic institution carried with it the demand that patients be released at the earliest possible moment, so that they not preempt facilities intended for treatment of others. In response to this demand, a few hospitals cast about for a means to get patients out of the hospital before they were completely ready to take up normal life. In some instances, special institutions were created on the hospital grounds; these operated somewhat like the trustee system of penitentiaries, that is, they kept patients under some sort of surveillance but gave them much freedom to carry on semi-normal activities outside the hospital grounds proper.

Meanwhile, the problem of dealing with patients defined as no longer requiring hospitalization, but still not ready to undertake full community responsibilities was seen as a task for institutions other than the state hospital. The social workers of county welfare departments were being called upon with especial frequency for this purpose. Welfare departments thus came to develop mental health units as one of their services. The original members of such units (including one of the present authors) found themselves on their own with virtually no guide lines to follow.

These social workers had to deal with ex-patients' special problems: their inability to care for their requirements; their need for board as well as room; their bizarre behavior which often unnerved normal individuals; and their need for supervision of medication.

Under such circumstances, the only alternative was to explore the boarding houses until one able to satisfy the specialized requirements of ex-patients was found. But when ex-patients moved in, the normal boarders quietly located elsewhere. There were, however, some compensations for the boarding house operator: the welfare department often assumed the financial obligations of the ex-patient's room and board, making him a fairly stable prospect; the welfare department usually quickly filled any vacancies and guaranteed a regular supply of boarders; and finally, the welfare department assumed responsibility for returning regressed patients to the state hospital.

As the halfway house began to assume the shape of a boarding house converted to the task of specializing in ex-mental patients, the experience of one operator tended to serve as a guide to others. Increasingly, operational procedures and various rules and regulations were standardized.

Included in the category of halfway houses are board-and-care homes, family-care homes, and boarding homes. Licensing regulations vary in each state, but an effort is made to control the living conditions necessary for health, an adequate diet, supervision of medication, physical well-being, and recreation.

Halfway houses are located in urban settings more often than rural settings because of convenience. Most ex-patients have little money and must often walk to shopping centers, relatives' homes, the county welfare department, and the mental health center. In a large city, the ex-patient can feel a sense of anonymity and merge into the population as a whole. Large old homes, new structures, and old hotels or apartment buildings serve well as halfway houses because they can accommodate a large number of people and often already possess the facilities necessary to care for ex-patients. Most halfway houses are started with private funds, but a few are sponsored by state, county, or federal funds.

The majority of residents in halfway houses come from state or private mental hospitals and are usually diagnosed as schizophrenics. Prior to admission, interested individuals who wish to live in the halfway house can visit for an afternoon or a weekend. Rules are often printed for the larger halfway house residents so all can understand what the management will tolerate. In the smaller homes the rules are explained informally.

The results of a recent, highly informative study of halfway houses was published by Harold L. Raush and Charlotte L. Raush.[15] They mailed questionnaires to 71 halfway houses in the United States that cared for individuals with psychological problems (this did not include ex-prisoners, alcoholics, or drug addicts). Although 57 answered, 17 did not meet the study's requirements; the 40 accurate replies served as the sample whose data supplied the factual material for the book.

In 1963, these 40 halfway houses were caring for 483 residents, with an average of 12 residents per house. Fourteen houses had 6 to 10 residents; 5 houses had 5 or less; 10 houses cared for 10 to 15; 4 houses had 16 to 20 residents; and 7 houses had 21 to 30 residents. Of the 483 residents, 407 had gone directly from hospital to halfway house, but 46 residents had never been in a hospital. Thirteen of the 40 halfway houses in the sample were affiliated with the Veteran's Administration. The study revealed that there were approximately twice as many men as women in the halfway houses; of the 40 houses, 15 had both men and women, 18 had only men, and 7 had only women.

As to the number of residents gainfully employed outside the halfway house, 9 houses reported 46 to 65 percent employed, 10 houses had 26 to 45 percent employed, and 11 houses had 25 percent or less employed.

Of the 34 houses that reported average length of stay, 11 houses put the average length of stay at 4 months or less, another 11 houses put the average at 4 to 8 months, 6 houses reported 8 to 12 months, and another 6 houses reported that their residents remained an average of a year or longer. In some houses a time limit is fixed, but in others the ex-patient is allowed to remain until he feels ready to leave.

Reports from twenty-five houses indicated where residents went to live after leaving the halfway house. In the Veterans Administration–affiliated houses, 18 percent returned to the hospital within one year, 37 percent went to live with their families, 17 percent made their way to another foster home, and 27 percent found a place to live in the community on their own. In the other 27 halfway houses (not affiliated with the Veterans Administration), 19 percent returned to the hospital within one year, 11 percent went to live with their families, 4 percent went to a foster home, and approximately 60 percent moved to another place in the community on their own. As the Raushes point out, the place to which residents move after the halfway house is dependent on the type of residents accepted by the halfway house in the first place.

In regard to follow-up, 31 of the 40 houses reported. Eight houses had set up a formal procedure for follow-up services, but 14 houses reported only social follow-up, such as visiting and invitations; 3 houses reported continuing therapy, and 6 houses referred ex-patients to clinics or offices.

As might be expected from their rather haphazard origin, halfway houses have been found to vary in almost every conceivable respect. Their members range from persons who have never been hospitalized to ex-patients who have been hospitalized for years. Some houses concentrate on high potential, others on high risk ex-patients. Some halfway houses only supply room and board, others take on a variety of additional services ranging from the supervision of medications to vocational help, work orientation, and minor forms of psychotherapy.[16]

In the opinion of the Raushes, the number of halfway houses will increase in the future. At the time they wrote their book (mid-1967), they estimated that about 100 halfway houses were operating in the United States. This estimate seems rather low, inasmuch as aftercare services have been an ongoing function of many county welfare departments in the United States since the early 1950s. Perhaps they ignored those aftercare services that lacked the official label of halfway house and the publicity, for much follow-up service is provided quietly by foster families and social'workers.

To accommodate the ever-increasing number of ex-patients in the community, larger halfway houses have been built in the past decade. Typical is the Jansen Home, a large board-and-care home which houses seventy-five to a hundred ex-patients. The staff consists of owner, administrator, counselor, recreational director, bookkeeper, accountant, cook, kitchen help, maid, and janitor. Ex-patients there often help with the bed making and some cleaning. Those who are employed in the kitchen or cafeteria receive a salary for their services. Supervision of medication is provided, and a staff member drives ex-patients in a large bus to the mental health clinic or outpatient department of the community hospital for scheduled checkups. Laundry service is provided for all ex-patients. Assistance with personal hygiene is given to those who need it. An attempt is being made to assist ex-patients in rehabilitation by counseling and education.

This halfway house is a new one, financed by private funds. The newly built structure consists of three stories of concrete blocks. Men and women are segregated by floor. The rooms are comfortable and are furnished with a bed, dresser, and closet space for each ex-patient. There are two, three, or four individuals to a room. Colorful drapes and bedspreads add a homey touch. A large cafeteria and kitchen provide for the meals; patients dine at small tables. For relaxation the house offers a large lounge, a T.V. room, and, for those able to participate in occupational therapies, a sewing and arts and crafts room.

A large proportion of the ex-patients who live in this and similar halfway houses are supported by social security and public assistance. Only a small proportion of ex-patients are able to pay their own way. Those ex-patients supported by public assistance may need a doctor's statement certifying that they require this type of care and supervision.

Most ex-patients tend to feel at home in the large board-and-care home just described, since, as a semi-institution, it is not very different from the mental hospital. Adjustment here is easier for the withdrawn person who has extreme difficulty establishing any kind of relationship with other people. Some withdrawn patients placed in small boarding homes have been unable to adjust, have become extremely anxious, and have had to be returned to the state hospital for a time. In the larger board-and-care homes, the ex-patient can be either anonymous to some extent or active. He can make friends with other ex-patients and take trips to town or just sit in the lounge and watch all the activities around him. He can exchange bits of gossip about the staff, ex-patients, or other professional personnel who visit the home. As a halfway house, the large board-and-care home is theoretically a stepping stone to the larger community. Many ex-patients, however, never leave the halfway house, preferring to remain within its safe confines. Sooner or later, researchers will discover that many halfway houses tend to become a new type of custodial institution with nuclei of chronicity—as groups of ex-patients in them preserve their own special culture that holds them in the house and away from the rest of society.

Boarding Homes

The whole field of mental illness suffers from an inclination to operate with an inflated language. Once a new term (such as therapeutic community or halfway house) appears, it tends to be applied to everything. All too often the same old practices continue with little change under the new name. Once the term halfway house grew popular, every place except his own home in which the ex-mental patient was domiciled tended to be called a halfway house.

In the view of the authors, however, the term halfway house should be applied only where the given institution specializes in handling the problems of ex-patients. The Raushes' survey of halfway houses quite evidently included boarding houses which could, but did not necessarily, receive ex-patients. In the present authors' view, it would be better to describe these simply as boarding homes.

There is some advantage in retaining the old designation of boarding home for the small board-and-care home that may or may not house ex-patients, but that in general, has patients who only require a bare minimum of complex specialized care. An example of the history of such a home is the following:

> Mrs. Gordon and her invalid husband lived in a spacious, three-story colonial house in one of the finer residential sections of town. With the loss of her husband's income, Mrs. Gordon sought to earn additional money and provide some meaningful occupation by taking into her home three elderly ex-patients with funds of their own from the state mental hospital. As long as she had to care for her invalid husband, Mrs. Gordon felt three more women would not add much more work; in addition, she felt in need of their companionship, since her husband had grown depressed and withdrawn as a result of his inactivity. Each woman had a room of her own overlooking the boulevard; meals were served either in the rooms or in the dining room. The ex-patients had the use of the entire home, and gradually grew well enough to assist Mrs. Gordon with preparation of meals. Their families were delighted with the spacious surroundings, the little attentions paid by Mrs. Gordon, and, above all, the improvement of the ex-patients. Mr. Gordon began to take an interest in the activities of the home and as a result his own health improved.

Boarding homes, both large (fifteen to thirty) and small (five to ten), provide a group living arrangement for non-patients and ex-patients who require a minimum of supervision. A representative of the management is available to supervise and help those who require it. The staff is small and some of the boarders may act as cooks, dishwashers, or cleaning women. These tasks are frequently assumed voluntarily, with a salary paid for services performed. Men and women may live in the house or it may be restricted to either men or women. An informal atmosphere is typical, with residents coming and going about their personal business: some go to their jobs; others go shopping; others visit friends or relatives; and some sit around over coffee in the kitchen. Medication may be supervised, and those ex-patients who must go to the clinic for scheduled appointments may be reminded of this.

The atmosphere in any boarding home of this size is created by the attitude of its caretaker. Those citizens in the community who have agreed to accept and care for the mentally ill are usually willing to give of themselves, are interested in helping the afflicted, and may have needs of their own to satisfy. A few may open a boarding home for the financial aspect but this is only part of the reason.

One couple, Mr. and Mrs. Sheldon, supervised twenty ex-patients (male). Mr. Sheldon worked as a maintenance man during the day and helped with the various chores after work. Their two children, a boy of ten and a girl of eight, attended school. Home was an old Victorian style house built in the 1890s by one of the first families of town. It was kept in good condition and the ex-patients helped in making repairs when needed. All ex-patients were made to feel like members of the family. They ate at a large table in the dining room. No demands were made on the ex-patients and they were free to come and go as they pleased. Since most were on public assistance, they often walked to the downtown district to shop or visit the county welfare department. Mrs. Sheldon was always at home and provided the supervision. She did all the cooking, washing, ironing, and mending for the men in the home. When the social worker visited, Mrs. Sheldon could usually be found ironing clothes in the living room while five or six of the men watched television or talked with her. The ex-patients seemed to idolize her. This room was the center of activities and all who stopped in were given coffee and doughnuts. After school the children came with their schoolmates; two cats were usually curled up on the old mantlepiece and a canary sang in the kitchen. Sometimes Mrs. Sheldon would play the old organ that she had bought at an auction. She took an interest in each of the men, corresponded with their out-of-town relatives, and discussed their needs and problems with the social workers. During the winter, she always requested long underwear so they would not catch cold. It was not surprising that few of the ex-patients in the Sheldon home ever returned to the state hospital.

A family care home offers a normal living experience in the community. Ex-patients who live with a family may work in the home, outside of the home, or not work at all if mentally unstable. Families, depending upon their capacity for tolerating deviant behavior, will accept patients with varying degrees of mental problems.

> The Richardsons, both of whom had been employed as ward aides in the nearby mental hospital, took two ex-patients into their home after they retired from their jobs at the hospital. These ex-patients, both men in their fifties, had spent over twenty years in the state hospital. They were opposed to the release and had begged to remain in the hospital. One man made strange gutteral sounds when he talked; the other had a serious facial tic. Several boarding homes had refused to accept them. When the hospital social worker appealed to Mr. Richardson, he remembered the two men and agreed to accept them in his home.
>
> With their knowledge of mental illness gained from past experience, the Richardsons were able to rehabilitate both men; eventually they moved on to living arrangements of their own. A long line of ex-patients have since lived in the Richardson home—some have eventually returned to their own families.

There are risks to the ex-patient in both the family care home and the halfway house. The chief danger in the family care home is that a family may exploit the ex-patient by obtaining considerable unpaid or underpaid labor from him. One must be careful, however, not to adjudge apparent exploitation too hastily. The ex-patient often knows that he is doing considerable menial service and at the same time is aware that he is receiving much solicitous consideration and care. In fact, he may be going out of his way to act like a contributing family member.

Some dangers of the halfway house were revealed by the

Chicago *Sun-Times* reviewers' tour of halfway houses in the Chicago area.

A tour last week of halfway houses for discharged mental patients turned up padlocked exit doors, unlicensed distribution of drugs, and supervision by untrained personnel.

On a surprise visit about 9 P.M. one night last week at the Kenbeach Apartment Hotel, 5107 N. Kenmore, the reporter-social worker team found a maintenance man in charge.

The janitor, Odell Hurst, said he was working a shift from 6 P.M. to 6 A.M. since the desk clerk was discharged a few days ago.

Asked what he would do if one of the residents needed medicine in the late hours, Hurst ushered the team into a locked office and opened a file cabinet containing some 60 bottles of pills. Seeing that some of the bottles contained tranquilizers, the team asked him how he would dole them out.

"I can't read that stuff," Hurst said. "All I know is I'm supposed to give it to them according to instructions."

One of the charges leveled by health officials in their court cases is that halfway houses officials are illegally administering medicine. Licensed sheltered-care homes are permitted to distribute medicine under a doctor's prescription; but there is no regulation for halfway houses.

At the nearby Traemour Hotel, 5427 N. Kenmore, the reporter-social worker team found one rear exit padlocked and another bolted from the inside.

A night clerk summoned the owners, Louis and Julius Pure, who led a tour through the six-story structure housing some 270 persons, a large percentage of them ex-mental patients.

Louis Pure said that a resident is paid to patrol the halls at night but added, "He must be asleep."

Fire inspectors have complained about the exit, Pure said, but he still keeps it locked until about 11 P.M. each evening.[17]

Nursing Homes

Elderly persons after discharge from a mental hospital who require nursing care are transferred to a nursing home if one is available. If possible a nursing home closer to the patient's family is chosen, so that they can visit more often.

The cost of care is paid by either the patient's own funds or public assistance. While the patient is in the state hospital, the application for public assistance (medical aid) is initiated and sent to the county welfare department, where eligibility is determined and a search for a suitable nursing home is made.

Lack of sufficient nursing homes in many communities has created problems for families and hospitals. Adult children are reluctant to commit their aging, senile, or mentally ill parent to a state hospital yet may be unable to care for them in their homes. Once the elderly patient has been admitted to the local community hospital, the children prefer to leave them there for months on end while a nursing home placement is sought. But the community hospital needs its beds for acute cases of illness and cannot be burdened with custodial cases. Pressure is placed on the family, who as a last resort may agree to commitment of the elderly patient to the state mental hospital. If additional nursing homes were constructed by the municipalities with tax-supported funds, most elderly senile and disturbed patients would not have to be committed to a state hospital at all.

Individual Living Arrangements

Those ex-patients who are single and fortunate enough to have a job waiting for them can return to an apartment in the community or live in the home of a friend. This type of patient often does not require or does not want aftercare service, preferring to make his own way. He may or may not avail himself of services at the community mental health center or of social clubs for ex-patients. His commitment may have been of a voluntary nature, with illness caught early and the period of hospitalization relatively short.

Another type of ex-patient who lives alone in a light housekeeping room or a room in a run-down hotel is the man or woman who has resisted all efforts to keep him in a halfway house under supervision. Some of these ex-patients walk the streets for lack of something better to do, are shabbily or bizarrely dressed, and carry their belongings with them lest someone in the building steal them away. A few harbor delusions of one kind or another and, outside of coming to the welfare department once or twice a year for eligibility review, want little to do with the social worker or the mental health clinic.

THE PROGRESS AND
REGRESSION OF EX-PATIENTS

Research by Freeman and Simmons on the adjustment of ex-patients in the community provides some information on the factors bearing on progress of the ex-patient.[18] They conducted a number of studies to determine the importance of tolerance of deviant behavior on the part of family members. Even if ex-patients were not performing adequately, it was found they did better if living with their parents than with a spouse. Furthermore, high-level performance was found to be associated with: middle class standing of the ex-patient; role of the ex-patient as head of the household; and expectations that he assume the responsibilities called for by his role. Low-level performance was found for ex-patients who: lived in homes with other males (who could assume their duties); and derivation from lower class strata and from families that did not expect much of them. In two subsequent research studies, Simmons and Freeman reported that return to the hospital was primarily the result of erratic behavior rather than of poor role performance. Whether high-level role performance kept the person out of the hospital despite erratic behavior was not clear.

A research project to determine community adjustment of patients released from a state mental hospital in Arkansas made a follow-up study of 326 out of 1,054 patients from two different Arkansas counties.[19] The total group included male and female, white and nonwhite, urban and rural persons. The majority of the patients were afflicted with schizophrenia, senile psychosis, general paresis, or psychosis with arteriosclerosis. The average length of stay in the hospital was twenty-seven months.

While in the hospital 34 percent died, after discharge from the hospital 13 percent died, and some patients could not be located.

The researchers found: no improvement in the sample's work regularity; poorer functioning than before among some after hospital treatment; and low ability to stay married or to get married. But they also found that: those who were married did better than single, widowed, or divorced ex-patients; the earlier in illness treatment was obtained, the better the chances of recovery; ex-patients' involvement in organized groups did not differ from that of the normal members of the community; some 26 percent of the ex-patients were as well adjusted or better adjusted than before their illness, 51 percent were not as well adjusted, 17 percent were much worse, and 6 percent were unable to function at all.

In *Women After Treatment,* the authors report the results of a research study, conducted by a group of social scientists and a doctor, to determine how well women functioned in the community after psychiatric treatment.[20] This study was conducted with a group of 287 women who had received short-term psychiatric treatment at the Columbus Psychiatric Institute and Hospital, Columbus, Ohio, from December 1958 through July 1959, and had then returned to the community. The majority of these women were Protestant, white, city dwellers, married, and in the lower and middle class strata. They suffered from psychoneurosis, functional psychosis, and organic impairment. Some 157 female neighbors were selected as a control group.

Evaluation of adjustment in the community, or "outcome," was based on: whether the patient was able to avoid rehospitalization; whether her performance level was adequate; and whether she was making a satisfactory adjustment as compared with normal women. This study employed methods seldom used before in mental health research such as: use of short-term but acutely mentally ill patients; use of psychiatric evaluation on each patient; and comparison of the performance of the mentally ill women with normal women in their community.

Questionnaires were devised as a means of gathering data. A series of interviews were conducted by psychiatric social workers with patients who were able to remain in the community over six months, with their household "significant others" (usually their husbands) and with the normal women and their significant others. If a woman returned to the hospital within six months, only her significant other was interviewed. As a method of judging performance of the women after release from the hospital, ratings were made on their ability to function in three areas—domestic, social, and psychiatric.

Results of the study revealed: that the majority of rehospitalized women (15 percent of the sample) experienced this contingency during the first six months after release; psychiatric and not social problems were the primary reason for rehospitalization; women who returned to the hospital in the six-month period suffered from chronic mental illness, organic ailments, and a low-level of social adjustment. Women who were rehospitalized after the six-month period suffered from a recurring, acute range of symptoms and few organic ailments, and enjoyed a higher degree of satisfactory role performance.

In comparing the ex-patients with their normal neighbors, it was found that the normal women performed much better in the psychological and domestic range; women who had received treatment had more psychiatric problems than their normal neighbors. There was a similarity between the two groups in role performance, role expectations, and ability to tolerate deviant behavior; and attitudes toward role expectations tended to follow the same pattern.

The 246 women who did not have to return to the hospital within the six-month period were found to function far better, especially psychologically, than those women who returned to the hospital within the six-month period. Diagnosis had a marked effect on adjustment after release—those patients with organic ailments were low performers, while those with psychoneurotic ailments were high performers. The performance of married women was found to be superior. Instrumental role expectation was related to the level of performance in domestic and social roles and ability to tolerate erratic behavior was related to psychological adjustment.

It was not possible to generalize with respect to category or treatment in this study in the opinion of its authors, since mental patients are sick in varying degrees. Some mentally ill patients require long-term hospitalization and should be afforded this care until there are adequate facilities in the community to assume this function. In addition, the study concluded that families of mentally ill persons should be given moral support and education in methods of caring for these patients at home. In the efforts to help the mentally ill patient, the study found that not enough attention has been paid to the needs of her family.

The Hospital as Custodial Institution

Since 1956, when the psychoactive drugs came into popular use in the nation's mental hospitals, the number of mental hospital patients has steadily decreased. Over the same period, the rate of readmission to state mental hospitals has been rising from 30 to 40 percent.

A number of reasons have been offered for the rise in readmissions. Many people who come out of state mental hospitals are not cured but have received, according to the hospital, maximum hospital benefit. Because they have not been cured, these ex-patients may make return trips several times. They subsist on tranquilizers and many become wards of the community for the rest of their lives. If they refuse to take their medication, they often become acutely ill and have to return to the hospital. Through the use of tranquilizers, the community has shifted into the role of custodian.

But the community is not yet ready to fulfill the role of custodian. Resources in the community have been steadily increasing to care for the ex-patient, but they cannot take the place of the hospital. On the hospital records, the discharged patients appear as cured, but this is not necessarily a fact. With so many people in the hospital, a certain number must be discharged if others are to be admitted. Ironically, in some instances the patient being admitted to the mental hospital is not as ill as the patient being discharged.

In Detroit, early in November 1969, an eighteen-year-old youth was convicted of killing a gas station attendant during an attempted holdup. He had recently been released from the state mental hospital. When interviewed by a reporter, the county prosecutor for Michigan's Genesee County made a vigorous attack upon the Michigan Department of Mental Health, laying on its doorstep responsibility for the youth's behavior. So many of the ambiguities that plague both mental hospitals and after-care facilities for the mentally ill ex-patient are typified by this case that it is worth quoting at length.

Genesee County Prosecutor Robert F. Leonard is incensed about the whole case. He blames the Michigan Department of Mental Health for the murder, shooting and robberies Smokey committed.

"I'm convinced that if the Department of Mental Health had done its job there would be one man alive today and another fellow who wouldn't have been shot," said Leonard.

"They turned him loose. They just refused to take him back, even acknowledging that he was dangerous.

"The mental health department appears to operate in a vacuum. They're by themselves. They're not concerned about the problems they're creating for society, for law enforcement."

Leonard said he didn't relish the idea of prosecuting a person so obviously psychotic. But the law left him no choice, he said.

What's more, somebody had to get Smokey Johnson locked up, he added.

Smokey's court-appointed lawyer, Ivor R. Jones, is disgusted with the way his client was treated by the mental health department and later by the State Department of Social Services.

"This kid was a walking time bomb," Jones exclaimed. "There's no question he's dangerous. He can look at you and smile, and then cut your throat."

Smokey Johnson was born June 17, 1951, the only son of Roger and Doris Johnson. They also have a 14-year old daughter, Valerie. The marriage broke up in October, 1955.

By 1965, when he was 14, Smokey Johnson had:

—Molested children in his neighborhood.

—Broken into a house and set fire to it in response to "voices" in his head. The house was destroyed.

—Spray-painted children.

—Stolen several cars and wrecked one.

—Been caught rifling purses in the girls' locker room at Brown City High School.

—Tried late at night to sneak into the bedroom of a woman who was serving as his foster mother. He was carrying a butcher knife in his teeth and was wearing her clothing and makeup.

When the Lapeer County Probate Court was asked to commit Smokey to a mental institution in 1965, the boy was examined by Dr. Ralph D. Rabinovitch, now director of the mental health department's Hawthorn Center in Northville.

Dr. Rabinovitch believed Smokey was suffering from schizophrenia, a mental illness that is characterized by detachment from reality and deterioration of the personality. The doctor believes so and testified to it at Smokey's murder trial.

"For his own protection and that of the community," wrote Dr. Rabinovitch in 1965, "I would strongly urge as early as possible hospitalization in an adolescent unit of a state hospital."

So, ultimately, Lapeer Probate Judge George D. Lutz ordered the youth committed to Pontiac State Hospital in August, 1965. Smokey entered that institution the following month.

During the next 18 months, Smokey escaped 14 times, according to Dr. Donald W. Martin, medical superintendent at Pontiac.

"He was one of the most difficult child cases we've ever had," he noted. "He was husky, aggressive, antisocial and considered by the staff to be quite dangerous."

Within a month of entering, Smokey joined with fellow inmates in a gang attack on a nurse.

Finally, the hospital gave up on him. His mother said they refused to take him back.

"There's got to be a way to keep this kind of person off the streets," Leonard declared, banging on his desk for emphasis.

"The Department of Mental Health has got to give more supervision to these people and show as much concern for the public as they do for making another bed available.

"But this [Smokey's case] is a classical case of a total foul-up," said Leonard. "Somebody's dead. Somebody's maimed. Here's a guy they knew was dangerous, but they let him go. Somebody's responsible.

"It's a clear case of indifference on the part of the mental health people." [21]

Not the least interesting feature of the case is the report that the youth had caused so much trouble while in the mental hospital that the staff refused to keep him. If the state mental hospital is unable to perform a custodial function for such cases, it is certainly evident that the community at large is not equipped to do so. Had he not committed murder and run afoul of the criminal law, this youth would most certainly have had other tours in the state's mental institutions simply because his illness persisted.

Recidivism

Patients return to the hospital because of lack of acceptance by the family, unemployment, too much idle time, excessive drinking, return of psychiatric impairment, failure to continue medication, increase in disturbance, or family stress.

The type of aftercare and kind of supervision afforded the ex-patient often affects the length of time he can remain in the community. Some ex-patients require constant supervision while others resent this as an invasion of their privacy. Frequent contacts by social workers in the community depend on the amount of money available for staff. Psychiatric resources such as mental health centers and clinics vary in each locality. And where the resources are available the ex-patient may want nothing to do with them. If the ex-patient is told where he has to live (and this is sometimes done) in order to control his environment, he may challenge this as interference with his civil rights.[22]

There are ex-patients who manage to function in the community while under provisional discharge and aftercare services, but regress as soon as the provisional discharge is terminated. Once the legal threat of commitment is removed, they stop taking their medication, their mental symptoms return, they may harass their families and neighbors, and finally they have to be returned to the hospital.

Why mental patients return to the hospital was the basis of a recent research project by Donald E. Spiegel and Patricia Keith-Spiegel, who studied 100 male patients at the Brentwood Hospital Veterans Administration Center, in Los Angeles, California.[23] After the readmissions rate had risen above 42 percent in the fiscal year 1966, they made a study of 100 patients who were readmitted consecutively. Of the patients readmitted, the reasons for discharge had been: maximum hospital benefit (31 percent), trial visit (47 percent), left against medical advice (16 percent), eloped (2 percent), and overstayed leave (4 percent).

Upon readmission, interviews were conducted with each patient; replies were recorded on a prepared interview schedule. Most of the patients (71 percent) had been short-term patients who had been in the hospital previously for less than one year. Forty-two percent were able to work after discharge, but 58 percent just "sat around"; more than half of the men who did work were either semi-skilled or unskilled. Sixty percent said there were no alternatives to rehospitalization and 62 percent returned willingly to the hospital.

Forty-two percent cited nervousness as a prime reason for returning to the hospital. Also among the multiple reasons contributing to their return were: poor physical health (31 percent), depression (31 percent), inability to find a job (31 percent), financial difficulties (26 percent), strange or frightening thoughts (26 percent), drinking problem (19 percent), fear of losing control of self (19 percent), loss of job (18 percent), need for medication (15 percent), suicidal thoughts (12 percent), behavior that disturbed others (12 percent), and being bothered by voices (6 percent).[24]

To live successfully in the community, 40 percent of the men felt a satisfactory job was essential, 27 percent placed first emphasis on successful treatment of their illness, 12 percent felt that improvement of their financial situation was necessary. The study as a whole indicated that most of the patients felt a need for community support.

There is a tendency to consider the ex-patient successfully rehabilitated so long as he does not have to be returned to the hospital. In the experience of the authors, however, few ex-patients who do not return to the hospital enjoy more than a marginally normal existence. Families do take a mentally ill member back home but often wearily resign themselves to putting up with his symptoms permanently; from then on he is kept permanently on tranquilizers. And the computers that register each ex-patient not readmitted as rehabilitated count up another "success." Many ex-patients placed in small boarding homes are supported by the welfare department and are emotionally sustained by the boarding house operator—in other words, they are treated as dependent. By no standard of normality do they enjoy more than a marginal adjustment.

Furthermore, the problems presented by the residents of many halfway houses remain to be intensively studied. With some frequency the halfway house reconstructs the type of patient culture that characterizes the chronic wards of the hospital.

NOTES

1. Milton Greenblatt, Richard H. York, and Esther Lucille Brown, *From Custodial to Therapeutic Patient Care in Mental Hospitals, Explorations in Social Treatment,* p. 116.

2. Otto Von Mering and Stanley H. King, *Remotivating the Mental Patient* (New York: Russell Sage Foundation, 1957).

3. See Barbara E. Phinney, "Volunteers in Hospital Programs for the Mentally Ill," in National Conference on Social Welfare, *Mental Health and Social Welfare* (New York: Columbia University Press, 1961), pp. 183–191.

4. Phyllis Rolfe, "The Psychiatric Team Comes to the Home" in *Mental Health and Social Welfare,* pp. 103–133.

5. Morris S. Schwartz and Charlotte Green Schwartz, *Social Approaches to Mental Patient Care,* p. 284.

6. Erving Goffman, *Stigma: Notes on the Management of Spoiled Identity,* pp. 93–94.

7. Ibid., p. 98.

8. *The Philadelphia Inquirer,* August 25, 1968, p. 23.

9. See Ida F. Davidoff, Agnes C. Lauga, and Robert S. Walzer, "The Mental Health Rehabilitation Worker: A New Member of the Psychiatric

Team," *Community Mental Health Journal* 5, No. 1 (1969): 46ff. This "in-between" specialist position was created in the Department of Psychiatry at the Albert Einstein College of Medicine in New York City.

10.   Jacob Christ, "Volunteer Training as an Education," *Mental Hygiene* 51, no. 3 (July 1967): 433ff.

11.   Simoń Olshansky, "The Vocational Rehabilitation of Ex-psychiatric Patients," *Mental Hygiene* 52, no. 4 (October 1968): 557.

12.   Ibid., p. 560.

13.   M. R. Yarrow, J. A. Clausen, and P. R. Robbins, "The Social Meaning of Mental Illness," *Journal of Social Issues* 11 (1955): 42.

14.   Ibid., p. 36.

15.   Harold L. Raush with Charlotte L. Raush, *The Halfway House Movement: A Search for Sanity.*

16.   Ibid., pp. 200–201.

17.   Basil Talbot, Jr., "Halfway Houses—Neglect Continues," Chicago *Sun-Times,* December 1, 1968, pp. 5, 30. Reprinted with permission of Chicago *Sun-Times.*

18.   Howard E. Freeman and Ozzie G. Simmons, *The Mental Patient Comes Home* (New York: John Wiley and Sons, 1963).

19.   Leta McKinney Adler, "Patients of a State Mental Hospital: The Outcome of Their Hospitalization," in Arnold Rose, ed., *Mental Health and Mental Disorder* (New York: W. W. Norton Co., 1955), pp. 501–523; Leta McKinney Adler, James W. Coddington, and Donald D. Steward, *Mental Illness in Washington County, Arkansas: Incidence, Recovery and Posthospital Adjustment* (Fayetteville, Arkansas: University of Arkansas, Research Series no. 23, July 1952); and Leta McKinney Adler, "The Relationship of Marital Status to Incidence of and Recovery from Mental Illness," *Social Forces* 32 (December 1953): 185–194.

20.   Shirley S. Angrist, Mark Lefton, Simon Dinitz, and Benjamin Pasamanick, *Women After Treatment, A Study of Former Mental Patients and Their Normal Neighbors.*

21.   Robert A. Popa, " 'Insane' Smokey Sent Away—to Prison," *The Detroit News,* November 2, 1969, p. 3.

22.   All such considerations form the basis for demands for comprehensive mental health proposals rather than the uncoordinated melange of institutions that exist in most places. See Robert Felix, "A Comprehensive Mental Health Program," in *Mental Health and Social Welfare,* pp. 3–21.

23.   Donald E. Spiegel and Patricia Keith-Spiegel, "Why We Came Back: A Study of Patients Readmitted to a Mental Hospital," *Mental Hygiene* 53, no. 3 (July 1969).

24.   Ibid., p. 435.

8

ALCOHOLISM

There Is a growing inclination to consider the problems of
mental illness, alcoholism, and drug addiction together. All
have tended to shift in professional and popular definition from
the sphere of delinquent behavior to that of illness. They are all
generally viewed as overlapping in various ways, though the
precise lines between alcoholism or drug addiction and mental
illness are not easily drawn.

Alcohol is used pathologically when it interferes with the
psychological and social functioning of the individual. If alcoholism only affected the individual, it would be serious but still
tolerable. From the beginning, however, it is a disaster to the
family. In the traditional American experience with alcoholism,
a familiar figure is the workman who spends his pay check on
alcohol, leaving his family without income. Such images played
a major role in the arguments of crusading organizations such as
the Womens' Christian Temperance Union, which did so much
to secure the passage of the Prohibition Amendment. Before
the rise of contemporary welfare institutions, such a family was
literally abandoned to starve: harried housewives took in washing and the children of alcoholics were objects of ridicule. Few

people are unaware of the cycle of violence which churns many alcoholics and their families: the alcoholic returns home drunk; he savagely beats and kicks his wife and children and smashes furniture and chinaware; he breaks down in tearful pathetic remorse, promising never to do it again; and he keeps his word with rock-like fidelity *until the next time.* One sometimes wonders how many thousands of times this has happened: an alcoholic lives gloriously for a few hours, spends his money on gambling and prostitutes, and brings venereal disease home to the family from his escapades. The kinds and forms of abuse of the family by the alcoholic seem endless.

While the examples of the devastations of alcoholism reviewed above are direct summaries of cases directly familiar to the authors, they are by no means intended to imply that alcoholism is a serious problem only in working-class circles. The authors have also had experience with a variety of middle- and upper-class persons (business men and a variety of professionals, physicians, lawyers, university professors, social workers, and so on) for whom alcoholism assumed nightmarish properties. Middle- and upper-class persons have the resources to pay for their habit; they and their families and associates are in a somewhat better position to keep alcoholism concealed for a time; and they are in position to seek treatment in a variety of discreet private institutions, keeping the phenomenon off the public records. Nonetheless, the behavior of alcoholics is very similar regardless of the social class of the afflicted. Alcoholism lowers inhibitions and releases psychologically repressed material in the individual's personality. The home life of middle- and upper-class alcoholics is characterized with great frequency by brutal symbolic and physical fighting. The authors know of cases where the alcoholism of middle-class and professional persons was the cause of (or excuse for) abusive personal attacks, theft, attempted rape, and the destruction of property.

Alcoholism does not only cause difficulties to the family. The alcoholic's loss of time from business and industry is a source of serious concern. Alcoholism is a major component in automobile and industrial accidents. It impairs the efficiency of professionals. And it is a major burden to law enforcement and welfare agencies.

TYPES AND PHASES OF ALCOHOLISM

The two categories of alcoholics as defined by the Alcoholism Subcommittee of the World Health Organization are "alcohol addicts" and "habitual symptomatic excessive drinkers," referred to as non-addictive alcoholics. In the opinion of E. M. Jellinek, one of the leading authorities on alcoholism, the disease conception refers only to the alcohol addicts. Both the alcohol addicts and the non-addictive alcoholics are characterized by excessive drinking that reflects underlying social or psychological problems. But alcohol addicts, after several years of excessive drinking, lose control, while non-addictive alcoholics do not. Jellinek observes that many excessive drinkers consume as much as or more than addicts over a period of thirty or forty years without loss of control. This suggests to Jellinek that a superimposed process (perhaps psychological, perhaps physiological) makes the difference between prolonged excessive drinking and addiction.[1]

Jellinek divides the course of alcoholic addiction into four phases, based on an analysis of over 2,000 male alcohol addicts' case histories.[2] All alcohol addicts do not necessarily display all the various symptoms of each phase, since each individual is unique and symptoms may overlap. The four phases, however, do represent the typical course of events that leads from social drinking to alcohol addiction.

1. *The pre-alcoholic symptomatic phase.* Most drinking begins in social situations. But the prospective alcoholic finds more than ordinary relief from the tensions of living in drinking, and therefore may deliberately frequent those social situations where liquor flows freely. At first these situations are occasional, but, within a period of from six months to two years, he falls into a pattern of daily drinking. From occasional drinking to unwind, the drinker progresses to

constant drinking accompanied by an increase in alcohol tolerance (and the need to drink more to achieve the desired effect).

2. *The prodromal phase.* This phase is characterized by sudden blackouts or amnesia, technically termed alcoholic palimpsests. The amnesia is not accompanied by loss of consciousness and is not necessarily due to an excessive amount of immediate alcoholic intake. The drinker develops a kind of drinking pattern and behavior which suggests that he cannot get along without the alcohol. Characteristic of the pattern are surreptitious drinking, preoccupation with alcohol, and avid drinking (gulping of first drinks). He may have a few drinks at home before going out for the evening, or, if he knows his companions well, he may bring along his own supply to fortify him until he returns home. Guilt feelings develop about his drinking behavior in reaction to his emerging dependency on alcohol; these are followed by an avoidance of reference to alcohol in conversation. Another warning symptom in the prodromal phase is the increase in the frequency of alcoholic palimpsests. The duration of the prodromal period varies from six months to four or five years and ends with alcohol addiction, at which point the drinker experiences loss of control over his alcoholic intake.

3. *The crucial phase.* The crucial or acute phase of alcoholism begins with the drinker's loss of control over alcoholic intake. He now requires only a single drink to set him off. Any consumption of alcohol sets into motion a chain reaction of compulsive alcohol intake; the drinker cannot stop until he becomes too ill to drink any longer. After a few days or weeks, he may go on another drinking spree. Although the drinker is unable to stop once he starts drinking, he is usually still able to decide when he will go on another drinking spree. If he wishes, he can remain sober for weeks at a time between episodes.

As he loses control, the drinker finds rationalizations for his drinking behavior; this is the beginning of an elaborate system of self-deception. When social pressures are brought to bear on his behavior, his rationalizations operate as a defense. To compensate for his loss of self-esteem he often displays grandiose behavior such as buying extravagant things for himself or his family. His family becomes part of the system of self-deception, and often one hears the exclamation, "He's so wonderful when he's sober!" But he often begins to isolate himself from his social environment, and marked aggressive behavior patterns may set in. Alternate periods of generosity and brutality may appear. Periods of remorse lead only to more drinking.

When pressure from family or friends becomes too great, the drinker attempts total abstinence, or change of his drinking pattern by setting up regulations as to when and where he can drink. This is seldom successful, however. In time he may drop his friends, quit his job, and center his behavior around alcohol. He begins to worry about how his present way of life interferes with his drinking, rather than about how his drinking affects his way of life. The addict begins to lose interest in outside activities. A reinterpretation of his interpersonal relations is accompanied by marked self-pity. He starts thinking about "getting away from it all" (geographically, not suicidally). Changes in family habits, brought on by the drinker's erratic behavior, cause the addict to develop unreasonable resentments. To avoid having his wife confiscate his supply of alcohol the drinker hides his bottles all over the house, in the garage, the basement, the attic, and even the dog house. Increased drinking leads to neglect of proper nutrition, first hospitalization, a decrease in sexual activity and accusations, possibly compensatory, of extramarital affairs against the wife. The crucial phase ends with the addict's need for regular morning drinking. Up to this point, heavy drinking has been usually limited to the evening, but now the addict must have a drink upon rising, another at mid-morning, and yet another following noon lunch; heavier drinking starts before dinner.

4. *The chronic phase.* As the addict continues to drink, alcohol increasingly dominates his life. Morning drinking

sets up a demand that breaks down his resistance until he becomes intoxicated during the daytime even on weekdays. Prolonged intoxication or benders follow and result in incapacitation, speech and thought impairment, and marked ethical deterioration. In 10 percent or less of alcoholics, true alcoholic psychoses may occur. By this time most of the alcoholic's friends have left him and he drinks with other persons involved in heavy drinking. When he doesn't have the money for his usual drinks he will substitute rubbing alcohol, canned heat, bay rum, shaving lotion, or vanilla; in general, he is quite prepared to consume any products with alcohol in them, even shoe polish. The addict suffers a loss of alcohol tolerance and develops indefinable fears and tremors when he is without alcohol. Without alcohol, he is also unable to perform simple mechanical acts. In an effort to control the fears and tremors his drinking takes on an obsessive character. Vague religious desires sometimes develop and the entire rationalization system collapses. The addict, at this point, sometimes admits defeat and is amenable to treatment.

EXTENT OF THE PROBLEM

To ascertain the number of individuals in the United States who use alcoholic beverages, a national survey was conducted by the Social Research Group of George Washington University in 1965. The study found that: 68 percent of American adults drink occasionally (this includes 77 percent men and 60 percent women); the percentage of women drinkers had risen in the past twenty years; infrequent to moderate drinkers constitute 56 percent of adults; heavy drinkers (including the problem drinkers) constitute 12 percent; heavy drinkers include a greater proportion of men (four men to one woman), are younger, have more money, entertain more, and have lower church attendance than those adults in the infrequent to moderate drinking category.[3]

Other facts regarding the drinking habits of Americans were revealed in the 1963 survey conducted by Harold A. Mulford.

According to the study: a greater proportion of adults who drink alcoholic beverages are under age thirty-nine; the smallest proportion of those who drink are over sixty years of age; a higher proportion of Catholics and Jews drink than any other group, with Baptists rating among the lowest; regionally, the highest proportion of adult drinking was found in the New England and Middle Atlantic states and the lowest proportion in the South Central States; adults who reside in larger communities, and have better jobs, higher income, and more education are more likely to drink; and 79 percent of single adults drink, compared with 72 percent of married people, 69 percent of those divorced, and 51 percent of widowed adults. Problem drinkers constitute 10 percent of the adult population; the proportion of problem drinkers is highest among males, in the Western states, among adults who reside in the large cities, among the unmarried or divorced, and among those with the least education and low-status jobs and among those with the most education and high-status jobs. The problems of drinking and heavy drinking are somewhat distinct. By religion the percentage of problem drinkers is lowest among the Jews, Lutherans, Congregationalists, Presbyterians, and Episcopalians.[4]

Although the exact number of alcoholics in the United States is not known, it is estimated that there were about 6.5 million alcoholics in the 1960s.[5] Some people think this estimate is too conservative, but it is difficult to arrive at an accurate figure since different standards have been used in various research studies. In 1969, the National Council on Alcoholism estimated that there are about 160,000 new alcoholics each year. According to the most recent 1971 estimates, there are approximately 9 million alcoholics in the United States.

Alcoholism has been related to arrests for criminal offenses. In court, the offender often cites the fact that he was under the influence of alcohol at the time as his reason for committing his illegal act. American taxpayers spend many millions of dollars each year to arrest the excessive drinker, bring him into court, and support him in either the workhouse or jail. Statistics compiled on a nationwide basis point up the gravity of the problem. In 1965, the Federal Bureau of Investigation reported that out of a nationwide total of 4,955,047 arrests, 2,225,578 or approximately 45 percent were for offenses of drunkenness, including vagrancy, disorderly conduct, and public intoxication.[6]

In the skid row areas of our large cities, a chronic alcoholic may be arrested twenty to thirty times a year for drunkenness and related offenses. An example of the repeated arrests of the same man is given by David J. Pittman:

> To illustrate, let us take the case of Portland, Oregon, for 1963; in this year there were 11,000 law violations involving drunkenness or the effects of drinking, but only around 2,000 different persons accounted for these arrests. Thus, these chronic court and police case inebriates are the men (rarely women) who are arrested, convicted, sentenced, jailed and released, only to be re-arrested— often within hours or days. They are the men for whom the door of the court or jail is truly a "revolving door." They are the men who inhabit Skid Rows, slums, and rooming house areas in every large American city.[7]

The association between violent homicide and alcoholic drinking by the offender was established by Marvin E. Wolfgang. He conducted a research study of 588 criminal homicides in Philadelphia and concluded that about 60 percent of the offenders guilty of violent homicide had been drinking before committing the crime. Of those individuals guilty of nonviolent (e.g., negligent) homicide, 50 percent had been drinking before committing the crime.[8]

Alcoholism is a causal factor in traffic accidents. The National Safety Council reports that in about one-half of automobile accidents fatal to drivers and approximately one-third of automobile accidents fatal to pedestrians, (adult) consumption of alcohol is a contributing factor. Recent research using alcohol tests on blood, breath, or urine has raised this estimate. In 1959, a study conducted in New York revealed that 75 percent of drivers involved in fatal accidents had been drinking and that, after being tested, these drivers had more than 0.10 percent blood alcohol levels (0.10 grams of alcohol per 100 cc. of blood).[9]

Characteristics of adults with the worst drunken-driving and drunken-accident records were tabulated in a research study by Indiana University's Department of Police Administration. The worst drunken-driving records included men in the 25 to 44 age group, women and men divorced, widowed, or separated, and those individuals who had drinking problems or drank frequently. The worst drunken-accident records included individuals who drank excessively about once a month and single men and women.[10]

The relation between accidents and alcohol in Minnesota in 1968 is described below.

A coroners' blood testing program on drivers and pedestrians killed in traffic was started under state law on July 1, 1967. Reports are sent to the Highway Department where they are reduced to cold statistics.

About half of all drivers killed on our state roads last year had been drinking, Staffeld said in his report. Over 48 percent of those tested had more than .05 percent blood alcohol concentration—the level at which most people show serious impairment of reflexes and judgment.

More than 42 percent of drivers killed were at or above .10 percent blood alcohol concentration—the level at which they are presumed intoxicated for the purpose of driving under Minnesota law.

Out of 1,057 road deaths, the blood tests were made on 265 of the 531 drivers killed—and 54 percent showed evidence of drinking. Some 43 percent were at or above the .10 percent that by law made them too drunk to drive.

Of the 122 pedestrians killed last year, 38 percent were tested and 24 percent showed evidence of alcohol. Half of the pedestrians tested were 65 or older.[11]

Industry is directly affected by alcoholism when the number of man-hours lost results in lower profits. Additional expenses to industry involve replacing trained workers, medical and hospital expenses, and the costs of disability. On the job, the alcoholic often quarrels with his co-workers, lowers production, suffers accidents, and is frequently absent from work. The failure of the alcoholic worker to do his share of the work lowers the morale of others. If he is a supervisor or executive, his wrong decisions, made under the influence, can affect relations with the customers and the public.

The cost of alcoholism to industry was estimated, in 1963, to be $2 billion per year. The National Council on Alcoholism arrived at this figure after consulting with several U.S. firms considered to be typically American. The estimate was the result of the following statistics: in 1965 alcoholics constituted about 3 percent (over 1.5 million) of a work force (industrial, business and government) of 55 million; their average salary amounted to $5,000; the cost of each alcoholic to his company was a minimum of one-fourth of his salary, or $1,250 a year (for lost manpower, training expenses, fringe benefits, inefficiency, and replacements).[12] In 1968 the Department of Labor estimated that alcoholism was costing the economy $4 billion a year.

"A typical study, made in Milwaukee by case workers and counselors, revealed that among people in the slums who were not working, 15 percent were alcoholics or heavy drinkers, affecting their employability," it said.

"In St. Paul, Minn., an alcoholism-counselor was added to the public employment staff to work especially with alcoholics," the statement said.

"In six months, 225 alcoholics were placed in jobs—and 75 percent of them are still at work and making good," it added.

There are an estimated six million alcoholics in the United States—roughly 3 percent of the population—who cost the economy $4 billion a year.

The nationwide system of federal-state employment offices already offers special help to alcoholics, who are officially designated as handicapped persons in job applications, the statement said.

"The department strengthened these efforts by drafting a comprehensive guide for counselors and interviewers dealing with alcoholics in the more than 2,000 local public employment offices," it said.[13]

PHYSIOLOGICAL EFFECTS OF ALCOHOL

Excessive consumption of alcohol over a long period may have damaging effects on the body. Brain damage is one of the most serious consequences. Alcoholic pyschoses constitute a major group of mental disorders related to alcoholic poisoning and organic brain damage. Korsakov's psychosis is a mental illness involving brain damage usually associated with alcoholism and deficiencies in the diet, and is characterized by peripheral neuritis, amnesia, disturbance of attention, and compensatory confabulation. Delirium tremens is caused by the withdrawal from excessive and prolonged intake of alcohol and is characterized by tremors, hallucinations, delusions, and occasionally convulsions; brain damage is often present and death may result. Hallucinosis is a condition in which the person hallucinates while in a clearly conscious state. In the alcoholic paranoid state which develops in primarily male chronic alcoholics, delusions of persecution appear; for example, a husband may be consumed with extreme jealousy because of delusions of his wife's infidelity. Alcoholics who also have mental disorders sometimes have deep-seated psychoses or certain anxiety-provoking problems that contribute to their excessive consumption of alcohol and their erratic behavior.

Malnutrition is another major consequence of chronic alcoholism. On a spree, the drinker tends to eat very little or not at all. As a result, prolonged drinking can lead to vitamin deficiencies, anemia, poor health, and a fatty liver. Cirrhosis of the liver is prevalent among chronic alcoholics; eight times more alcoholics have it than nonalcoholics.

Other bodily ailments resulting from excessive use of alcohol are polyneuropathy (a degenerative disease of the nerves), characterized by burning sensations in the soles of the feet and pain in arms and legs; pellagra, caused by a deficiency of the B-complex vitamin niacin, resulting in skin lesions, gastrointestinal symptoms, and occasionally mental aberrations; and "beer heart," a heart condition caused by a deficiency of vitamin B_1 which is manifested in a weakening of the heart muscles, heart enlargement, and swelling of legs.

THE CAUSES OF ALCOHOLISM

Three different categories of factors or causes may play a role in the development of alcoholism: physiological, individual developmental (psychological), and social.

Physiological Causes

The simplistic approach to alcoholism is the notion that alcohol causes alcoholism: hence, no alcohol, no alcoholism. But men have been manufacturing alcohol in one form or other for thousands of years, and only a relatively small proportion of those with access to it have become alcoholics. So the possibility must be considered that the physiology of some persons makes them particularly susceptible to the disease.

The clearest case for the role of physiological factors in the development of alcoholics would be provided by the existence of hereditary tendencies. It is true that the children of alcoholics often become alcoholics. The disease, however, also occurs in the children of abstainers.[14] Moreover, alcoholism is much less frequent among those children of alcoholics raised apart from their home environments.[15]

A variety of allergic, nutritional, and hormonal theories of the physiological basis of alcoholism have been proposed. W. D. Silkworth argued that since the physiological changes introduced by consumption of alcohol resemble those of hayfever, there may be a common foundation.[16] Nutritional theories of alcoholism were first experimentally explored by R. J. Mardones, who examined rats deprived of vitamin B-complex and given a choice between water and an alcohol solution. In contrast to a control group with a sufficient amount of vitamin B, the experimental rats increased their intake of the alcohol solution.[17] J. J. Smith approached the problem from a different point of view by suggesting that alcoholism was caused by pituitary deficiency resulting in adrenal-cortex exhaustion.[18] All of these possibilities have been explored and debated at some length. An excellent summary is to be found in Harry Milt's *Basic Handbook on Alcoholism.*[19]

These studies and others stimulated by them remain inconclusive. For this reason, the American Medical Association quite appropriately lists the following physiological theories of alcoholism as hypotheses:

1. Alcoholism is caused by a metabolic disturbance which results in a craving for alcohol.

2. Alcoholism is caused by an abnormal sugar metabolism

3. Alcoholism is caused by any of a variety of endocrine deficiencies including hypothyroidism, hypopituitarism, hypoadrenalism, and hypogonadism.

4. Alcoholism is caused by dietary or metabolic deficiency of vitamins or minerals.

5. Alcoholism is caused by glandular dysfunction, that is, liver deficiency, hyperinsulinism, or "asynchronization" of all the endocrine glands.

6. Alcoholism is caused by sensitivity to some foodstuff, the symptoms of which are specifically relieved by use of alcohol.

7. Alcoholism is caused by defective function of an "alcohol appestat" in the hypothalamus, causing a thirst for ethanol.

8. Alcoholism is caused by imbalance of acetylcholine and receptor sites in the ascending reticular formation of the brainstem.[20]

At the present stage of research, the evidence seems to weigh against any notion of the exclusive cause of alcoholism by physiological factors. That there is differential physiological sensitivity to alcohol, however, seems indicated, with the strong possibility that physiological factors may contribute to alcoholism's development. It has been noted that in the development of alcoholism, different individuals move through its various stages at different rates. In the movement from one stage to another, rates may vary from a few months to many years. It is possible that physiological factors may play some role in the differential rates.

Individual Developmental Causes

Most attempts to explain alcoholism have adduced psychological factors. Ever and again, when persons in the early stages of alcoholism are examined, alcohol appears to be employed by the individual to make up for some deficiency he experiences in himself. And when studies of the possible parental influence on alcoholism have been conducted, childhood conditions that might be interpreted as potentially causing the individual difficulty in coping with life problems often seem to be associated with later alcoholism: inconsistently affectionate mothers, parental conflict, deviance (particularly sexual) on the part of the mother, low esteem of the father for his wife, role evasions by either parent, parental inadequacy, anti-social behavior on the part of the parents.[21]

Freud believed that the personality arises through a number of distinct phases. The individual's pleasure impulses are first focused on sucking (oral phase). One of his first adjustments to society is represented by sphincter control, and he is both socialized and rewarded in the course of this adjustment (anal stage). Then, if he is to reach maturity, he eventually learns, through a series of subphases, to focus his pleasure on a legitimate object of the opposite sex (genital phase). While everyone experiences all these phases to some extent, major crises along the way may cause an individual to regress to and become fixated on a premature phase of development.

R. R. Knight, a proponent of the Freudian psychoanalytic approach, believes that the alcoholic's behavior pattern is characteristic of the oral stage.[22] The alcoholic tends to be very dependent and passive, yet demanding. He is unusually interested in mouth activities. According to Knight, insufficient mothering is partly responsible for alcoholism, in which the individual continues to seek those forms of gratification that he lacked in infancy.[23]

Others subscribing to a psychoanalytic point of view, however, derive alcoholism somewhat differently. Some psychoanalysts have maintained that regression to an oral phase may be a component in homosexuality. In this context the individual, realizing the general social repugnance to homosexuality, may drink to conceal his homosexual inclinations, perhaps even from himself.[24]

In fact, there are a number of other ways in which persons

subscribing to a Freudian perspective have attempted to explain alcoholism. To the majority of these, characteristics acquired in the course of individual development seem most plausibly to explain alcoholism.

Among the personal traits to which alcoholism has been theoretically linked are excessive anxiety, tension, repression, regression, fixation, immaturity, frustration, aggression, a low level of personal control, impulses toward self-destruction, homosexual fixation, inability to stand tension, poor integration, guilt obsession, sense of emotional deprivation, and inability to accept or give love.

It has been both asserted and denied that a distinctive alcohol-prone personality can be discerned. This ambiguity in part is bound up with inconsistencies in the conception of personality. If, as is often the case, personality is viewed not as the presence or absence of any single trait but as a peculiar ensemble of traits, one could argue that alcoholism has psychological causes without accepting the notion that there is such a thing as an alcohol-prone personality.

But the problems represented by a potentially alcohol-prone personality do not end here. A considerable number of theories of personality have been advanced. While there are many points of convergence among them, they differ in their notions of both how personality arises and the peculiar ensemble of traits that distinguish it. Hence, they tend to account for alcoholism from different biases. A few examples will illustrate the manner in which explanations for alcoholism may reflect alternative theories of personality.

The theory that the personality of the alcoholic is characterized by unconscious self-destructive urges has been set forth by Karl Menninger.[25] In his opinion, the alcoholic's strong urge to destroy himself results in his addiction to alcohol. Menninger views the alcoholic pattern as a progression: in the oral stage the alcoholic is frustrated; this frustration leads to rage directed at his parents, but the rage is suppressed because of guilt feelings; eventually, the rage is replaced by feelings of inferiority and worthlessness, and addiction to alcohol results.

The Adlerian theory of personality regards the alcoholic personality as an inferior-superior type. The alcoholic, from this point of view, drinks to compensate for a sense of weakness or inferiority,[26] At the beginning of addiction, the alcoholic may feel extremely inferior: he may be a loner, shy, overly sensitive, and depressed; or he may compensate for weakness with a superiority complex characterized by a longing for power and boastfulness. Adler maintained that, as the result of overindulgence in childhood, the adult may be unable to cope with societal demands and may resort to alcohol to resolve his inferiority feelings.

The number and variety of approaches to the alcohol-prone personality is so great that a few persons have been tempted to take an eclectic approach to the problem. Representative of such an approach is that of R. J. Cantanzaro, who lists the following thirteen characteristics of the alcoholic: emotional immaturity; a high level of anxiety in interpersonal relationships; feeling of isolation; low self-esteem; low frustration tolerance; a tendency toward grandiosity; ambivalence toward authority; perfectionism and compulsiveness; feelings of guilt; sex-role confusion; angry overdependency; and inability to express angry feelings adequately.[27]

At the present stage of research, perhaps the safest approach to developmental causes of alcoholism can be summarized as follows: 1. There is no conclusive evidence of an alcohol-prone personality (that is, a single ensemble of traits invariably associated with the affliction). 2. Psychological factors of a variety of sorts, however, seem to be strongly associated with alcoholism. 3. While physiological and sociological factors also play a role, psychological factors seem to be most important. George N. Thompson's summary seems to be eminently just:

> At the present time we can state only that emotional factors add to the problem of alcoholism and are related to the other factors that are stated. Alcoholism is probably in general due less to a specific psychiatric syndrome than it is the result of multiple factors. Among these are the biologic, the social, the psychologic and the cultural, and among psychologic factors are certainly to

be considered the emotional factors. . . . In the majority of cases
it is probable that the emotional factors or emotional disorders
are the most prominent causes.[28]

Social Causes of Alcoholism

Each individual is born into a milieu with its own various customs of alcohol use. The practices of alcohol use by the individual's family, peer group, religious institutions, social stratum,
and society as a whole inevitably affect his inclination to control
or abuse the use of alcohol.

FAMILY. The family is the most immediate representative of
wider society for the individual. Of course, the family is also
inseparable from his personal development, so that its influence
is often critical in establishing the psychological roots of alcoholism. Furthermore, family patterns of alcoholism might
signify the existence of genetic components in the disease or in
the inclination toward it.

When Jellinek examined the results of various studies of
more than 4,000 alcoholics, he found that 52 percent had been
reared by one or two alcoholic parents.[29] In M. Bleuler's study
of upper-class alcoholic patients, he found a much higher percentage of alcoholics among their relatives than among the
general population.[30] And W. McCord and J. McCord found
that, of a sample of 51 alcoholics, 22 percent of their sons also
became alcoholics, while only 12 percent of the sons of a sample
of 125 non-alcoholic fathers became alcoholics.[31]

In our affluent society, with several automobiles per family,
more teenage drivers, and a rising rate of venereal disease
among teenagers, more attention is now being paid to teenage
drinking.

Teenage drinking is often felt to be associated with delinquency. But a research study conducted in Massachusetts indicates that there is no difference between normal and delinquent
high school students as to the proportion who drink. The important factor, rather, was *how* the students drank.[32] The drinking patterns of teenagers reflect those of their parents and vary

according to ethnic background, religion, age, sex, economic status, and so on.

It was noted earlier that when the children of alcoholic parents are raised outside their parental homes, they are less likely to become alcoholics in adulthood. This seems to indicate that the higher rate of alcoholism among those raised in the homes of alcoholics is a product both of the fact that these children learn to use alcohol in a manner that tends to lead to alcoholism, and the fact that the home environment creates special tensions in the individual which he tends to resolve (or attempts to resolve) by alcohol, in somewhat the same manner as his parents.

The drinking patterns of peer groups may reinforce or con-travene the drinking practices of the family. Perhaps most youth peer groups display drinking practices parallel to those of the groups' parents. In studies of the drinking patterns of more than 8,000 high school students, the number of those using alcohol varied from 30 percent in Michigan to 80 percent in New York. Though all of those who drank reported having been drunk at one time or another, less than 6 percent had as much as one drink a day. Drinking was reported to be for plea-sure, for social purposes, or for experimentation. The patterns among youth were similar to those among adults: more boys than girls, more urban than rural students drank.[33] The drinking patterns among the boys with delinquent behavior, however, was quite different from the patterns found by Maddox. Among 500 delinquent boys at the Massachusetts Reception Center, 28 percent were abstainers, 34 percent moderate drinkers, 13 percent heavy social drinkers, 9 percent relief drinkers, and 7 percent addictive drinkers.[34] In cases of this sort, there may be a sharp difference between peer group and home drinking patterns.

As the individual grows older, peer group drinking patterns can be anticipated to vary more widely from those of the family. In a survey of drinking behavior among 16,000 college students in twenty-seven colleges, some 74 percent drank, and while there were no alcoholics in the group there were heavy and problem drinkers. Around 6 percent had drinking problems serious enough to involve loss of friends, injuries or accidents, and failure to meet obligations.[35]

RELIGION. Religious attitudes toward alcoholism vary from enjoining abstinence as a religious obligation (Islam, Mormonism, and some Protestant sects) to the employment of some forms of alcohol in religious rituals (Catholicism and Judaism). Most Moslems and Mormons do not drink because of their religions' prohibition of alcohol. Mulford's survey found that among religious denominations, Jews had the highest percentage of drinkers—90 percent. Catholics had 89 percent and Lutherans had 85 percent. Sixty-one percent of Methodists drink and 48 percent of Baptists.[36] But the rates of heavy drinking and alcoholism by religion are somewhat different: Protestants (other than Methodists and Baptists) have the heaviest rates, followed by Catholics, with Jews showing the lowest rate.

CLASS AND STATUS. In Mulford's survey, it was discovered that, contrary to popular belief, the well-to-do and better educated drink more than the lower strata. Eighty percent of those who have attended college drink, compared to 46 percent of those who did not complete high school. Of those earning more than $10,000 a year, seven out of eight are drinkers, compared to one out of two of those earning less than $3,000 a year. Hollingshead and Redlich found interesting class contrasts in the first treatment of alcoholism. Some 67 percent of alcoholics in the two highest classes were first treated by private practictioners or in private hospitals; some 65 percent of alcoholics in the lowest class were first treated in the state hospital, and the remaining were first treated in public clinics.[37] Class differences in the forms and duration of treatment of alcoholism were also found.

ETHNIC GROUP. Different cultures vary widely in the types and forms of their alcohol use. Transposed pluralities from other societies often find it useful to band together in their new home for mutual protection and promotion of their common interests.

Such ethnic enclaves tend to preserve many elements of their original culture, including customs of alcohol use. However, the ethnic group is operating in the framework of a majority culture that tends to erode the culture of the ethnic group. This may bring ethnic drinking patterns into line with the majority culture or create conditions where they vary from both.

Italians in Italy drink wine at their meals and on many other occasions and generally for pleasure. But drunkenness is uncommon. Most Italian-Americans drink, although they do not by any means restrict themselves to wine. They drink not only at their meals but socially and for pleasure, and children are early initiated to the practice. Yet they also have a low rate of alcoholism and of arrests for problem drinking. But in the successive generations, the rate of hard liquor consumed and amount of intoxication tend to increase.[38]

Universally among Jews, drink plays a ritualistic role in most religious observances and holidays. But the Jews produce few alcoholics. Younger generations, however, have tended to adopt the drinking patterns of middle-class Americans (cocktail parties, drinking at receptions, business luncheons, and so on). Excessive drinking is almost directly related to the degree of departure from religious orthodoxy.[39]

In France about 90 percent of the adult population drink; their average daily intake of wine is about three-fifths of a quart for men, about one-fifth of a quart for women. Farmers consume more alcohol than urbanites and the poor more than the well-to-do. French alcoholism is high by comparison with most western countries. Excessive daily drinking without intoxication occurs, but with negative effects on health and life span. Heavy daily drinking with almost continuous inebriation also appears. Somewhat similar drinking patterns appear in Argentina, Chile, Portugal, and Spain. French-Americans, however, do not display unique drinking patterns.[40]

Among American ethnic groups, the Irish have one of the highest rates of alcohol use, heavy drinking, and alcoholism. It is generally assumed that the nineteenth-century Irish brought their drinking patterns to America. But while heavy drinking occurs in Ireland, the rate of alcoholism is not high. The Irish may represent that type of ethnic situation in which interaction with the wider culture has elevated the alcoholic rate.[41]

Among Chinese-Americans in New York City's Chinatown, drinking was found to be widespread but with little isolation and very little lone drinking. Drinking there occurs primarily in connection with family ceremonies (births, weddings, rites for the dead) and national and religious celebrations. Although little boys are introduced to drinking early, intoxication is frowned upon. Drunkenness in women is particularly disapproved.[42]

Various social factors, here only sketchily reviewed, cannot by themselves cause alcoholism. They may, however, in conjunction with physiological and psychological factors, certainly have an impeding or facilitating role.

THE TREATMENT OF ALCOHOLISM

Obviously, the treatment of alcoholism cannot be undertaken except on a hit-or-miss basis until the problem of causes is solved. As noted above, much uncertainty about the status of causes of alcoholism still remains. To some extent, the history of the treatment of alcoholism may illuminate its causes.

Throughout most of the history of western society, alcoholism was attributed to moral defect. Hence, the problem of treatment took the form of setting up ethical and legal controls. The nineteenth century gave rise to the anti-saloon league, composed of women who smashed saloons and gave morally uplifting speeches to the public. During this period, ministers attempted to persuade people to attend church and treated the alcoholic as one who needed to repent and be saved. The treatment of the alcoholic was based on moral education and religious inspiration.

There were repeated efforts in the late nineteenth and early twentieth centuries to control the consumption of alcohol. The Eighteenth Amendment, which enacted Prohibition, was the climax of these efforts. Not repealed until 1932, this national experiment in attempting to control alcohol by legislation was one of the fiascos of modern times. Its failure proved that legislation against mores is impossible. Millions of people went into the home-brew business and the underworld took over the manufacture and sale of alcohol, creating all kinds of problems for the law enforcement agencies.

Over and beyond moral uplift, religious salvation, and legislation, some private clinics did attempt to use the resources of modern psychology. One device employed the behavioristic concept of the conditioned reflex through aversion therapy. Everything that the alcoholic patient ate or drank was drenched with alcohol, so that he eventually vomited at the sight of it. This gave the alcoholic a period of grace in which to reconstruct his life. But after three to six months, this conditioning wore off.

There is little evidence that psychotherapy was being generally used to treat the alcoholic before World War II. The varieties of treatment described below have all been instituted since.

Facilities and Services

The various services and facilities available for the treatment of alcoholism include: state hospitals; special state alcoholic programs; outpatient clinics; general hospitals; community mental health centers; private psychiatric hospitals; general practitioners; and psychiatrists in private practice.

STATE HOSPITALS. From the time of their origin the state hospitals have treated alcoholics. According to the National Institute of Mental Health, approximately one out of five admissions is alcoholic. All 245 state mental hospitals in the United States admit alcoholics even when this is presumably forbidden, and in some state mental hospitals alcoholism is the single largest category of admissions, reaching 40 percent in Maryland. Some state hospitals have extensive detoxification services and about 15 percent have separate treatment programs for alcoholics.

SPECIAL STATE ALCOHOLISM PROGRAMS. Special state programs for alcoholism were first established in the 1940s and have continued to develop since. As of 1967, some forty states had special programs. These vary from mere public education programs to comprehensive programs funded for community-based outpatient services and, in a few cases, inpatient services.

OUTPATIENT CLINICS. Outpatient clinics for the treatment of alcoholics were first established in the 1940s and numbered around 125 by the mid-1960s. Most outpatient clinics are supplied by funds from state alcoholism programs. Their directors are usually psychiatrists and often serve on a part-time basis. Psychiatric and medical consultation is made available in outpatient clinics. Extensive use is made of psychotropic drugs and a few operate detoxification facilities.

GENERAL HOSPITALS. General hospitals have always admitted unconscious patients, but, except for a few Canadian and American hospitals which have long offered care to alcoholics, most have turned away non-acute cases as noisy, weak-willed, and immoral persons disruptive of hospital routine. A few wealthy patients under the care of private physicians may have been admitted for detoxification, but usually under some euphemism such as "gastritis." In the 1950s this all began to change. In 1957 officials at San Francisco's Mount Zion Hospital began to accept alcoholics simply as sick people and they were found to be no more disturbing than ordinary patients.[43] The success of this experiment led many other hospitals around the country to change their attitudes toward alcoholics. A research project led by Morris Chafetz at Massachusetts General Hospital demonstrated the importance of the attitudes of hospital personnel from the time of first admission to the emergency ward services of the general hospital.[44]

COMMUNITY MENTAL HEALTH CENTERS. Community mental health centers, founded by federal legislation, are still too new to have standardized alcoholic services. A few have set up formal arrangements with some alcoholic facility, but most give alcoholism low priority.

PRIVATE PSYCHIATRIC HOSPITALS. Around 90 percent of all private psychiatric hospitals admit some alcoholics. According to a 1966 survey, however, alcoholism accounts for only about 6 percent of their patients.

GENERAL PRACTITIONERS.   Most general practitioners encounter alcoholism in their course of practice. What they knew about it until recently depended on their on-the-job experience. Most have confined themselves to treating the physical damage resulting from the excessive use of alcohol and have avoided the psychological and psychiatric aspects of the affliction. One aim of the various state alcoholism programs has been the education of medical practitioners in broader forms of treatment.

PRIVATE PSYCHIATRISTS.   A 1966 survey of psychiatrists in private practice revealed that they conceptualize the problem of alcoholism in somewhat the same manner as psychiatrists in alcoholism programs: some 70 percent see it as a personality disorder; 15 percent as a disease; and 13 percent as both a symptom and a disease. Of 190 psychiatrists surveyed, over 100 saw two or fewer problem drinkers a month, and 24 saw ten or more a month. At the time of the survey fewer than 1,000 persons with serious drinking problems had been seen by the 235 psychiatrists with prominent reputations in private practice.[45]

THE CLERGY.   The traditional definition of drinking as a sin cast the problem of alcoholism into the lap of the clergy. Typically its method of handling the problem was to call upon the "sinner" to repent, seek divine aid, and be saved. A few alcoholics were in fact rescued, but most slid back into "sin" after a time. Clergymen still counsel excessive drinkers among their flocks, but they increasingly utilize contemporary psychiatric and sociological knowledge and often refer their charges to appropriate treatment facilities.

ALCOHOLICS ANONYMOUS.   AA is a voluntary fellowship of ex-alcoholics gathered together to firm up their resolve and extend aid to others.

It is a close-knit fellowship of individuals prepared to come any hour of the day or night and counsel a potential back-sliding brother seized by an overpowering desire to drink. It is very similar to a religious sect, although without a specific religious message or program. It was in fact founded in the 1930s by two alcoholics who had joined the Oxford Group in a vain attempt to cure themselves of alcoholism. (The Oxford Group, or Buchmanism, was a religious movement emphasizing Christian fellowship or sharing and public confession of sins with absolute honesty, purity, love, and unselfishness in small groups. The movement is named after its founder, Frank Buchman. There is little question that its major features were taken over by AA.) AA has grown rapidly since then and now has more than 7,000 chapters, with one in most large communities. As time has gone by, AA has operated less like a withdrawn sect and now cooperates with other therapists. Modeled after AA are Al-Anon, established to help the wives and husbands of alcoholics, and Al-Ateen, devoted to aiding the children of alcoholics to understand their parents' problems.

LOCAL NON-GOVERNMENTAL AGENCIES. Among the more prominent of the local non-governmental agencies which have developed programs for alcoholics and their families are the Salvation Army, the Volunteers of America, and various church-sponsored missions. A number of special privately operated hospitals for alcoholics have played a role as research and training centers. And halfway houses for alcoholics have made their appearance as institutions intermediate between the hospital and the community.

INDUSTRIAL PROGRAMS. Although industry has long been reluctant to concern itself with alcoholism among its employees, on the grounds that it had no right to interfere in their private lives, employers are in a position to note alcoholism in its early stages. Moreover, it is in the interest of industry to reduce absenteeism and to avoid, if possible, the replacement of skilled employees lost to alcoholism. Since World War II, many large firms have begun to set up alcoholic programs for those employees in need of such service. At the present time more than 200 American firms maintain their own company programs, usually as part of their health and industrial relations programs. They are often able to catch the problem early, before the individual's health and financial resources are depleted. And they have a powerful incentive—the threat of loss of livelihood—at their disposal. It is estimated that there is a 50 to 70 percent recovery rate in company programs.[46]

Parallel to industry's interest in alcoholism is the increasing inclination of insurance companies to include treatment of alcoholism in their health insurance policies. Treatment is covered by many commercial insurance companies, state disability insurance programs, union plans, Blue Cross, and Blue Shield.

Methods of Treatment

The evidence suggests that alcoholism is a complex product of possibly physiological and certainly psychological and sociological factors. Furthermore, alcoholism is not one disease, but rather a category of afflictions, the common property of which is excessive use of alcohol resulting in a variety of physiological and possible psychological consequences. This complexity bears upon the problem of treatment, for characteristically some things work in some cases, but not in others. The best results seem to be brought about by a combination of treatments. For purposes of review, however, it is simplest to break down the kinds of treatment into physiological, individual developmental (psychological), and social.

PHYSIOLOGICAL TREATMENT.   The various types of physiological treatment of alcoholism are primarily directed toward detoxification, mitigation of withdrawal symptoms, and the treatment of the deleterious physiological effects of prolonged alcohol use. Without adequate medical care for acute intoxication and severe withdrawal symptoms, the patient may not survive. Until recently, alcohol substitutes such as chloral hydrate and paraldehyde were employed to mitigate withdrawal symptoms; but today's new tranquilizers (such as reserpine and meprobamate), together with the control of fluid and electrolytic balance, permit most patients to recover from delirium, hallucinations, and tremors relatively quickly.

Among the chronic disorders due to prolonged excessive use of alcohol are: alcoholic polyneuropathy (involving weakness, numbness, pain, paresthesis, and a number of other symptoms); Wernicke's encephalopathy (characterized by ataxia, ocular abnormality, and mental confusion); Korsakoff's psychosis (a severe impairment of memory and learning); alcohol amblyopia (visual failure); alcohol cerebellar degeneration (ataxia of stance and gait); cerebral atrophy; gastrointestinal disorders; liver ailments; hepatic failure resulting in periodic disorders of consciousness; and pancreatitis.[47] Most of these disorders are partly complicated by nutritional deficiencies.

While detoxification and treatment of the conditions resulting from prolonged alcohol use do not cure alcoholism proper, they are often necessary preliminary steps for such treatment. Once detoxification and the mitigation or partial reversal of chronic disorders are accomplished, however, drug therapy is frequently employed to start the patient on the road toward control of his actual alcoholism.

Inasmuch as tensions and anxieties often trigger drinking, tranquilizing drugs seemed to be a logical substitute for alcohol. While they are often highly effective, the alcoholic tends rapidly to become addicted to them, exchanging one form of dependence for another that may be worse in the long run.

Aversion therapy has been updated with drugs. Nausea-producing agents such as emetine or apomorphine, administered with an alcoholic beverage, are intended to develop a conditioned reflex aversion to alcohol in any form. Disulfram (Antabuse) and citrated calcium carbimide (Temposil) are also widely used. A patient regularly taking them finds that the ingestion of alcohol produces a pounding headache, flushing, and nausea.

Like the older forms of aversion therapy, however, the conditioning developed with the assistance of drugs only lasts for a short time. It may, however, provide a kind of breathing space during which other modes of treatment may be advanced.

Among the more daring experiments in drug therapy are those using lysergic acid (LSD). Roughly the same procedure is followed as that employed by Grinker and Speigel in their technique of narcosynthesis. However, instead of administering to the patient amytal sodium or some other "truth serum," the experimenter administers lysergic acid. This sends the patient on a "trip" under the observation of the experimenter, who then has access to and is potentially able to manipulate all sorts of psychological material that would under ordinary circumstances be repressed. Although some investigators have reported successes, such research is too limited at present to permit safe conclusions.

INDIVIDUAL DEVELOPMENTAL (PSYCHOLOGICAL) TREATMENT. In one respect the conception of alcoholism has not changed much. In the past as in the present its causes were thought to lie primarily in the individual. However, the manner in which the psychological causes of alcoholism must be handled has been revolutionized. It is generally agreed to be useless to harangue, denounce, or admonish the alcoholic, to aggravate his sense of guilt, to call upon him to repent, or to exhort him to firm his resolve, strengthen his will, and to hold fast to the good.

If the alcoholic drinks in the first place out of a sense of inadequacy, weakness, inferiority, or guilt, it is hardly plausible that he will be inclined to give up drinking by intensifying these feelings. Exhortations intended to firm up the individual's resolve may only have the effect of increasing his guilt and sense of helplessness.

Psychotherapy is a general label for a wide variety of procedures which attack the problem of alcoholism at the level of the individual's conscious and emotional experience. Trained professionals seek to raise the level of the individual's insight into his own problems, while at the same time giving him whatever counseling and guidance will help bring his drinking under control. When psychotherapy is successful, it is presumably because of a transformation of attitude and emotion on the part of the patient that renders drinking behavior irrelevant.

The specific form that psychotherapy takes varies with the resources of the patient (in general only the well-to-do can afford the expensive individual services of a psychiatrist or other professional); the training and theoretical persuasion of the therapist (his conception of personality and its disorders dictates where he looks for the source of the trouble and how he thinks it may be treated); and the diagnosis in the special case (for example, whether the particular patient is analyzed to be neurotic or psychotic determines the type of procedures deemed appropriate for treatment). Regarding the last factor, it is widely assumed that if in a given case the alcoholic is neurotic his problems are accessible to psychoanalytic procedures; if, however, he is psychotic, psychoanalysis is not of much help.

SOCIOLOGICAL (GROUP THERAPEUTIC) TREATMENT. In contrast to individual therapy—one therapist working with one patient—groups of patients may be treated by teams of therapists. Group therapy has many variations, and a group of patients may meet with one or with several therapists (psychiatrist, psychologist, internist, social worker, perhaps a clergyman, and so on).

There are many arguments for group therapy. It involves a saving where financial resources are indaequate for individual therapy; it prevents contrary and independent counsel, diagnosis, and therapy; and it makes possible the sharing of various staff perspectives.

Group therapy presents the patient with a social situation. If a given clinic has trained internists, psychiatrists, nurses, social workers, psychologists, vocational rehabilitation counselors, occupational therapists, and clergymen of various faiths available, the patient is provided with teams that bring to bear on the therapeutic process perspectives appropriate to many of the aspects of everyday life.

Even at the level of individual treatment, some consideration of the social factors in the rise of alcoholism make themselves felt. Alcoholics Anonymous, for example, which started out by concentrating on the single individual alcoholic, has come to accept the necessity of considering the family as well. Moreover, Al-Anon, which uses the techniques of AA to work with the wives and husbands of alcoholics, has tended to transform the alcoholic's former debilitating social situation.

The family of the alcoholic came increasingly to be taken into account as it was found that the circumstances that drove the individual to drink often did not stop with his individual medical and psychological problems. Moreover, the drinking itself frequently became, over time, the basis for family tensions which played back upon and reinforced the drinking complex. Hence, if the individual were started on the route to control of his drinking problem but if his family situation were left unchanged, the simplest way out for the individual often was to return to drinking. Similar considerations apply to a wide variety of economic and vocational problems which may have been factors in the rise of alcoholism in the first place and which became worse as a result of it. For the many problem drinkers with such varied individual problems, the principal services required are emergency care of both the medical and psychiatric type; inpatient care; partial hospitalization, including both day and night treatment; outpatient clinic care; halfway houses; and the services of a variety of welfare, rehabilitation, and vocational workers.

An example of a comprehensive treatment program for alcoholism is provided by the Georgian Clinic of Atlanta. The Georgia Commission on Alcoholism was established in 1951. The first major component of its program, the Georgian Clinic, was opened in 1953. Since 1956, under the direction of Dr. Vernelle Fox, it has provided a range of services including twenty-four-hour care, day programs, and outpatient services. For treatment, it relies primarily on therapeutic groups intended to help the patients attain a better understanding of themselves. The program has been described by Dr. Fox as follows:

> After physical evaluation, the patient undergoes psychiatric, social and vocational screening in an attempt to determine his recovery potential. Medical management and treatment prescription is begun immediately and continued throughout the contact. A series of orientation procedures follows: the patient sees appropriate films, attends personal interviews and counseling sessions,

and participates in group meetings. Each week, there are 69 group meetings, together with 16 staff group meetings. A network of occupational, recreational and vocational activities designed to aid self-expression is woven into the program. The patients themselves form a therapeutic community, earlier members sponsoring the newer and more frightened. This "acceptance attitude therapy" is an important factor in orienting and strengthening the new patient. After leaving the clinic, all patients are urged to attend group meetings regularly for at least two years in the outpatient clinic, or at a local chapter of Alcoholics Anonymous or a community-based clinic, and to continue indefinitely if possible.[48]

Because the clinic views the alcoholic's most common problems as relating to others, it thinks of treatment as extending over a long period and encourages the patient to think of a minimum of two to three years. Discharge planning is undertaken with this in mind. When they leave, most patients are transferred to outpatient status, and those from outside the Atlanta area are referred to one of the four outpatient clinics. While formal evaluation had not been made of the program, Dr. Fox stated that two-thirds of the patients who remain with the treatment for a length of time "recover their socioeconomic status in the community with complete sobriety or recover sufficiently, with continuous supportive therapy, to maintain their jobs and families without welfare assistance." [49]

The Georgian Clinic's claims for recovery are unusually high. In general, therapists divide alcoholics into three major types with differential recovery rates: psychotic alcoholics (constituting 5 to 10 percent of all alcoholics, who suffer severe chronic psychoses and are usually in state mental hospitals); skid row alcoholics (impoverished "homeless men," who account for 3 to 8 percent of all alcoholics); "average" alcoholics (men and women usually still married or living with their families and holding jobs, who account for about 70 percent). The prognosis for chronic psychotic and skid row alcoholics is poor—perhaps about 10 percent are aided by ordinary therapy. The so-called "average" alcoholic fares somewhat better. Complete cure, in the sense that he might learn to drink moderately, is generally viewed as nearly impossible. Permanent abstinence is the goal of most treatment. Less than 20 percent of all treated patients have been able to maintain complete abstinence for more than three to five years. But rehabilitation—conceived as the achievement by the patient of an adequate family life, a good work record, and a respectable position in the community, with control over drinking most of the time—can be expected in about 60 percent of the cases.

By Public Law 91–616, Congress passed the Comprehensive Alcohol Abuse and Alcoholism Prevention, Treatment, and Rehabilitation Act of 1970. This established within the National Institute of Mental Health the National Institute on Alcohol Abuse and Alcoholism, charged with systematic reporting to the President and Congress of recommendations on the control, treatment and abuse of alcoholism. The Institute was also charged with the conduct of programs for the prevention, treatment and rehabilitation of alcoholics among Federal civilian employees and for Federal assistance for State and local programs. The act authorized appropriations of $40 million for the fiscal year ending June 30, 1971, $60 million for the year ending June 30, 1972, and $80 million for the year ending June 30, 1973 for grants to states to assist them in carrying through alcohol programs. By spring 1971 a dominant factor in the field of alcoholism was the brisk competition for available alcoholics among the hundreds of programs established under this new act and funded by the National Institute on Alcohol Abuse.

NOTES

1. E. M. Jellinek, *The Disease Concept of Alcoholism.*
2. Ibid.
3. Ira H. Cisin (Paper presented before American Association for the Advancement of Science, Washington, D.C., December 1966).

4. Harold A. Mulford, "Drinking and Deviant Drinking, U.S.A., 1963," *Quarterly Journal of Studies on Alcohol* 25 (1964): 634–650.

5. V. Efron and M. Keller, *Selected Statistical Tables on the Consumption of Alcohol, 1850–1962, and Alcoholism, 1930–1960* (New Brunswick, N.J.: Rutgers Center of Alcohol Studies, 1963).

6. U.S. Federal Bureau of Investigation, *Uniform Crime Reports for the United States, 1965* (Washington, D.C.: U.S. Dept. of Justice, 1966).

7. David J. Pittman, "The Chronic Drunkenness Offender: An Overview," in *Conference Proceedings on the Court and the Chronic Inebriate* (Washington: U.S. Dept. of Health, Education and Welfare, 1965), p. 6.

8. Marvin E. Wolfgang, *Patterns in Criminal Homicide* (Philadelphia: University of Pennsylvania Press, 1958), p. 166.

9. *Accident Facts* (Chicago: National Safety Council, 1966).

10. Robert F. Borkenstein, Richard F. Crowther, Robert P. Shumate, Walter B. Ziel, and Richard Zylman, *The Role of the Drinking Driver in Traffic Accidents* (Bloomington, Indiana: Indiana University, Department of Police Administration, 1964).

11. Donald J. Giese, "Report on Drinking," *St. Paul Pioneer Press,* May 25, 1969, p. 5.

12. Lewis F. Presnall, cited in *Business Week* (September 21, 1963).

13. Labor Department Release, *The Denver Post,* December 8, 1968, p. 12.

14. Juha Partanen, Kettil Bruun, and Touko Markkanen, *Inheritance of Drinking Behavior* (Helsinki: Finnish Foundation for Alcohol Studies, 1966).

15. E. M. Jellinek, "Heredity of the Alcoholic," *Quarterly Journal of Studies on Alcohol* (New Haven: Yale University Center of Alcohol Studies, 1954). And Anne Roe, "Children of Alcoholic Parents Raised in Foster Homes," *Quarterly Journal of Studies on Alcohol* (New Haven: Yale University Center of Alcohol Studies, 1945).

16. W. D. Silkworth, "Alcoholism as a Manifestation of Allergy," *Medical Record* 145 (1937): 249–251.

17. R. J. Mardones, "On the Relationship Between Deficiency of B Vitamins and Alcohol Intake in Rats," *Quarterly Journal of Studies on Alcohol* 12 (1951): 563–575.

18. J. J. Smith, "A Medical Approach to Problem Drinking," *Quarterly Journal Studies on Alcohol* 10 (1959): 251–257.

19. Harry Milt, *Basic Handbook on Alcoholism,* pp. 46–55.

20. Paraphrased from American Medical Association, *Manual on Alcoholism,* pp. 15, 16.

21. W. McCord and J. McCord, *Origins of Alcoholism* (Stanford: Stanford University Press, 1960); L. N. Robins, Wm. Bates, and P. O'Neal, "Adult Drinking Patterns of Former Problem Children" in Pittman and Snyder, *Society, Culture and Drinking Patterns.*

22. R. R. Knight, "The Psychodynamics of Chronic Alcoholism," *Journal of Nervous and Mental Diseases* 86 (1936): 538ff.

23. See also G. Lolli, "Alcoholism as a Disorder of the Love Disposition," *Quarterly Journal of Studies on Alcohol* 17 (1956): 96ff.

24. Morris E. Chafetz, "Practical and Theoretical Considerations in the Psychotherapy of Alcoholism," *Quarterly Journal of Studies on Alcohol* 20 (1959): 281ff.

25: Karl Menninger, *Man Against Himself* (New York: Harcourt Brace, 1938).

26. H. Ansbacher and R. Ansbacher, *The Individual Psychology of Alfred Adler* (London: Routledge and Kegan Paul, 1946).

27. R. J. Cantanzaro, "Psychiatric Aspects of Alcoholism" in David Pittman, ed., *Alcoholism* (New York: Harper and Row, 1967), pp. 37–41.

28. George N. Thompson, ed., *Alcoholism*, p. 458.

29. E. M. Jellinek, "Heredity and Alcohol," *Quarterly Journal of Studies on Alcohol* (1945): 105–113.

30. M. Bleuler, "Familial and Personal Background of Alcoholics" in Oskor Diethelm, *Etiology of Chronic Alcoholism* (Springfield, Ill.: Charles C Thomas, 1955).

31. W. McCord and J. McCord, *Origins of Alcoholism*.

32. Edward Blacker, Harold W. Demone, and Howard E. Freeman, "Drinking Behavior of Delinquent Boys," *Quarterly Journal of Studies on Alcohol* 26 (1965): 223ff.

33. G. L. Maddox, "Teenage Drinking in the United States" in Pittman and Snyder, eds., *Society, Culture and Drinking Patterns*.

34. E. Blacker, H. Demone, and H. E. Freeman, "Drinking Behavior of Delinquent Boys," ibid., pp. 223–237.

35. Robert Straus and Seldon D. Bacon, *Drinking in College*.

36. Mulford, "Drinking and Deviant Drinking."

37. Hollingshead and Redlich, *Social Class and Mental Illness*, pp. 280, 281.

38. G. Lolli, E. Seriani, G. Goldner, and P. Luzzato-Fegiz, *Alcohol in Italian Culture*.

39. Charles R. Snyder, "Culture and Jewish Sobriety," in Pittman and Snyder, eds., *Society, Culture and Drinking*.

40. R. Sadoun, G. Lolli, and M. Silverman, *Drinking in the French Culture*. Rutgers Center for Alcoholic Studies, Monograph No. 5, 1965.

41. R. F. Bales, "Cultural Differences in Rates of Alcoholism," *Quarterly Journal of Studies on Alcohol* 6 (1946): 480–499; R. F. Bales, *The "Fixation Factor" in Alcohol Addiction: An Hypothesis Derived from a Comparative Study of Irish and Jewish Social Norms* (New York: Harvard University Press, 1964).

42. N. L. Barnett, "Alcoholism in the Cantonese of New York City" in O. Diethelm, ed., *Etiology of Chronic Alcoholism* (Springfield: Charles C Thomas, 1955), pp. 179–227.

43. Mark Berke, Jack D. Gordon, Robert I. Levy, and Charles B. Perrow, *A Study on the Nonsegregated Hospitalization of Alcoholic Patients in a General Hospital*, Hospital Monograph Series 7 (Chicago: American Hospital Association, 1959).

44. Morris E. Chafetz, Howard T. Blane, Harry S. Abram, Joseph Golner, Elizabeth Lacy, William F. McCourt, Eleanor Clark, and William Meyers,

"Establishing Treatment Relations with Alcoholics," *Journal of Nervous and Mental Disease* 134 (1962): 395ff.

45. Raymond M. Glasscote, Thomas Plaut, Donald Hammersley, Francis O'Neill, Morris Chafetz, and Elaine Cumming, *The Treatment of Alcoholism: A Study of Programs and Problems* (Washington, D.C.: American Psychiatric Association, 1967), pp. 22–26.

46. Kenneth A. Rouse, *What to Do About the Employee with a Drinking Problem* (Chicago: Kemper Insurance Group, 1964).

47. For a compact review see American Medical Association, *Manual on Alcoholism.*

48. Vernelle Fox and Marguerite A. Smith, "Evaluation of a Chemopsychotherapeutic Program for the Rehabilitation of Alcoholics," *Quarterly Journal Studies of Alcoholism* 1 (1959): 767ff.

49. Raymond M. Glasscote, Thomas F. A. Plaut, Donald W. Hammersley, Francis J. O'Neill, Morris E. Chafetz, and Elaine Cumming, *The Treatment of Alcoholism,* p. 52.

9

DRUG
DEPENDENCE

Drug dependence, like alcoholism, is often associated with mental illness. Earlier, it was noted that all three problems were once viewed as moral lapses and have since become redefined as illnesses. The three problems form a kind of continuum, in which mental disorder is now largely viewed as an illness, while drug dependence is still widely considered a form of delinquency.

Opium and its derivatives played the major role in the rise of U.S. legislation dealing with drugs. Hence, our review can conveniently begin with it.

Opium cultivation was known in ancient Mesopotamia, Egypt, Persia, Greece, and Rome, and formed an important item of the pharmacopoeia of those civilizations. From the Middle East, opium was transported to India and China by Arabian traders. Following the introduction of tobacco in the Far East, opium was smoked together with tobacco as a prophylactic against various diseases. By the eighteenth century, opium-smoking had become so widespread in China that an imperial edict against it was issued. However, Dutch, and later English, traders smuggled so much opium in from India that the imperial government's attempts to control the traffic were futile. The confiscation of a large quantity of opium in 1839 by the Chinese government precipitated the Opium War, and eventually the British forced the reluctant Chinese government to legalize the opium trade.

With a sort of poetic justice, China became one of the main suppliers of opium to the rest of the world. In England and other European countries in the late eighteenth and early nineteenth centuries, opium-eating became a fad among artists, poets, and writers. Among its famous users were De Quincy, Poe, Coleridge, Swinburne, and Baudelaire.

In the United States, exposure to opiates occurred in the nineteenth century, in large measure through its use in patent medicines. The hypodermic method of administering morphine developed as an anesthetic during the Civil War, increased mass exposure, especially since the addictive qualities of the drug were unknown at the time. Opium-smoking was introduced by Chinese immigrants in the larger cities on the Pacific and Atlantic coasts, and eventually spread out of the Chinatowns to other urban areas.

The Pure Food and Drug Act of 1906 required the accurate labeling of all drugs, driving many opiate patent medicines off the market. In 1909, Congress banned the importation of opium except for medicinal purposes.

From 1900 to 1920, legislation was passed in the attempt to control the drug traffic. At that time, the number of illicit users of narcotics was much greater than at present, estimated to be about 1 in 400 persons; current estimates run between 1 in 2,000 and 1 in 4,000.[1]

The Harrison Act of 1914 set up penalties for illegal possession of narcotics. Its sentences varied from two to ten years imprisonment for the first offense, five to twenty years imprisonment for the second offense, and ten to twenty years imprisonment for any further offenses. This act, with its subsequent amendments, regulates the manufacture, production, importation, sale, compounding, dispensing, and giving away of opium or coca leaves (which contain cocaine) and their salts, derivatives, and preparations. Other provisions of the law state that doctors, wholesale and retail dealers, institutions, hospitals, and those prescribing or dealing in drugs for medicinal purposes must obtain a license and keep an accurate record of the drugs sold, bought, and used. Illegal sale of narcotics carries with it a fine of $20,000 plus five to twenty years imprisonment for the first offense and ten to forty years for any future offenses. Any individual guilty of selling narcotics to a minor (under eighteen years of age) is ineligible for parole and probation, even in his first offense, and can be sentenced to prison for life.

The increasing number of drugs produced through modern chemistry has affected the quality of experience and the potential for addiction. New developments have forced the extension and new passage of legislation controlling narcotics. Congress, in an effort to combat drug abuse, passed the Drug Abuse Control Amendments of 1965 and placed its regulatory powers under the Federal Food and Drug Administration. The purpose of the Drug Abuse Control Amendments was to curtail illegal peddling and misuse of counterfeit drugs, amphetamines, and barbiturates, as well as other stimulant and depressant drugs. This amendment prohibits the manufacture, processing, or compounding of these drugs except by certain drug firms designated for legal distribution. A strict record of the drugs must be kept by the manufacturer, distributor, and seller. The user is restricted to only five refills of the prescription, subject to his doctor's approval. Penalty for illegal manufacture and sale of barbiturates carries with it a fine of $1,000 to $10,000 and a prison sentence of from one to three years. A person found guilty of selling such drugs to persons under the age of twenty-one may be sentenced to a period of five to six years in jail and be fined up to $15,000.

On April 8, 1968, the Department of the Treasury's Bureau of Narcotics and the Food and Drug Administration's Bureau of Drug Abuse Control were transferred to the Department of Justice and merged as the new Bureau of Narcotics and Dangerous Drugs. The most recent legislation on the penalties under federal law for the illegal sale and possession of dangerous drugs states:

Anyone who possesses dangerous drugs illegally is subject to a penalty of not more than one year imprisonment and/or $1,000 for a first or second offense and not more than three years imprisonment and/or a $10,000 fine for a third offense; an offense of possession with intent to sell, manufacture, or sale of dangerous drugs is subject to a penalty of not more than 5 years imprisonment and/or a $10,000 fine. The growing abuse of drugs by teenagers is a particularly tragic and disturbing aspect of the entire drug abuse problem. Therefore there are special penalties for violators over 18 years of age who sell or give drugs to anyone under 21 years old. For a first offense, the punishment may be imprisonment for not more than ten years and/or a fine of $15,000. A second offense carries a penalty of not more than 15 years imprisonment and/or a $20,000 fine.[2]

NATURE AND EXTENT OF
DRUG ABUSE

The term "drug dependence" rather than "drug addiction" has been accepted by the World Health Organization as well as by the National Research Council of the National Academy of Sciences. The World Health Organization defines the term "drug dependence" as "a state of psychic or physical dependence, or both, on a drug arising in a person following administration of that drug on a periodic or continuous basis."[3] It classifies the various types of drug dependence as: the morphine type, the barbiturate-alcohol type, the cocaine type, the *Cannabis* (marijuana) type, the amphetamine type, the *khat* type, and the hallucinogen type.

One common characteristic of all these types is psychic dependence. Psychic dependence involves a psychic drive in the individual that makes it essential for him to use the drug on a chronic or periodic basis, either to obtain pleasure or escape from his problems. Physical dependence, which may or may not be present, is characterized by acute physical disturbances in the individual when use of the drug is suspended.

Other terms frequently referred to in discussions of drug

abuse are "tolerance," "drug addiction," and "drug habituation." By tolerance is meant the ability of the body to adapt to progressively larger doses of the drug, making yet larger amounts necessary to achieve the desired psychic effect.

Drug addiction refers to physiological dependence on the drug, the person addicted finding the withdrawal symptoms intolerable. Drug habituation refers to psychological dependency on the drug, an increasing inability to face life without it despite the fact that the particular drug may have no major physiological withdrawal effects.

The addict uses drugs to produce a desired physical and psychic state. From this standpoint, the major types of drugs break down into the following categories: those which induce a general feeling of well-being (the opiate derivatives); those which either heighten or depress the physical and psychic level, hence sometimes described as the "up and down" drugs (the amphetamines and barbiturates); and those which sharpen or destroy physical and mental sensations (the hallucinogens).

In advanced stages of drug addiction, the individual may come to depend upon a wide variety of drugs to move from one state or situation to another. Judy Garland is a well-known illustration.

> One of our frequent topics of conversation was pills. Rather than force her to stop taking them altogether, I asked her to cut down gradually. She had built up a strong tolerance for pills, and often took enough to kill the uninitiated. . . .
>
> Often, when Judy was depressed, she took ups, and her heart would pound alarmingly. Then she'd gulp sleeping pills to calm down. I told her how ruinous this was to her health and how difficult it was living with her when she was stoned on pills.
>
> Her real problem was lack of sleep. At most, she slept three or four hours in a 24-hour period. And, of course, there were the tranquilizers and the sleeping pills, along with Ritalin, a powerful "uppy" and anti-depressant.
>
> Like a child in need of a favorite toy, Judy felt totally insecure without a bottle of Ritalin in her purse. She needed enormous

doses to perform. Later, she required powerful doses of Seconal to sleep after the performance.

She took pills to sleep, pills to wake up, pills to give a good performance, pills to counteract other pills.[4]

When she died, the autopsy revealed that her body had at last failed to rally from a heavy dose of sleeping pills.

Narcotics

Narcotics are those drugs which are used, medically, as anesthetics or soporifics. Generally referred to in this category are opium and its derivatives—codeine, paregoric, methadone, heroin, and morphine—obtained from the resin of the pod of the opium poppy. Synthetically prepared narcotics include dolophine and demerol.

HEROIN. Heroin, also called "smack," "scag," "junk," "H," or "horse," is the narcotic most widely used by addicts. Rarely used in its pure form, it is usually cut by the dealer with dextrose, quinine, or other white crystalline substances. It is this practice of cutting that causes so many accidental deaths from overdose, since the user can never be certain of the proportion of pure heroin in each dose.

The four different ways of taking heroin are orally, sniffing (called "snorting"), injection into the skin (called "skin-popping"), and injection into the bloodstream (called "mainlining"). Mainlining is the method most frequently used by hard-core addicts because it takes a smaller amount of heroin to get the desired effect, and it works more quickly. The initial "rush" is usually followed by a period of somnolence, which lasts until the drug begins to wear off and the user begins his frantic search for the next "fix," or for the money to obtain it. Besides the dangers of overdose, heroin addicts are frequently subject to hepatitis and other infections from unsterile needles, and to malnutrition because the drug reduces all appetites, including hunger.

The most immediate consequences of narcotics addiction are the biological, psychological, and social costs to the addict. The narcotic user is "hooked" when he develops a tolerance for the drug. Withdrawal symptoms appear about eighteen hours after discontinuance of the drug, and are characterized by sweating, shaking, chills, diarrhea, nausea, and body cramps. Drugs come to occupy his whole life; family responsibilities, work, education are thrust aside. Since the addict may require $100 to $300 for a day's supply of heroin, he often cannot support his habit without turning to some form of crime: theft, other crimes against property, or, in the case of women or male homosexuals, prostitution. The life span of a junkie on the street is about ten years.

Hallucinogens

The hallucinogens, so called because in varying dosages they tend to produce distortions of physical and sensory reality, occur both naturally and synthetically. Certain natural hallucinogens, such as peyote, psilocybe mushrooms, and, to a certain extent mescaline, as well as marijuana and hashish, have been used for centuries in various cultures for their hallucinatory and euphoric effects.

The synthetic hallucinogens—LSD-25 (lysergic acid diethylamide) and DMT (dimethyltryptamine) are the best known—originate in clandestine laboratories, although small amounts are synthesized for legitimate research. Often referred to as "acid," "sunshine," "cubes," "Big D," and "trips," most of these drugs are disguised as common objects: sugar cubes, chewing gum, hard candy, mints, crackers, wafers, blotter paper, postage stamps, aspirins, vitamins, antacid tablets, beads, and other forms.

LSD seems to be the most dangerous of the hallucinogens; marijuana, which is perhaps the least dangerous (though its full clinical effects are not established), is certainly the most popular.

LSD.   LSD is one of the most dangerous drugs being abused today. It was first prepared synthetically in 1943 by Dr. Albert Hofman, a chemist for Sandoz, Ltd., a Swiss pharmaceutical corporation. This acid was found to be present in ergot, a fungus that grows as a rust on the rye plant. Dr. Hofman discovered

LSD's hallucinogenic effect when he accidentally inhaled a sufficient amount.

LSD frequently alters sense perceptions, although alterations vary with the individual user and the quality and quantity of the drug taken. Flat objects may appear three-dimensional, colors more brilliant, and stationary objects mobile; the senses of taste, smell, hearing, and touch are more keen; one sensory impression may be merged into another, so that colors may appear to have taste or music may appear as a color. The user may think he can float or fly in space; he may feel both sad and happy, or depressed and elated at the same time. Individuals respond differently to the drug and refer to their experiences as either good or bad "trips."

LSD is so powerful that one ounce is sufficient to produce 120,000 average doses. The usual dose is so tiny it can hardly be seen with the naked eye. The effect lasts from eight to ten hours and often longer, and there have been some reports of spontaneous "flashes" (recurrence of effects) months after the last trip. It is possible to develop a tolerance for LSD if the same amount is taken on a daily basis, although such frequent use is rare.

The hallucinogens in general and LSD in particular have been promoted as a means of expanding consciousness under the slogan "turn on—tune in—drop out." Under the influence of LSD, the individual may feel invincible; there have been reports of persons who stepped out of upper stories of buildings or in front of speeding automobiles to prove it.

A five-year-old girl who accidentally swallowed a sugar cube that had been soaked in LSD was still suffering effects nine months later, and it took over five months for her IQ to return to normal. There is also some indication that LSD may cause chromosome breaks in unborn babies, but the evidence is not conclusive.

LSD, in short, may cause serious temporary or permanent mental changes, nervous breakdowns, episodes of violence and self-destruction, and perhaps genetic changes in unborn children.

The risks reported for the more powerful hallucinogens, particularly LSD, include psychosis, suicide, personality changes, the release of aggressive impulses, habituation, warped social outlook, and reduced effectiveness. But research is lacking as to the frequency of psychosis caused by LSD and other powerful hallucinogens. A study of seventy post-LSD psychiatric admissions in a Los Angeles medical center (representing 12 percent of all the admissions in a six-month period) showed that one-third were psychotic on admission and two-thirds required more than a month of hospitalization. Suicide inclinations are hard to distinguish from the bizarre behavior occurring under LSD, such as supposing that one can jump from windows and fly. Proven cases of crime associated with hallucinogens appear to be minimal, although recently several particularly gruesome murders have been reportedly linked to hallucinogen-using "cults." It should be pointed out, however, that persons who exhibit bizarre or psychotic behavior while under the influence or following the ingestion of hallucinogens may well be border-line mentally ill individuals for whom the drug is simply a catalytic agent that pushes them over the edge.

There has been a lack of studies with regard to the role of hallucinogens in vehicle accidents. Although the use of hallucinogens seems to establish dependency, a loss of social and work efficiency, and increase in divorce, the samples in these studies have been small.

MARIJUANA.   Introduced into the United States in about 1920, marijuana has been habitually used by millions of people all over the world for the psychological effect it produces. Its use has been most prevalent in Africa and Asia. In India it was long used as a household remedy, for religious ceremonies, and for its euphoric effect. In China it was used to relieve pain during surgery. In the United States during the first decades of the twentieth century it was prescribed as a fairly effective remedy for migraine headaches, and was known medically as "fluidextract Cannabi indicae."

Marijuana is the dried leaves and flowering tops of the Indian hemp plant *Cannabis indica,* var. *sativa,* which grows wild throughout most of the United States and in Africa, India, Southeast Asia, the Middle East, and Mexico, and is cultivated in all of those areas. It is usually smoked in a pipe or in cigarettes called "joints" or "reefers." It can also be eaten, combined with foods; this method is said to produce a more intense and longer-lasting "high," although it is not frequently used because of the large amounts of the drug required. In the United States marijuana is referred to as "grass," "pot," "boo," "tea," "shit," and occasionally "Mary Jane."

Also derived from the same plant is hashish, commonly referred to as "hash." Hashish is obtained by scraping off the waxy resin produced by the leaves to protect themselves from the hot sun; this resin is then packed into bricks and smoked in pipes, either pure or mixed with marijuana. The effects of hashish are more intense and of longer duration than are those of marijuana.

Marijuana, when smoked, acts on the central nervous system. The user may develop a feeling of well-being, become excited or depressed, experience a distortion of time and distance, feel very hungry and/or thirsty, and become unusually talkative or drowsy. When the dosage is increased, it may produce feelings of deep anxiety, erratic behavior, and aggressiveness. According to the American Medical Association, the effects of marijuana are felt in a few minutes after inhaling the smoke and can last (rarely) as long as twelve hours. A variety of effects are achieved through the use of marijuana, depending on the dosage, whether the marijuana is pure or mixed, whether it is smoked or eaten, the social setting at the time of use, and, of course, individual physical and psychological responses.

In the opinion of the American Medical Association, using marijuana does not cause physical dependence; neither does it produce in the user physical or mental changes of long duration. The possibility of psychological dependence, however, is present. If an individual uses marijuana continuously in order to avoid painful experiences, to achieve social acceptance, or to lessen anxiety, he is dependent on the drug. But if he stops using marijuana, he does not become physically sick.

While the AMA's opinion summarizes current knowledge about marijuana, some students feel that further study may reveal long-term effects of the drug. Dr. Donald R. Jasinski, chief of clinical pharmacology at the Federal Addiction Research Center in Lexington, Kentucky, maintains that the active ingredient in marijuana has now been isolated and is known as Delta 9, tetrahydrocannabinol (THC). In small doses, THC causes elation, euphoria, relaxation, and a sense of well-being. As the dose is increased, it causes reactions similar to those experienced by users of LSD.[5]

Some law enforcement officials have maintained that marijuana use leads to criminal acts, distasteful behavior, and the risk of later heroin use. While studies made over seventy years ago in India and North Africa have linked psychosis with heavy use of cannabis and have linked dependency with apathy and reduced effectiveness, these findings have not been supported recently or in the United States. Moreover, although many heroin users have early experience with marijuana, there is no one-to-one association. Nor has any linkage of marijuana use and criminality been established.[6]

No discussion of marijuana would be complete without taking into account the considerable movement sponsored by many eminent persons to legalize the use of the drug. Dr. Norman Zinberg, professor of psychiatry at Harvard Medical School, sums up much expert opinion in his argument that there is no valid medical evidence to prove the effects attributed to the drug. He has predicted that laws against marijuana will disappear within five years. Professor John Kaplan of Stanford University Law School has predicted that New York will be the first state to legalize it. No less an authority than former Attorney General Ramsey Clark has urged the repeal of the laws against marijuana on the grounds that it erodes credibility when young people do not experience the negative effects attributed to it. Clark opines that this experience tempts young people to discount the dangers of heroin and LSD as well. Meanwhile the country has to wrestle with the discrepant ways in which the various states respond to use of the drug. A youngster apprehended with a marijuana cigarette in New York may well receive a suspended sentence while in Texas he could receive thirty-three years in prison.[7]

Amphetamines, Barbiturates, and Cocaine

The amphetamines are stimulants and often go by such names as "speed," "dexies," "pep pills," "ups," "A's," "bennies," "drivers," "crossroads," and "footballs." These include amphetamine capsules, amphetamine tablets, amphetamine-barbiturate combinations, and dosage forms of methamphetamine and phenmetrazine tablets. The barbiturates are depressants, and are often referred to as "downs," "barbs," "goofballs," "redbirds," "yellow jackets," and "blue heavens"; the last three names refer to the colors of commercially produced barbiturate capsules. The barbiturates include pentobarbital capsules, secobarbital capsules, amobarbital capsules, amobarbital with secobarbital, phenobarbital tablets, and a variety of other combinations.

AMPHETAMINES. Amphetamines, which are non-narcotic, stimulate the central nervous system. Therapeutically, they are prescribed by doctors to curb the appetite in individuals on medically supervised reducing diets; for treatment of mild depressions; for treatment of narcolepsy, in which the person has an uncontrollable desire to sleep; and, paradoxically, to calm down hyperactive children. Most widely used of the amphetamines are benzedrine, often called "bennies," dexedrine, referred to as "dexies," and methedrine, known as "meth," "crystal," and "speed."

In 1927, amphetamine sulphate (benzedrine) was produced synthetically in the United States; the old benzedrine inhaler, which was used to alleviate head congestion associated with colds, was produced by the Smith, Kline and French laboratories in 1932. Because of increasing problems of abuse, it became necessary to discontinue the use of benzedrine, and modern inhalers do not contain it. Amphetamines are increasingly being abused by various groups of people: by housewives trying to lose weight or relieve fatigue; by college students cramming for examinations; by long-distance truck drivers needing to stay awake; and by athletes preparing for tournaments or various sporting competitions.

Others abuse amphetamines for the thrill of the "up" feeling, for a narcotics substitute, and for the effect achieved when mixed with other drugs or alcohol. Usually amphetamines are taken in pill form, but some inject it into the vein ("speeding") to achieve more rapid effects. This method can result in hepatitis, abcesses, personality disorders, psychotic conditions, and even death from sudden increase in dosage.

Although the abuse of amphetamines does not cause physical dependence in the user, it does create a condition of tolerance necessitating larger doses to achieve the desired effect. Psychological dependence may occur with accompanying breakdown in personal, family, and community relations.

Physical effects observed in amphetamine abusers are restlessness, sleeplessness, profuse perspiration, excitability, and unclear or rapid speech. Persons who have taken heavy doses over a long period of time may develop acute psychoses accompanied by auditory or visual hallucinations. Sudden withdrawal of the drug can cause severe depression and suicidal tendencies.

The stimulant amphetamines tend to elevate the mood and produce a state of well-being in the user; but "when carried to an extreme, the psychotoxic effects of large amounts of drugs of the amphetamine type may lead to aggressive and dangerous antisocial behaviour." [8]

BARBITURATES.   The best known of the sedative drugs, barbiturates act as depressants which relax the central nervous system. Therapeutically, sedatives are prescribed by physicians for patients with insomnia, high blood pressure, before and during surgery, and in cases of epilepsy and mental illness. Used in a variety of illnesses, they tend to sedate or calm the patient and induce sleep. Short-acting barbiturates, such as nembutal and seconal, are the drugs abused most frequently. Long-acting barbiturates include luminol, amytal, and butisol.

Barbiturates, like amphetamines, can be legally obtained only by a physician's prescription. Abusers may circumvent this restriction by going to several different physicians and persuading them that the drug is urgently needed. Some physicians are lax in their supervision of patients and approve refill of prescriptions by phone; a few physicians are cynically aware of what they are doing and charge exorbitant fees for their services. Drug abusers develop into extraordinarily skilled "con artists" who resort to all kinds of devious methods and rationalizations to procure their supply. One young woman of twenty-three, known to the authors, was addicted to alcohol as well as drugs; she would telephone a physician at 3:00 A.M. to plead for a prescription for barbiturates, mentioning the name of another doctor, recently deceased, from whom she had obtained her previous prescription.

When barbiturates are abused (taken in higher dosage without supervision of a physician), the effects are similar to those of alcoholic intoxication: the user develops slurred speech; he is confused, staggers, becomes drowsy, develops hand tremors. He becomes highly irritable, uses poor judgment, is highly emotional, and may become physically assaultive. Increased and prolonged use of barbiturates can result in physical dependence and increased tolerance. For the physically dependent user, sudden withdrawal of the drug can result in nausea, cramps, convulsions, delirium, severe mental disturbances, and in some cases death. Psychological dependence brings preoccupation with drugs and the consequent effects on the user's interpersonal relations.

In the United States, barbiturates are one of the main causes of accidental poison deaths. Because barbiturates are easy to obtain and because many people think of them as just another sleeping pill, they may forget when they took the previous dose and a fatal overdose may result. According to the American Medical Association, more suicides, whether intentional or unintentional, have been caused by barbiturates than by any other substance.

COCAINE. Cocaine, which is used medically as a local anesthetic, is obtained from the erythroxylon coca plant. It was known by the Incas of Peru, who mixed the leaves with lime and vegetable ash and chewed them for their euphoric effects; this practice is still carried on by the Indian peoples of the Andes. Cocaine crystals can also be inhaled ("snorted") or injected into the blood stream by a hypodermic needle. The effect is similar to that of benzedrine. The ecstatic sensations of physical and mental power are eventually succeeded by deep depression as the effects of the drug wear off. The user may feel as if insects were crawling over his body and typically develops paranoiac fantasies. "Coke-heads" often carry weapons and are capable of violent attacks on people while under the influence of their delusions.

EXTENT OF DRUG ABUSE

Attempts to estimate the extent of drug abuse face special difficulties. As in the case of any illegal practice, the only accurate figures are those provided by addicts known to the authorities. However, when the definition of a practice as illegal does not have full public support, the amount of unreported cases is unusually large. When, moreover, exposure of a practice carries social stigma, the motives for concealment are especially strong.

Another factor standing in the way of accurate reporting of drug abuse is the rapid proliferation of non-narcotic drugs in the postwar period. The older reporting facilities were primarily oriented to the users of narcotics whose social circumstances were generally different.

Finally, the rapid proliferation of new drugs occurred in considerable measure in middle- and upper-class circles. The various institutions developed for detection and control of narcotic use in lower-class circles were not well adapted to the detection or handling of them in higher socioeconomic groups. Moreover, middle- and upper-class users do not have to resort to crime to sustain the habit with the same frequency as lower-class users. They are in a position to conceal the problem longer.

Narcotics

The number of known narcotics users fell to its lowest point in the twentieth-century United States during the World War II years, at which time the number was estimated at about 20,000. After World War II, this figure rose to about 60,000. The official figures, however, are undoubtedly too low. When the New York City Department of Health undertook an intensive narcotics registration project, there was a sharp rise in the number of known addicts, leading to estimates that about 1 in 80 persons in the city is addicted. Moreover, at Bellevue Hospital it was found that for every chronic heroin user known to the police, at least one other was not. Hence it was conservatively estimated in 1968 that there were about 50,000 addicts in New York and about 100,000 nationally.[9] On a CBS news broadcast on March 12, 1970, Dr. Stanley Yolles, former director of the National Institute of Mental Health, was quoted as estimating that there are at least 100,000 to 150,000 hard narcotic addicts in the nation.

Hallucinogens

LSD. After the hallucinogenic properties of lysergic acid diethylamide (LSD) were discovered in 1943, a variety of researchers began to experiment with its possibilities. In the 1960s, LSD received tremendous publicity at the hands of Dr. Timothy Leary, a former Harvard researcher who established himself as charismatic leader of the psychedelic cult. In the opinion of Donald Louria, Leary and other members of the cult have deliberately confused LSD and marijuana use. This has led to such gross exaggerations as the statement in the March, 1966 edition of *Life,* that over a million doses of LSD would be taken in the United States during the year; a *Playboy* interview in which Leary asserted that more than 15 percent of the college students use LSD; and the statement before a Senate investigating committee that 40 percent of the students at Stanford University had been taking hallucinogens. More trustworthy studies indicate that the experiments with LSD in colleges vary by area, from less than 1 percent to about 10 percent in areas of highest use. Louria calculates that the countrywide maximum is perhaps 3 percent or less for college students, indicating that perhaps less than 120,000 (or as low as 30,000) students in college have had experience with LSD or other powerful hallucinogens.

MARIJUANA. In 1950, a United Nations survey estimated that there were about 200 million persons in the world using some form of marijuana. It was introduced into the United States in the 1920s and reached sufficient extent in the 1930s to be included in the narcotics legislation, although it has none of the properties of the true narcotics and has never been conclusively proven to be a dangerous drug. Despite its illegality, its use has greatly increased since the World War II period, reaching epidemic proportions in the 1950s and 1960s. According to the September 1969 issue of *Time,* a conservative administration task force estimated that at least 5 million Americans have used marijuana at least once. Dr. Stanley Yolles estimates that it has been used by at least 12 million, perhaps even as high as 20 million. But he also estimates that perhaps about 65 percent of these are merely casual pot smokers.

In the opinion of David Ausubel, the spread of marijuana can be attributed to its adaptability to the needs of aggressive, status-deprived adolescents in revolt against conventional society and against socioeconomic, racial, and ethnic deprivation. It is cheaper and less dangerous than the opiates and was even used by American soldiers stationed in India and Burma during World War II. Use was originally highest among persons in the entertainment field (jazz musicians) and minority groups (particularly blacks and Latin-Americans), but it is now definitely a middle-class, suburban phenomenon as well. In contrast to opiate addicts, marijuana users prefer to use the drug in social gatherings.[10]

Marijuana is used most by young people between the ages of eighteen and thirty, in all strata of society. The danger, especially for the young, is that experience with one drug may lead to the use of other and more potent drugs, either through acquaintances or via the dope peddler.[11]

Pentagon officials recently admitted that use of marijuana among American soldiers in Viet Nam is quite widespread. Testimony was given before a senate investigation committee in the summer of 1970 that large percentages (possibly as high as 35 percent) of some units have used the drug, and that units have gone into combat "stoned," firing, at times, at other American soldiers or at American helicopters. In fact, 35 percent is probably a conservative estimate. Marijuana is cheap and easily obtainable in Viet Nam, and quantities of it have been entering the United States with returning GI's.

It was reported over ABC-TV news on April 27, 1971, that some 60 percent of the American soldiers in Viet Nam have used drugs while on duty there. An addict in Viet Nam is able to support his habit on approximately $10 a day, compared with an estimated $100 a day in the United States. The consequences of the influx of returning soldiers addicted to hard drugs are only beginning to be felt.

Most of the marijuana used in the United States, however, is either home-grown or Mexican. The Mexican trade is estimated to retail at about $100 million a year. The Mexican farmer receives about $2 a kilo; the marijuana then passes through a variety of hands until it sells to the consumer for about $300 a kilo, or "brick," or about $20 to $35 an ounce. On September 22, 1969, a massive search for marijuana smugglers by American agents—called "Operation Intercept"—was set in motion at the Mexico–California border. Every car, airplane, and boat was thoroughly searched. A massive traffic jam developed with cars waiting as long as six hours to get across the border; business was off on both sides of the border by as much as 40 to 60 percent. Though some marijuana was confiscated, speculation was that the real purpose of Operation Intercept was to dramatize the significance of controlling the smuggling, to force the price up enough to slow its use, and to persuade the Mexican government to eradicate the production of marijuana at its source. In a special feature of NBC-TV news, two dealers in marijuana were asked their opinion of the campaign; they felt that driving up the price would not stop the traffic but could possibly make it profitable enough to be taken over by the underworld. Another widely noted effect of Operation Intercept and the "tight market" on marijuana was to markedly increase the use of hard drugs among habitual marijuana users. The price of marijuana in hard times is about that of small doses of heroin. This is often cited as one reason for the recent spread of heroin among suburban youth.

Amphetamines

No exact figures are available, but during the same period that experimentation with potent hallucinogens has increased, there has been increased use of stimulants. The number of illicit users of amphetamines is estimated to be in the millions, most taking stimulant pills such as dexedrine, amphetamine sulphate, and methedrine, but also, among the young, intravenously injected methamphetamine.

THE CAUSES OF DRUG ABUSE

The three possible types of factors that may play a role in drug dependence are: physiological, individual developmental (psychological), and social.

Physiological Causes

Since each person responds somewhat differently to various chemical substances, it would seem reasonable to posit differential physiological sensitivity as a possible factor in the incidence of drug dependence. A large number of people use mood-altering drugs without becoming dependent on them. Moreover, from all outward appearance, individuals with approximately the same psychological and social risks may become addicted at different rates. While no one at present seems prepared to argue that physiological factors alone may cause drug dependence, this is one of the areas of the problem that deserves further research. As in the case of alcoholism, if such physiological risk categories could be established, they could be important factors in prevention programs.

Individual Developmental
(Psychological) Causes

Whether or not physiological makeup contributes to drug dependence, psychological makeup is generally agreed to play a role. The same kinds of psychological factors believed to effect alcoholism are also cited to explain drug addiction. Also, as in the case of alcoholism, arguments have been made for a drug-prone personality type. For example, the heavy drug user has been described as a narcissistic type, self-oriented, mistrustful of others, insecure, unloved, alone, unhappy with his life, sensitive, and escapist, preferring to take refuge in drugs and opt out of society.[12] Peter Laurie was most impressed by the level of anxiety experienced by addicts and the uniformly low opinion they held of themselves and their abilities. The addict seldom has a job, a home, or a spouse.[13]

Ausubel has classified opiate addicts, based on predisposing personality factors, as follows:

1. *primary* addiction, in which opiates have specific adjustive value for particular personality defects;

2. *symptomatic* addiction, in which the use of opiates has no particular adjustive value and is only an incidental symptom of behavior disorder;

3. *reactive* addiction, in which drug use is a transitory developmental phenomenon in essentially normal individuals influenced by distorted peer group norms.[14]

Primary drug addiction, in Ausubel's classification, is broken down into two subgroups—inadequate personality, and state of anxiety and reactive depression. The inadequate personality characterizes the greater number and the less hopeful of the addicts. One of the main features of the inadequate personality type is motivational immaturity, that is, an inability to identify with normal adult goals. This type tends to be passive, unreliable, and unable to defer gratifications. Other characteristics of this type are an inability to accept distasteful tasks and a lack of capacity for self-criticism. Clinical evidence, Ausubel argues, has proven that the inadequate personality is a characteristic of the majority of drug addicts. Adolescent heroin addicts under treatment at Bellevue Hospital were found to present characteristics' of the inadequate personality, such as lack of motivation in their studies, inability to concentrate, passivity and dependence, and narcissism, as well as strong attachment for their mothers and inclination to fantasy-adjustive techniques.

Anxiety and reactive depression characterize a smaller number of opiate addicts. Such types have a better prognosis. This type is characterized by continued striving and high aspiration, low self-esteem, and overreaction to environmental situations that results in fear and depression. This group has a higher educational level, with the majority having attended or completed college. Such an addict has often held professional or semi-professional jobs, and achieved acceptable economic and marital adjustment. He uses the drug for its sedative effect and its ability to reduce anxieties. He can get by with a smaller dose and his job and personal activities can go on as usual. Addiction risks are high when such persons work in the medical or related professions where drugs can be obtained without risk of apprehension.

Symptomatic drug addiction, in Ausubel's classification, occurs in aggressive antisocial psychopaths. The individual refuses to conform to ethical standards of society, has a contempt for other people, is delinquent, remorseless, aggressive, and hostile. This type of addict feels he is getting even with society through drug addiction, which he knows is socially disapproved. The symptomatic drug addict has often been delinquent since childhood, and the crimes he commits are not necessarily due to his consumption of drugs.

Reactive drug addiction is described by Ausubel as primarily an "adolescent phenomenon." It provides a way of gaining acceptance into the peer group and a means of expressing aggressive, anti-adult feelings. Although about 15 to 20 percent of adolescents are not in the reactive addiction group (anxiety neurotics and inadequate personalities), the greater number in the reactive addiction group are average youngsters experimenting with drugs in the course of their development. This type of drug addiction is "usually a transitory, self-limited phenomenon with no serious or lasting consequences." [15]

Social Causes

Complex societies sustain a multiplicity of social patterns. Hence, some indication of the role of social and cultural factors in drug use and abuse is provided by the incidence of practice in various social strata, age and sex categories, occupations, and educational levels.

CHANGING PATTERNS OF DRUG USE. According to a variety of early surveys in the nineteenth century, drug users numbered about two-thirds women, more whites than Negroes, more upper-class than middle-class individuals, a higher percentage of physicians than of most other professions, and older (the average age of the users being forty or older) rather than younger individuals.[16] Today, these patterns do not apply. The nineteenth-century addictive pattern may have been due, at least in part, to the fact that many people, women in particular, became addicted through use of medicines prescribed to alleviate pains of migraine headaches, menstruation, and other typically "female ailments." Since persons of the higher socioeconomic classes had, as always, greater access to medical care, it follows that they would also have had greater access to (addictive) medicines.

Major contemporary trends in drug addiction are toward a concentration in large urban centers, in the slum areas of the cities (although it is by no means confined to the lower economic classes), with heavy concentration among minority groups such as Negroes and Puerto Ricans.[17] Also, there has been a trend toward earlier use. The average age of the male patient treated at the Lexington Addiction Research Center has dropped about eight years, and use of morphine has decreased but use of heroin has increased.[18] The ratio of addiction by sex is about nine men to every one woman; and women tend to become addicted at a somewhat later age. Around one-third of the drug addicts treated at Lexington have at least a high school education. The educational attainment of addicts roughly corresponds to that of the general population. The incidence of opiate addiction among physicians has been estimated at around one in 100 physicians, comparable to the rate of one in 3,000 in the general population. Jazz musicians have also been reported to have high rates of drug use.[19]

THEORIES OF SOCIAL CAUSATION. Personality and psychological need theories of opiate addiction have been directly challenged by Alfred R. Lindesmith. He argues that the decisive element for addiction is the conscious connection of withdrawal symptoms with cessation of drug use.[20] In support of this point, Lindesmith notes that some individuals get "hooked" even though they had not voluntarily taken opiates at all, as in the case of individuals treated with narcotics for illnesses or accidents.[21] Nor can euphoria be the determining factor, since some users have never experienced it and after long use the euphoria vanishes anyway. So far as it plays a role, Lindesmith argues that the euphoria is like the bait on the hook, rather than the hook itself.[22] It has also been noted by students of drug addiction that many addicts are actually hooked on the use of the *needle*, i.e., they get a kick from sticking it into their veins. Some former addicts who are otherwise "clean," report that occasionally they will shoot up with some innocuous solution simply for the pleasure of shooting.

From this perspective, the habit of using drugs is learned. The individual must know how to administer it and recognize its effects.[23] Howard S. Becker has argued that three things are essential if one is to smoke marijuana with pleasure: to smoke it in a way that would produce the effects, to recognize the effects, and to interpret them (feeling dizzy, thirsty, or hungry, misjudging distances, feeling a tingling sensation in the scalp) as pleasurable.[24] Most drug addicts are initiated into the act by friends, acquaintances, or even marital partners. It is often done for "kicks" and to express contempt for "squares." [25] And there may be a variety of other motivations, such as relief of pain, inducement of euphoria, attempt to achieve acceptance by the group.[26] The pressure to participate in group practices may be powerful.[27]

THE TREATMENT OF
DRUG DEPENDENCE

The Narcotic Addict Rehabilitation Act of 1966 inaugurated a fundamental change in policy toward addicted persons charged with narcotic offenses under the law. The act provided for the voluntary commitment by addicts to hospitals for treatment, rather than to prisons. This new act views the addict as in need of medical care rather than punishment. It was hoped that these more generous provisions would stem the rise in the number of narcotic addicts in the United States. The present estimate is 100,000 to 150,000 persons.

Under this law, an addict accused of a non-violent federal offense can, if he wishes, be committed to the care of the Surgeon General of the Public Health Service for treatment and rehabilitation. If convicted of a violent offense, the addict can be committed to the care of the Attorney General for a treatment period of up to ten years, but not for a longer period than the original sentence he faced upon conviction. If not charged with any offense, the addict can be committed for treatment to the Surgeon General through his own application or that of a relative.

Other provisions call for intensive aftercare services for the addict upon his return to his community; federal support to states and communities for training programs; and construction and staffing of new addiction treatment centers.

According to Jonathan O. Cole, there are no special treatment facilities for nonopiate drug dependence.[28] Withdrawal detoxification of patients depending on barbiturates, most other sedatives, and some tranquilizers often requires closer medical supervision than opiate withdrawal. If dependence is undetected, convulsions, delirium, and deaths may occur. Cole believes that abusers of LSD and other hallucinogens who develop psychiatric symptoms can probably be handled adequately with conventional psychiatric methods.

Since opiate addicts have often been forced to resort to crime to sustain their habit and have as a result often landed in jail or prison, prison hospitals have had to detoxify them and the period in jail or prison has been drug-free. There is no good evidence that, without additional intensive treatment and re-habilitation, this keeps them drug-free, other than the fact that repeated imprisonment may be a factor in "aging out," whereby older addicts gradually abandon their use of drugs. Close parole supervision after imprisonment is a factor in slowing relapses. Involuntary commitment, in Cole's opinion, is essentially similar except for the difference made by facilities of psychiatric hospitals and psychiatric aftercare clinics. When voluntary commitment is accepted by the patient in lieu of trial and imprisonment for noncompliance, the differences between this and imprisonment or involuntary commitment is more apparent than real, although the addict may be less stigmatized by this approach to his problems.

There are, in Cole's view, four major voluntary treatment settings: medical psychiatric, Synanon-type programs, Addicts Anonymous, and religious programs. A number of hospitals admit heroin addicts for detoxification without additional treatment; addicts occasionally accept this to avoid trial and imprisonment, or even seek hospitalization to bring the cost of their habit down. The Synanon-type program utilizes ex-addicts and group pressures and conducts therapeutic community programs to help addicts face their problems. Addicts Anonymous employs group meetings and interpersonal support after the model of Alcoholics Anonymous. Religious programs primarily rely on spiritual incentives as a motive for abstinence.

Physiological Treatment

The drug addict, like the alcoholic, must be detoxified before other treatments can begin. Moreover, with drug addicts, physiological alterations produced by the use of drugs may be the foundation of psychological craving. The withdrawal period is normally completed in three to four weeks. It is known that elevated body temperature, a high blood sedimentation rate, and increased cold pressor response may persist for five to six months after withdrawal from opiates. But the relation of these physiological conditions to psychological craving for heroin is not known.

Methadone is a long-standing opiate which, in daily oral doses, provides a substitute addiction that makes heroin ineffective. In the treatment program at Lexington, Kentucky, methadone is substituted for the narcotics used by addicts and reduced rapidly in amount. If the patient is also addicted to barbiturates, a similar but slower reduction is also carried out. The average time of withdrawal varies from a week to a month. As of September 1969, around thirty methadone maintenance programs were operating in the country, including two in Minneapolis, Minnesota. Around 100 patients are being treated at the Mt. Sinai Hospital clinic in Minneapolis. The value of the program has been argued as follows: "A former addict says that the average heroin user needs $100 to $300 a day to support his habit. For the most part, that money comes via theft, which means that by rehabilitating the 100 Minneapolis addicts, the Mt. Sinai clinic has wiped out from $365,000 to $1,095,000 in annual crime." [29]

Also of possible value is cyclazocine, a drug which, if taken in doses as large as 4 milligrams, can successfully prevent heroin from having any effect. Much value could potentially be derived from a cyclazocine-like drug with longer action so that the patient would not have to come to the clinic as often. Moreover, it would open the possibility that a patient, on cyclazocine, trying heroin or other drugs several times without effect would tend to extinguish his conditioned response to this addiction.

It is particularly important that the therapist, who has no coercive control over the addict, know whether he is abstaining from the drug. Nalorphine is a narcotic antagonist which, when periodically injected in the patient, provides evidence of readdiction. Addicted patients show dilation of the pupils; nonaddicted patients show constriction of the pupils. Urine testing is also employed for monitoring abstinence. Thin-layer chromatography and various other methods can be used to check addicts for the presence of opiates. Nalorphine and urine testing are chiefly tools of the therapist to keep the addict abstinent.

Developmental (Psychological) Treatment

Many types of therapists have worked with addicts on an individual basis: psychiatrists, psychologists, social workers, ministers, ex-addicts, and so on. Depending upon the therapist's presuppositions about the nature of personality and his diagnosis of the underlying personality problems of the particular addict, such therapy can vary from advice and counseling intended to increase individual self-awareness to various depth therapy attempts to bring to the surface repressed material. In the February 15, 1969, issue of *The New Yorker,* Emily Hahn presents an account of her addiction to opium, acquired in Shanghai in 1935; she was cured of her addiction by a refugee German doctor who employed the techniques of narcosynthesis. Among the recent devices of individual therapy for heroin addiction are the use of LSD with hypnotherapy to produce short-run favorable changes in the attitudes of addicts.

Sociological (Group Therapeutic) Treatment

As in the spheres of mental illness and alcoholism, group therapy for addiction is a rather vague notion covering a wide variety of activities involving a number of addicts and one or more therapists of various sorts. Group therapy can vary from lectures, discussions, film programs, public confessionals, psychoanalytically oriented forms of group psychotherapy, and psychodrama to the kinds of group activities sponsored by Addicts Anonymous and Synanon.

When group therapy expands to the point where it tends to involve all phases of life and not merely special group meetings, it becomes more or less coextensive with what is sometimes called "milieu therapy" or what Maxwell Jones calls "therapeutic community" procedure. The Synanon society constitutes a therapeutic community of ex-addicts.

The Synanon organization was founded by Charles E. Dederich, a former business executive, who had resolved his own alcoholic problem and was fired with missionary zeal to help others. A group of alcoholics and drug addicts collected around him, some moving into Dederich's home and others to various apartments in the vicinity. They held lengthy discussions of their mutual problems, eventually reforming their emerging society around persons who had thrown off the addiction and gradually working out a system of educational and therapeutic communities. Dederich himself visualized the society as constituting a family-like structure, affectively important for its members. The daily program that developed comprises some type of work, a noon education seminar, group sessions in which individuals freely talk out their problems to achieve emotional catharsis and bring to light repressed impulses, and various training procedures. In the view of Dederich, therapeutic agents trained by Synanon are uniquely qualified by their lengthy histories of criminal experience and knowledge of the crime problem from the inside. They have had the emotional experience of rejecting one way of life for another and understand how painful such conversions are; furthermore, they are familiar with the Synanon social system and with emotional as well as rational understanding of how to help others.

Among the major forces at work in Synanon, according to Lewis Yablonsky, are the involvement of the ex-addict in a social setting of persons who understand him and provide him with realistic opportunities for achievement and prestige, the creation of a new social role supported in the ex-addict's own community; the development of ability to relate, communicate, and work with others; a system of controls; and the consolidation of self-identity and empathy.[30]

Special living arrangements have increasingly been found important to ease the transition of the ex-addict to life in the wider society. Synanon houses, to be sure, represent a stage between the hospital and the wider community. The development of other halfway houses for ex-addicts has also occurred. Moreover, since male addicts have either lost or had never acquired adequate skills to support themselves, vocational rehabilitation is often necessary. Family and social service agencies may need to work not only with addicts but also with their families, helping them secure all the medical, social, and legal aid they require.

Daytop Lodge is a voluntary treatment program serving drug addicts placed on probation by the local courts in Brooklyn, New York. It is headed by a Synanon-trained ex-addict and staffed chiefly by ex-addicts. It receives support from the City of New York and operates a program modeled on that of Synanon.

The California Rehabilitation Center of Corona, California is a treatment program under the corrections system of the state. Its inpatient treatment program is modeled on Maxwell Jones' therapeutic community notions, with not only group therapy meetings but also an integrated work therapy, social, and vocational training program. On return to the community, patients are supervised by specially trained case workers.

The Fort Worth and Lexington United States Public Health Service Hospitals have detoxification programs combining individual and group psychotherapy with educational and vocational rehabilitation programs.[31] The treatment program at Lexington is divided into four phases. During the first, narcotics are withdrawn. Next, the patient is transferred to an orientation and evaluation unit, to be seen individually and in groups by a psychiatrist, a psychologist, a social worker, and a vocational and education officer; the purpose is to diagnose his disorder and determine the next phase of treatment. In the third phase the patient is transferred to a continued treatment unit and possibly administered both individual and group psychotherapy and a variety of educational and vocational training programs. In this phase, there is no single program but a variety of possible programs, ranging from mere physical and custodial care to intensive treatment of a variety of sorts. In the fourth phase, the patient is transferred to his home community to receive follow-up help from its agencies. This is the least developed phase of the program. About 10 percent stay drug-free for the first year after release.

Methadone maintenance treatment appears in two forms: gradual outpatient withdrawal with methadone being administered in decreasing doses over several months; and prolonged maintenance on relatively high dosages in a single supervised daily dose. Some thirty programs at present rely on the second practice.

Many states have long possessed laws authorizing drug curricula in the grade schools. Minnesota, for example, has had legal provisions for drug training since the 1920s. However, these provisions were largely unused as long as drug abuse remained primarily an adult problem. With the spread of drug use among school-age children, which reached epidemic proportions in the late 1960s, authorities on all levels have grown alarmed. In New York City, in 1969, 224 teenagers appeared among the 900 persons who were known to have died of heroin overdoses.

Across the country, programs to provide drug education to children have been underway. In December 1969, four San Francisco high schools introduced an experimental "crash pad" service to help high schools assist students suffering from drug effects. In Huntington, West Virginia, the Union Women's Club and city police joined forces to supply 10,000 pamphlets on drug abuse to children. In Ohio some 100 physicians, pharmacists, and psychiatrists donated free time to the Cincinnati Free Clinic to treat young people suffering from drug depression. In the fall of 1969 the Los Angeles City Unified School District provided for drug information in the health courses from grade seven on. From New York to Arizona, Wisconsin to Louisiana, Florida to Oregon various kinds of pilot programs, crash programs in drug education, and specialized services have been undertaken. Lectures by policemen, narcotics agents, even former addicts have been employed. Currently in Minnesota drug education is occurring on four levels: primary, intermediate, junior and senior. Three model school pilot programs are underway.

In the spring of 1970, President Nixon called for $135.6 million in education and research funds for the fiscal year July 1, 1970 to June 30, 1971 for the creation of a national clearing house for drug abuse and education. This was intended to provide a center for the reference of problems and coordination of drug education programs. The talents of major authorities in the drug abuse field such as Stanley F. Yolles, Richard H. Blum, Marvin R. Levy, Sidney Cohen, Godfrey M. Hochbaum, Helen H. Nowlis and many others have been enlisted in this enterprise. With the establishment of the National Clearing House for Mental Health Information, increasing coordination and standardization have appeared in the various drug education programs, but it is too early to ascertain the success of these efforts.

Three classes of opiate addicts have a somewhat better prognosis than others: patients who have become addicts in the course of treatment by medical practitioners; physicians and other medical addicts; and older heroin addicts. The younger addict and the lower-class ghetto addict are generally rather poor risks.

The basis for the differential risk seems to rest in considerable measure on the social anchorage of the two groups. The person who becomes addicted in the course of treatment for some real or functional ailment and the professional who becomes addicted usually have a family, home, job and social standing that are threatened by their addiction. These persons, too, are often middle- or upper-class in social derivation and tend to respond to the usual types of dynamic psychotherapy.

On the other hand, those addicts from lower strata and ghetto areas are without money, jobs, skills, and permanent ties. Furthermore, they are from a social group that does not have much faith in the professional therapist.

The special case is represented by the older heroin addict. Undoubtedly, the change of the individual's physiology that comes with aging makes some difference in the need for the drug. It is also possible that, if he survives, the addict very slowly tends to acquire some kind of system of ties which provide a motive for breaking the habit. It is certainly true that as the individual grows older it is not as easy to maintain the life of petty crime needed to sustain the heroin habit. In any case, the process of aging plays a role in the ease with which an individual can break the drug habit.

With respect to all types of addicts, mere institutionalization without aftercare or rehabilitation has little permanent results. Those classes of addicts with a better prognosis respond reasonably well to institutionalization, plus dynamic therapy and some aftercare. For the average addict, the only successful programs are those that combine strong group support, support and assistance by the treatment agency, and aid in living and vocational adjustment. Among the programs that have claimed substantial success are Synanon, Daytop Lodge, the California Rehabilitation Center, and New York City's intensive parole.

By the fall of 1970, some thirty centers around the country were utilizing substitute addiction to methadone to keep the individual free from heroin. They were serving about 4,000 people. Many private physicians were also maintaining addicts on this drug.[32] Methadone permits the addict to satisfy his habit in a legitimate manner and does not put him under any pressure to resort to crime to sustain it. In methadone treatment centers of this sort, the method of handling heroin addiction approximates that used in England.

NOTES

1.   Donald B. Louria, *The Drug Scene,* pp. 3, 4.

2.   *Drug Abuse Control* Amendments to the Federal Food, Drug, and Cosmetic Act, *United States Code,* Title 21.

3.   Nathan Eddy, H. Halbach, Ing. Harris Isbel, and Maurice H. Seevers, *Drug Dependence: Its Significance and Characteristics,* Bulletin, World Health Organization 32 (1965): 721–733.

4.   Mickey Deans, "Her Husband's Story of Judy Garland," *Look* (October 7, 1969), pp. 85–87.

5.   In an address to the 77th Annual Minnesota Welfare Conference in Minneapolis. Reported by the Minneapolis *Tribune,* March 18, 1970, p. 1.

6.   Richard M. Blum, "Mind Altering Drugs and Dangerous Behavior," President's Commission on Law Enforcement, *Task Force Report: Narcotics and Drug Abuse,* 1967, pp. 23ff.

7.   An excellent summary of the case was made by Lloyd Shearer, "Pot and Justice," St. Paul *Pioneer Press,* Parade Section, March 7, 1971, p. 18.

8.   Eddy, Halbach, Isbel, and Seevers, *Drug Dependence,* p. 729.

9.   The present section primarily follows Louria, *The Drug Scene,* pp. 6ff.

10.   David P. Ausubel, *Drug Addiction: Physiological, Psychological, and Sociological Aspects,* pp. 93–95.

11.   Ibid., p. 729.

12.   Kenneth Leech and Brenda Jordan, *Drugs for Young People: Their Use and Misuse,* p. 73.

13.   Peter Laurie, *Drugs: Medical, Psychological and Social Facts* (Baltimore, Md.: Penguin Books, 1967), pp. 36–37.

14.   Ausubel, *Drug Addiction,* p. 39.

15. For a detailed discussion of this classification breakdown, see Ausubel, *Drug Addiction,* pp. 33–56.

16. Alfred R. Lindesmith and John H. Gagnon, "Anomie and Drug Addiction," in Marshall B. Clinard, ed., *Anomie and Deviant Behavior* (New York: The Free Press, 1964), pp. 142–163.

17. H. J. Anslinger and William F. Tempkins, *The Traffic in Narcotics* (New York: Funk & Wagnalls Co., 1953), p. 281; Isidor Chein, Donald L. Gerard, Robert S. Lee, and Eva Rosenfeld, *The Road to H,* chapter 2.

18. John C. Ball, "The Onset of Heroin Addiction in a Juvenile Population," Addiction Research Center, National Institute of Mental Health, Lexington, Kentucky, July 29, 1966, mimeographed, p. 6.

19. Charles Winick, "Physician Narcotic Addicts," *Social Problems* 9 (1961): 174–186; Charles Winick, "The Use of Drugs by Jazz Musicians," *Social Problems* 7 (1959–60): 240–254.

20. Alfred R. Lindesmith, "A Sociological Theory of Drug Addiction," *American Journal of Sociology* 43 (1938): 599ff.

21. Alfred R. Lindesmith, *Opiate Addiction,* p. 72.

22. Alfred R. Lindesmith, "Basic Problems in the Social Psychology of Addiction and a Theory," in John A. O'Donnell and John C. Ball, eds., *Narcotic Addiction* (New York: Harper & Row, 1966), p. 102f.

23. Bingham Dai, *Opium Addiction in Chicago* (Shanghai: Commercial Press, 1937), p. 173.

24. Howard S. Becker, "Becoming a Marijuana User" *American Journal of Sociology* 59 (1953): 235–243, and Howard S. Becker, *Outsiders: Studies in the Sociology of Deviance* (New York: Free Press, 1963), pp. 41ff.

25. Harold Finestone, "Cats, Kicks, and Color," *Social Problems* 5 (1957): 3–13.

26. John A. Clausen, "Social and Psychological Factors in Narcotics Addiction," *Law and Contemporary Problems* 22 (1957): 38ff.

27. Isidor Chein and Eva Rosenfeld, "Juvenile Narcotics Use," *Law and Contemporary Problems* 22 (1957): 52–69.

28. Jonathan O. Cole, "Report on the Treatment of Drug Addiction," in Narcotics and Drug Abuse, pp. 135–142. The present section primarily follows Cole.

29. St. Paul *Pioneer Press,* September 14, 1969, p. 2.

30. Lewis Yablonsky, *The Tunnel Back: Synanon* (New York: Macmillan, 1965).

31. John A. O'Donnell, "The Lexington Program for Narcotic Addicts," *Federal Probation* 26 (March 1962): 55ff.

32. American Medical Association, *Perspectives in Long Term Care* 1, no. 4, p. 1.

10

TOWARD AN
INTEGRATED
THEORY

In the post-World War II period mental illness, alcoholism, and drug dependence have increasingly been viewed as national problems. To be sure, concern about alcoholism and drug addiction reached the national level earlier, culminating in the Drug Act of 1914 and the Volstead Act of 1919. There is little doubt, granting the mood of the times, that had Americans believed they could legislate insanity out of existence, they would have tried that too.

All in all, the attempts to legislate drug use were fairly successful; the attempt to legislate the use of alcohol was a disaster. The former legislation was more or less in tune with the mores of the time; the latter was not. Thousands of Americans who would not otherwise have dreamed of it went into the manufacture of various forms of alcohol. Bootlegging enlisted the talents of upstanding individuals in every American community. Rum running and large-scale manufacture and traffic in alcohol was increasingly organized by the underworld. And by the 1933 repeal of Prohibition, there were more speakeasies in the United States than there had been saloons before the Volstead Act.

Hard drinking has always been a part of the open, gregarious, dominantly male society of the American frontier. In the early twentieth century these traditions were still strong, despite the multiplicity of temperance groups seeking to reverse them. Use of the "hard drugs" tends to be individualizing, isolating, and contrary to this gregarious tradition. Americans, in fact, have always tended to look at the lone drinker as suspect. Hence, the treatment of the possession of drugs as a felony was in accord with social practice. The number of drug addicts began to drop sharply once drug use was officially defined as criminal; where drug use did appear, it long tended to be confined to ghetto areas where the underworld organization of the drug traffic made them available, and to specialists like physicians who had privileged access to them.

During the Great Depression, Americans were too preoccupied with the general socioeconomic crisis to worry much about alcoholism and drug addiction. Millions of Americans simply did not have the money to sustain any extensive use of alcohol, even if they were so inclined. Nor was the drug traffic particularly profitable during this time. Moreover, mental illness has a way of receding at such times, as if personal crises are displaced by social crises.

But with America's entry into World War II and the war-induced prosperity, the old hard-drinking patterns that had always typified the society of American males reappeared with new intensity among GIs and workers in war industries. The international traffic in illicit drugs, however, fell to an all-time low. Like all social crises, the war tended to suppress manifestations of mental illness. Combat, to be sure, produced thousands of "battle fatigue" casualties. But one had no way of knowing how many of these would have become mentally ill without the special stresses of combat.

Meanwhile, many new drugs had been synthesized, and in the postwar period the problem of alcoholism reappeared with new vigor and drug abuse assumed enterprising new forms. Once the inhibiting pressure of external crisis was withdrawn, mental illness seemed everywhere to reappear. A number of presidential task forces have reviewed all three problems—mental illness, alcoholism, and drug addiction. Special programs with respect to them have been sponsored by recent presidents. New national legislation has been enacted. Both the theory and the mechanisms for dealing with these problems have been undergoing change. These theoretical and practical developments are best evaluated against the background of the conceptual resources of sociology on the one hand, and the general trends in recent American society on the other.

Human social life exists to an unusual extent in the consciousness of its members. In contrast to the instinctually programmed social life of nonhuman creatures, human social life can only assume forms that are learned or invented, for man is the terminal creature in a series of species whose instincts have been replaced by intelligence. Ironically, man became more socially dependent for survival at the very time he lost his instincts for any special form of social life. His progress from infancy to maturity marks the longest period of complete dependency of any higher species.

Man's loss of instincts occurred concomitantly with his expansion of intelligence. While instincts adapt a creature in advance to survival in a particular environment, loss of these instincts forces him to come to individual terms with his environment. New features of the environment that permit enlargement of the creature's life are discovered. For this reason, man has penetrated more different environments than any other single species.

A creature cannot lose its instincts for being social in particular ways without simultaneously losing its instincts for special forms of individuality. Because his individuality is not instinctively fixed, man has become the most highly individualized of all creatures. He learns and invents a self in endlessly varied modalities.

The fact, however, that man must learn and invent his own personality and social system does not mean that the basic problems of collective life can remain unsolved. Three types of problems that human collectivities must solve are the mastery of nature, socialization and social control.

By mastery of nature is meant those activities by which men utilize the energies and materials of the physical world in a life-promoting manner. Science, technology, and economic systems are the primary institutional complexes devoted to this task.

By socialization is meant those activities by which men transform presocial activities and materials into social form. Since the human individual is not born social, he can only become so by his own doing. His emotions must be shaped into a set of responses appropriate to his social system, if he is not to be repeatedly at odds with the persons with whom he interacts. He must acquire the basic skills and knowledge essential to interhuman life. The whole range of education, then, is devoted to socialization. There is, moreover, good reason to extend the concept of socialization to cover various other matters that are not social, until they are defined in a manner making them so. Diseases, accidents, and illnesses are not in themselves social, but they may become occasions for new patterns of activity. And the problems that form the ultimate core of religion, the trans-routine problems of the meaning of life and of death, the meaning of the universe, and so on become occasions for collective action. The complex of socialization includes family, educational, health, welfare, and religious institutions.

Finally, since interhuman behavior must be taught and learned and is always close to the consciousness of its bearers, it is peculiarly subject to challenge. Differential learning by the young and differential interpretation by their elders continuously produce variations, between which choices must be made. Some must be made binding or mandatory. If people are to accomplish collective tasks, some plans and arrangements must be given preference over others. Decisions must be made as to differential task performance. In short, social control is an unavoidable problem for human collectivities. Among the major types of control tasks are the development of decision-making mechanisms, enforcement of rules, resolution of conflicts, and preservation of social arrangements from outside challenge. Political, law enforcement, legal, and military institutions conduct various tasks of social control.

Institutions are mankind's learned or invented solutions to its collective problems. They are the human counterpart of the instinctual arrangements of nonhuman species. Groups are the specific organized patterns of interpersonal activity that put institutions into practice.

But the organization of interhuman life does not stop with the formation of institutions and groups to solve the problems of mastery of nature, socialization, and social control. Since any given plurality must solve all three problems, the manner in which one problem is solved inevitably affects the solution of the others. What is done in the sphere of mastery of nature has consequences for socialization and social control, and vice versa. For individuals moving from problem to problem, solutions in one sphere of life must be modified to fit solutions in others. In the process, all sorts of compromises become essential. In the formation of a complete way of life (that is, of a community), it is the many points of interadjustment between group and group that make community possible.

In terms of these distinctions, we can locate our particular problems. True, some persons make a living by supplying the alcoholic and drug demands of the community, and others make a living by treating the mentally ill, alcoholics, and drug addicts, thus giving the problem an economic dimension. Nonetheless, the problems presented by mentally ill, alcoholic, and drug addicted members of the community primarily belong to the spheres of socialization and social control.

CONTRASTING ORIENTATIONS TO HUMAN SOCIAL LIFE

While sociologists are in rough agreement about the components of social life (groups, institutions, communities, and so on), they are not in complete agreement as to their comparative importance and the relation they bear to one another. This differ ential evaluation ultimately determines the manner in which mental illness, alcoholism, and drug dependence are explained. Sociology has long been polarized by the different orientations of the holists and the elementarists.

Holism is the position in social science that treats society as an entity with unique properties of its own and capable of operating as a causal agent. The term holism was derived from the status assigned in explanation to the whole. Contemporary functionalism, the most prominent of the current forms of sociological holism, treats the autonomous social system itself as the primary agent of social life. The complete or autonomous social system is the functionalist's term for society. Groups and institutions are viewed as partial social systems that derive their significance from their service to the whole. In estimating the significance of any particular aspect of social life, the functionalist inquires into its system-determined relation (its functional significance) to the whole.

Elementarism is the position in social science that treats interhuman behavior as the decisive component of social life. The term elementarism is derived from the fact that its proponents do not conceive society as a special entity but rather look for its peculiarities in some more basic item or element. This approach is like the cell theory of biology or the atomic theories of chemistry or physics. In elementarist thought, society is, at best, a fictitious entity or an economy of speech. Society does nothing, only people do things. A sociological analysis is only complete when one can account for who does what. One of the most important types of elementarism is social behaviorism. (Its several subdivisions are of no special importance to this analysis.)

The functionalist treats the social system (society, community) as not only an entity, but as an entity whose entire reason for existence is to yield a set of values. Many functionalists have insisted that in any given social system, there can be only one legitimate value system. The social behaviorist, on the other hand, conceives society as a general strategy of collective life. The immediate strategies of people to solve their problems are groups and institutions. A community is a secondary strategy, arrived at by modifying particular group strategies. Such a secondary strategy is almost never characterized by a single value system, but rather by a multiplicity of values reflecting numerous compromises. The functionalist has a monolithic conception of social life; the social behaviorist has a pluralistic conception of social life.

The functionalist treats the group as a subsystem of the social system. So far as a group is not a harmonious cog in the social machine, according to the functionalist, it is dysfunctional and ought to be adjusted to eliminate strain. The social behaviorist treats the group as a primary strategy of collective life, designed to solve collective problems. He finds no a priori reason why any given group, without special adaptation, should be harmoniously integrated with other groups in the society as a whole. He recognizes that, in adjusting group to group, the immediate efficiency of any one group may be reduced. Thus, the natural relation to be expected between group and community is one of dynamic interadjustment. Unless the group is modified it interferes with others; but too much interference with any group destroys the purpose for which it arose in the first place.

When, from his standpoint of the whole, the functionalist turns to such problems as mental illness, alcoholism, and drug dependence, he treats them as functional if they promote the social system's objectives, dysfunctional if they do not. They are seen as problems of social control. The social behaviorist, on the other hand, sees them as one more variation in the ceaseless ways men explore the possibilities of experience. From his perspective, mental illness, alcoholism, and drug dependence are problems of socialization.

TRENDS IN CONTEMPORARY SOCIETY AND THE CRISIS OF SOCIALIZATION

In the colonies, the North had begun to evolve into a world of towns and cities, the South into a world of plantations resting on slavery. In their Revolution, the people of the United States won the possibility of crossing the Appalachians and beginning the great movement westward that dominated our nineteenth-century experience. When the two systems of social life that were developing came into conflict in the Civil War, the victory of the North ensured the dominance of the town and city pattern.

In servicing the frontier, the eastern seaboard rapidly evolved into the industrial and financial hub of the new nation. Meanwhile, into the vacuum created by the constant movement of people west, increasing numbers of immigrants were drawn. With the rise of large-scale industry after the Civil War, the tide of immigration grew. The cities, bursting at their seams, developed into vast congested aggregates, within which thousands of ethnic ghettos formed. By the end of the nineteenth century, the frontier had been conquered. No longer a nation of small towns, America was on the threshold of becoming a nation of vast urban complexes. The nation was also changing from one of small businesses into one of giant industrial concerns. The majority of Americans had not reconciled themselves to any of these three transformations. They still clung to an individualistic frontier ethic; they experienced their cities as great corrupt aggregations of ethnically and religiously alien masses; they fought large-scale industrialization by banding together in labor unions, by forming chambers of commerce to prevent small business from being gobbled up by big business, and by pressing for various kinds of antitrust legislation on a national level.

A number of properties of nineteenth-century American society might have been correlated with mental illness, alcoholism, and drug addiction. Slavery, for example, had systematically deprived the imported blacks of their African heritage. To make slavery work, it was necessary to destroy the Negroes' political, religious, and general social system, as well as his very family life. Abolition did not, however, restore to the former slave a viable system of institutions. These blacks, comprising about 10 percent of America's population, were destined to suffer a wide spectrum of social, economic, and political deprivations that turned them into a high risk group with respect to mental illness, alcoholism, and drug addiction.

Nineteenth-century Americans were highly mobile; constantly uprooted from their primary groups, they were subject to a variety of special tensions. In the West's isolated frontier towns were aggregates of transients, homeless men whose chief form of entertainment was hard drinking in the saloons. The drinking traditions of the American frontier were a major source of America's continuing problems with alcohol abuse. For persons pulled from the countryside into the city, there were unusual opportunities for access to liquor and drugs. Meanwhile, in the country at large during the nineteenth century, patent medicine salesmen filled their nostrums with opiates that led to addiction among many of their customers.

But despite the components of nineteenth-century American society which increased the risks of mental illness, alcoholism and drug addiction, the complex of local institutions was still relatively intact. Most families remained anchored in their local institutions. Families were still large and took care of most of their dependent members. Family and religion were closely interlocked. With great frequency, religious groups took the lead in seeking to control alcoholism. And even within the cities' ethnic ghettos, the complex of primary institutions was strong. The rising incidence of mental illness, alcoholism, and drug addiction among ethnic groups tended to characterize second and third generation immigrants, over whom ghetto institutions lost control.

Twentieth-century America, after two world wars, has emerged as one of the most powerful and technologically advanced nations of the world. The trend toward mass production and consumption has continued unimpeded, and large-scale organization has increasingly typified all areas of life, with industry, labor, and government leading the way. More and more individuals find themselves tiny cogs in huge organizational machines over which they have virtually no control. All this, however, is a familiar story. The changes in the institutions of socialization are of special interest.

The democratization of the family is nearly accomplished. More and more women work outside the home. Children begin school (with nursery school) earlier and continue longer. Divorce has increased. The family has lost its former capacity to take on additional dependents. The average family, moving once every five years, loses the stabilizing influence of anchorage in the context of a traditional community. Moreover, with families moving as often as they do, kinship ties are repeatedly severed. The individual family, in short, at times approximates a kind of freely floating social atom.

Religion has lost many of its traditional forms and the contemporary clergyman operates more and more like a social worker or social scientist. While church membership, if anything, has risen, attendance has tended to fall. With the mobility of families, the old semipermanent linkage of family and church is a thing of the past. Upwardly mobile families often change their churches as they change status. Strong forces tend to homogenize religious messages and programs of the major American denominations of Protestantism, Catholicism, and Judaism. In addition, religion is no longer able to operate as the primary welfare institution of society outside the family itself.

Health and welfare institutions have been transformed and separated from close connection with the family and religion. The large-scale hospital and clinic and the scientifically trained specialist have moved to the center of medical practice. Moreover, local institutions have proven to be inadequate to welfare tasks that have increasingly been taken over by the state and national government.

The family, religion, and health and welfare institutions of twentieth-century American society no longer form a single interlocked complex.

UNPROGRESSIVE PROPERTIES
OF SOME CURRENT
SOCIOLOGICAL APPROACHES

One of the most striking properties of current sociological discussions of mental illness, alcoholism, and drug dependence is the general tendency by many sociologists to describe them as forms of deviance. Typical of this approach is the formulation of Simon Dinitz, Russell R. Dynes and Alfred C. Clarke:

> Human deviance is just as characteristic of society as conformity is. Every human group, no matter how cohesive, stable, and well integrated, must somehow respond to such problems as mental illness, violence, theft, and sexual misconduct, as well as to other similarly difficult behaviors. Problems of deviance inevitably are defined as being a real or perceived threat to the basic and core values of the society.[1]

Norms are conceived as the standards against which deviation is defined, measured, and sanctioned. These standards, in turn, are described as the "should's and should not's in society."[2] Traditional folk societies are said to possess a single set of internalized, integrated norms with immediate sanctions and with a conception of deviant behavior as part of total behavior. By contrast, modern industrial societies are said to possess a complex set of loosely integrated norms, with uncertain and delayed sanctions and a view of deviant behavior as characteristic of the total person. In accord with this tradition of dividing historical societies into two general types, social change is seen as a movement from folk to industrial society.

Seven types of normative changes are said to occur in the social development from folk to industrial society: norm breakdown; norm conflict; the rise of unattainable norms; the appearance of discontinuous norms; the persistence of impotent and sanctionless norms; the appearance of evasive norms; and the appearance of stressful norms. These types of normative change are conceived to have brought about the change from deviance to deviants.

Five types of deviants are isolated by Dinitz, Dynes and Clarke: freaks, sinful men, criminals, sick men, and alienated men. Among the interpersonal reactions excited by all these deviants they list: fear, anxiety, tension, pity, sympathy, anger, hostility, revulsion, and feelings of aggression. Presumably the amount and intensity of any given reaction vary with the type of deviant. Interpersonal sanctions exercised against these deviants include: withdrawal of affection, shunning, rejection, isolation, ostracism, ridicule, laughter, and gossip. Among the institutionalized responses to these deviants are: protection and rehabilitation for freaks and sick men; punishment, excommunication, and banishment for sinners; and punishment and imprisonment for criminals. Presumably, alienated men have not been defined as deviants long enough to have encouraged special institutionalized reactions. All forms of deviance are assumed to be negatively evaluated or stigmatized by society. The most general result of the stigmatization process is the deviants' assimilation of society's negative assessment, leading them to low self-esteem.[3]

The influence of contemporary functionalism on this formulation appears at every point. Society, be it of traditional or contemporary type, is viewed as an entity, the object of which is to make available a basic set of "core values" pursued in accordance with a special set of rules or "norms." The dichotomous approach to society, developed in the theories of Ferdinand Tönnies (Gemeinschaft *v.* Gesellschaft) and Emile Durkheim (societies based on mechanical solidarity *v.* societies based on organic solidarity), is invoked in the folk society–industrial society contrast. Moreover, all events in a society are evaluated from the presumed standpoint of the whole and in terms of their contribution to the needs of the whole. Deviance seems to be a euphemism for dysfunctional.

When one characterizes a person or his behavior as deviant, and deviance as a property antagonistic to the core values of society, one may be making a generous contribution to the misfortunes of the unfortunate. In American sociology since W. I. Thomas, one position has been very familiar—that the manner in which one defines a matter is a component of its social reality. In contemporary sociology, this perception has been revitalized in Robert Merton's imaginative euphemism, "self-fulfilling prophecy." The way one defines a situation may be an important factor in bringing it about. When, as in the present case, cripples are defined as freak-type deviants, one cannot but wonder why the social scientist should be inclined to add his own contribution to their misfortunes. This is doubly interesting, inasmuch as, under the concept of "stigmatization," many of the same students of social problems bracket insights contained in Thomas' notion of "definition of the situation" and Merton's notion of "self-fulfilling prophecy."

It would be quite unfair to assume that the social scientist obtains a fine sense of self-importance when he speaks assuredly in the name of society as a whole and isolates those persons who fail to live up to his notion of society's core values as deviants. It certainly offends most normal sensibilities to treat persons with diseases, birth defects, brain damage, or any of a variety of crippling defects as deviants. But such are the absurdities to which commitment to a theoretical position can lead. If one believes society to be a whole with a single value system, and if one is critical of anything that stands in the way of the highest possible realization of this single value system, anything short of this becomes dysfunctional.

The conception of individuals as deviants defines them as problems of social control. Much that is unprogressive in the response to mental illness, alcoholism, and drug addiction is directly traceable to the persistence of this notion. When society defined the mentally ill as moral or mental monstrosities, its inclination was to bury them indefinitely in custodial institutions, behind bars, and often subject to fewer considerations than those given criminals. Some students, opposed to the plea of insanity as ground for mitigating responsibility for criminal acts, have correctly observed that the conditions endured by the mentally ill often entail greater punishment than normally administered to persons convicted of criminal acts. The conception of alcoholism as deviance led to futile attempts to control it by punitive legislation. Furthermore, society has increasingly come to realize that treating drunkenness as a misdemeanor contributes in the long run to the very problems that inclined the individual toward alcoholism in the first place. Some responsible opinion holds that many persons in authority in the United States apparently learned little from the disaster of Prohibition; for they may at present be repeating a similar drama in their handling of drug abuse.

In America two rather distinct patterns of drug abuse are apparent: use of the opiates (particularly heroin), and use of other drugs.

The nineteenth- and early twentieth-century American was pragmatic, outgoing, sociable. Alcohol was characteristically used as a facilitating agent in social occasions. Drug use, like lone drinking, did not fit this social pattern. This is probably the major reason why the problem of alcoholism, although quantitatively much greater (there are perhaps as many as 6 million heavy drinkers in America, while there are probably not more than 2 million heavy users of drug of all sorts), has caused much less concern. The opiates particularly do not lend themselves to use as a social facilitating agent, as does alcohol. Hence, opiate legislation, which not only imposed severe criminal sanctions on traffic in drugs but also made the possession of opiates a felony, corresponded with contemporary mores. The number of opiate addicts declined rather steadily to World War II. Illegal traffic in opiates was organized during this period by the underworld in much the same manner as it had organized the liquor traffic during Prohibition.

Heroin has chiefly been supplied by the underworld in city ghetto areas, which have supplied a disproportionate number of addicts. It is an expensive habit and the addict, who may require anywhere from $100 to $300 a day to purchase his supply, can often only support his habit by crime. When, during the autumn of 1969, a major campaign was undertaken in Washington, D. C., against pushers and other suppliers, the price of heroin rose sharply and, to the astonishment of law enforcement officials, the crime rate in the city tripled.

The mass society of the twentieth century has brought a different range of experience into focus. Millions of persons experience themselves as alone in the mass of their kind, while modern technology has created a push-button world. Modern chemistry has synthesized thousands of new drugs. Modern men find themselves endlessly bombarded by the mass media with advertisements of pills for just about everything: birth control pills, pills to ease pain, pills to relax, pills to pep one up, pills to sleep. Many contemporary physicians seem almost routinely to prescribe tranquilizers. The public consumes pills by the ton. Furthermore, many new drugs lend themselves to socially facilitating uses in a variety of situations. Some forms of twentieth-century drug use, then, are comparable to the uses of alcohol. Moreover, the extensive consumption of sedatives, tranquilizers, and excitants is by no means confined to the lower classes but spread throughout American society.

Under these circumstances, parents' difficulties in understanding the extensive use of drugs by their children is rather astonishing. It conjures up the picture of parents, with cocktail in hand and sleeping pill laid out at bedside, discussing with alarm their children's experiments with marijuana. Dr. Stanley Yolles estimates that from 25 to 40 percent of young people have tried marijuana, and on the East and West Coasts and near the large cities the figure is 50 percent. At the Woodstock Musical Festival, held during the summer of 1969, it was estimated that 90 percent of the 400,000 young people attending openly smoked marijuana. The use of drugs has spread into not only the high schools but even to the elementary schools.

A surprising number of straight students are turning on too. The children of U. S. Senators George McGovern and Alan Cranston have been arrested on marijuana charges, as have the sons of California Assemblyman Jesse Unruh and Actor Darren McGaven. One of Vice President Spiro Agnew's daughters was suspended from Washington's exclusive National Cathedral School for three days last spring after an investigation was held to determine if she had been smoking pot.[4]

A United Press International dispatch, describing the Miami area as a narcotics supermarket, found an active traffic in drugs in Miami's schoolyards.

Larry, 13, used to wrap and deliver newspapers to earn a dollar for movies and ball games. Now he wraps and delivers reefers to keep himself in "pot and speed."

Larry is one of hundreds of youths peddling narcotics, to be swallowed, smoked, inhaled or injected, in Miami schoolyards. Five years ago, the same kind of kids got high on beer.

Larry's "turned-on" companions have found that drugs are much easier to get than beer and they are twice as kicky.

Larry isn't a product of Miami's slums. He lives in a palm-shaded suburb of a tourist-oriented city that narcotics agents say has one of the worst drug problems in the world.

One of the few things the Chamber of Commerce doesn't brag about is Miami's status in the narcotics business or the 26 persons who have died this year from drug overdoses.

Miami is a national import center for cocaine. It's the regional distribution point for heroin, marijuana, LSD and illicit barbiturates.

At the air conditioned junior high school where he is a "B" student, Larry roams the halls between classes taking orders. If pressed, he'll deliver during the lunch hour, but he'd rather do it after school on the motor scooter his accountant dad bought him for the paper route.

Larry's business earns him $100 a week, enough to support his drug purchases and still leave him pocket money. He planned next year to take on smack—heroin—and triple his income.

Once a week, Larry rides his scooter to a wooden fishing pier wedged in a row of tourist motels at the north end of Miami Beach. Here Larry restocks his merchandise.

If you blinked you lost Larry among the young look-alikes who, pressed together by sheer numbers, moved like a human river along the sand. It was the evening rush hour—800 kids looking for something to turn on the night.[5]

Dr. Richard Blum and his associates at the Institute for the Study of Human Problems at Stanford University give the following portrait of the college student drug user.

The student who has some familiarity with drugs—meaning, principally, the amphetamines ("pep pills"), marijuana and LSD—is likely to be a middle-class or upper-middle-class male majoring in the humanities or the social sciences at a college or university in or near an urban center. He probably disagrees with his parents' politics and is himself a left-wing activist.

He is likely to have moved several times during his childhood and early adolescence. He probably characterizes himself as non-religious in the traditional sense. Sports are of little importance to him, as are campus clubs and groups.

He is dissatisfied with his courses and teachers and what he sees as the irrelevance of his education, with the institution's administration, with the society he grew up in and the world as it is.[6]

After the daughter of the fifty-seven-year-old television star, Arthur Linkletter, leaped to her death during a bad trip on LSD, her father, in an interview with the Los Angeles *Times,* gave the following account:

Faced with minor problems, she sought relief with LSD six months ago—but didn't find it. Instead she had a fearsomely bad "trip" which left her hallucinating long after the drug should have worn off. She told her brother she feared it was destroying her mind.

Friday she tried it again and, overwhelmed by fears unimaginable to the normal mind, she sought surcease again—and found it in a moment's panicky plunge from her kitchen window, Linkletter said.

Diane was a pretty girl, with talent and promise, who hoped to have a Hollywood career.

"She was a loving, happy girl from a family which was always very close and caring," said Linkletter.

"She was not in an abyss of melancholy. She was young. Still in her teens, it seemed. And, like all young people, she had problems. Emotional problems. Boyfriend problems. Career problems.

"And always there was the family name to contend with—you know how hard that can be. You're prejudged by everyone. All of my kids have had to adjust to it, having that name riding on top of them.

"Diane was very loving and happy—but very emotional.

"She was a girl who was not psychotic, not under treatment, a happy girl, with no money troubles. She had problems that teens have had since time began. But LSD gives them a way of avoiding facing up to those problems." [7]

The use of drugs by young people is frequently attributed to two things: the generation gap and the availability of drugs. Typically, Arthur Linkletter has asserted that his daughter's death was not suicide, but murder by the persons who make LSD available. But while a generation gap exists with respect to many things, it certainly cannot be in the push-button consciousness that tends to characterize all Americans in this world of technological miracles. The use of drugs by the young to turn on or off is merely their version of the almost universal use of sedatives, tranquilizers, and stimulants by their elders. And if in the teeth of such an obvious trend in mores, one reiterates the drama of the Volstead Act, Americans will indeed have learned little.

One of the major risks in the persistent tendency by many sociologists to classify mental illness, alcoholism, and drug addiction as forms of deviance is that by their very labelling they tend to maintain the stigma that is so prominently a part of the problem. Moreover, the tendency to evoke punitive sanctions with respect to these problems tends to give genuine therapeutic efforts a negative denotation, as if they were a substitute for punishment.

PROGRESSIVE FEATURES
IN THE SOCIAL RESPONSE

Most Americans (and most sociologists) are not prepared to view illness as a form of deviance. When they grow ill they do not particularly appreciate being viewed as goldbricks. They take a rather dim view of employers who interpret their illnesses as malingering absenteeism. They are well aware of the fact that feigned illness may be a device to avoid responsibility, but see in this no reason to withhold sympathy and assistance to the genuinely ill.

Americans frequently observe that it is in times of illness and misfortune that one discovers the value of one's family and one's friends, or the humanity of one's employer. And while most persons are familiar with instances of illness as a burden, social relations are normally deepened and ties are strengthened in the process of giving and receiving help. From this perspective, illness, far from representing a form of deviation, is one of the primary reasons for social life in the first place. Illness does not always diminish, and may in fact enrich and deepen the range of social life.

One of the major social trends of the twentieth century is the view that mental disorder, alcoholism, and drug dependence are forms of illness. Mental disorder was assimilated to the forms of illness first and drug dependence is the last to show the effects of this transformation. Even in the early 1950s, alcoholics were being denied treatment at most general hospitals as moral delinquents and troublemakers. And drunkenness is still a misdemeanor, for which the drinker can be thrown in jail or shipped off to the workhouse.

In the 1960s the application of the psychotropic drugs for dealing with the opiates developed. At the same time, the increasingly widespread use of drugs has led to a situation where illicit manufacture and traffic in drugs burgeons; and in many instances, the individual may be damaged more by the drug laws than by drugs. At the time of writing, the possession of marijuana, for example, is classed by the federal drug laws as a felony punishable by two to ten years in prison and up to $20,000 in fines for the first offense. A chaotic situation exists in the state laws applying to possession of marijuana. While more research is necessary, many students are of the opinion that the smoking of marijuana is a mild intoxicant, is non-habit forming, and is far less damaging than alcohol. There seems little question that the new legislation proposed by the Nixon administration, which would make the possession of marijuana a misdemeanor, will be passed. The United States seems to be moving somewhat in the direction of the English method of handling opiates.

In Britain in 1926, the Rolleston Committee defined opiate addiction as an illness and legitimated administration by physicians of heroin and cocaine to addicts after offers had been made to withdraw the individual from drug use. The number of known addicts in England has been far less than that in America. In 1960, a committee reported 454 known addicts out of a population of 50 million. Moreover, the addict was not forced into the position of having to resort to crime to support his habit and often held down a respectable job. The British committee reported that the illicit trade in morphine, heroin, and other drugs was almost negligible. In 1962, Edwin Schur conducted a two-year study of narcotic addiction in Britain and America; he thoroughly condemned the American system and extolled the British system.[8]

But even while Schur was writing, the situation in England was changing. In 1961, 56 new cases of drug addiction were reported. The rate of new cases increased each year with an increase of 522 in 1966, a greater increase in one year than in the previous 25. There are at present about 2,000 known heroin addicts in Great Britain, still proportionately far below the 100,000 to 150,000 addicts in the United States, but far too many to encourage self-congratulation on the part of the British. Hence the British have consulted the American way of handling drugs (the American rate remained fairly constant over the same period), and they have introduced much more stringent legislation against the drug traffic than in their previous history.[9]

Among the factors in the English problem apparently are the power of the international drug traffic's organization and changes in postwar British society. British society has lost some of its former conventional rigidity, its population has become more mobile, its lower classes have risen to a position of greater power. Under the British system of socialized medicine, some doctors, according to Louria, have been overprescribing opiates. Six were particularly at fault. In 1962, one physician prescribed 600,000 tablets of heroin, or 6 million milligrams, which in the United States would permit approximately 200,000 individuals intravenous doses. The same doctor on one occasion prescribed 900 tablets to a single addict. Some physicians, in short, were operating as drug pushers.

Moreover, according to Louria, the practice had grown up

among British patients of obtaining more drugs than they required and selling their unused drug supplies to non-addicts for food or other goods. Once the non-addicts had become "hooked," they presented themselves as addicts and applied for drug supplies on their own. If allowed to continue without interruption, this practice results in a drug addicts' proselytizing cult. Contrary to reports, British addicts do not generally work to capacity and by and large have poor work records. The net result is that drug addicts sit around in the taverns all day waiting for their daily supply of drugs, with little to do other than recruit others to the cult. English opiate addicts were found to be much more broadly distributed among the social classes than their American counterparts. They were also found to make far more general use of drugs. The illicit international drug traffic has been expanding and the use of the nonopiate drugs is rapidly increasing.

In contrast to American practice, the British in the past made no concerted effort to rehabilitate their drug addicts. They have recently begun to enact much more stringent legislation to control the illicit drug traffic. It is quite possible that the British will find some value in a rehabilitation policy modeled on American procedure, to counteract the tendency among British addicts to form self-perpetuating cults. In the long run, the British and American systems of meeting the problem will probably borrow more from each other.

In any case, the American Narcotic Addict Rehabilitation Act of 1966 established a new national policy for the treatment of narcotic addiction, based on the view that narcotic addiction is symptomatic of an emotional illness that should be treated, and that it is not a criminal circumstance in itself. The act provides for civil commitment and aftercare services for narcotic drug addicts. The NIMH encourages and provides support to nonprofit private and governmental organizations for the construction, staffing, operation, and maintenance of community-based treatment programs for narcotic addicts.

The general trend, in short, in all three areas of mental disorder, alcoholism, and drug dependence is to treat them as symptomatic of emotional illness and to develop community-based programs comprising the following types of services:

Inpatient treatment, including, in the cases of alcoholism and drug dependency, withdrawal.

Outpatient services.

The establishment of special living arrangements, such as halfway houses or placement where indicated with qualified families.

Aftercare services such as vocational and educational programs.

Partial hospitalization services.

Prevention services, including consultation, education and community organization programs.

Diagnostic services, including, in the case of drug dependence, techniques for detection of opiates and other drugs.

There are some inclinations toward combining all three types of problems into a single package, making their treatment the objective of a single integrated community-based program.

INTERRELATIONS

When one treats mental problems, alcoholism, and drug dependence as modalities of illness, it is essential to keep in mind that all users of alcohol and drugs are not pathological. The use or nonuse of alcohol and various drugs by most individuals is determined in considerable measure by the practices of the special social groups with which they associate. Edwin Sutherland made this argument (differential association), and has been followed by numerous other criminologists, to refute the idea that criminal behavior usually has special psychological or psychopathic causes. Sutherland felt that those persons who resorted to crime for psychological reasons constitute a minor part of the crime problem. Most criminals are as "normal" as most non-criminals. Persons assimilating the problems of mental illness, alcoholism, and drug dependence to criminality could be expected to apply to them the differential association theory.

The argument that alcohol and drug use also is usually a product of differential association has been advanced under the concept of special subcultures. The social practices with respect to drug use by jazz musicians, hippies, and youth in urban ghetto areas and various youth groups have been examined as a product of their special subcultures.

If an individual associates with groups that use drugs or make heavy use of alcohol, his practices will probably correspond to the group norm. In the opinion of Alfred R. Lindesmith, this is all that is essential to produce addiction, which occurs the instant the individual associates the distress he experiences at the time with a drug's withdrawal.[10] But while delinquent gangs often tolerate drug use, studies of juvenile gangs have not revealed drug use to be a major group activity.[11] Moreover, most delinquent gangs disapprove of excessive use of drugs by their members, since it interferes with their effectiveness in carrying out thefts, robberies and other types of criminal activity. If the leader of a delinquency gang gets "hooked," he is deposed as no longer trustworthy.

It is certainly clear, however, that learning in a context of differential group association plays some role in mental illness and drug and alcohol abuse. The studies that have been reviewed establish the role of learning in alcohol and drug abuse beyond any question. The role of learning in mental illness is not quite as self-evident.

Pirandello's play, *Enrico IV*, perceptively fastens on the manner in which inadvertent psychological problems may be seized upon and then become a counter in an individual's strategies of control over his social environment. The play's presumed madman, who conceives himself as the historical Holy Roman Emperor Henry IV, arrives at his state following a psychic breakdown after sustaining an accidental blow to the head during a historical pageant, in which he had assumed the identity of this historical personage. His family found it easier to accept the madman's delusions than to contradict them; they kept him in a room furnished in the period, dressed his keepers in the costume of the time, and responded to him as if he were in fact the emperor. The play counterposes the penetrating social and psychological insights of the presumed madman to the stereotypes and banalities of the "normal" persons about him. It is eventually revealed by the presumed madman that, while he had in fact been out of his head for a time, he had eventually come to his senses only to discover that the charade enacted for his benefit gave him enormous control over the people around him, for, within the sphere of his presumed delusion, they had yielded to him an almost imperial control over their actions. Hence, he decided to maintain the illusion as a way of maintaining control over his family and associates.

One of the most familiar properties of large numbers of mentally ill individuals is the ambiguity of much of their behaviors. Typical are: the mother who goes into mental collapse every time her son or daughter becomes serious about his or her girl or boyfriend; the wife whose "case of nerves" is the basis of a tyranny over her husband; the husband whose outbursts keep his wife and children in a state of abject surrender. It is often difficult to decide where the feigning of the symptomology of mental illness leaves off and where the illness proper begins.

Furthermore, the social worker responsible for aftercare services of the mentally ill often sees a given patient before and after his tours through the state mental institution. While this is generally viewed as an antitherapeutic sentiment, he often gets the impression that after each tour in the institution, the patient has managed to expand and deepen his command over the symptomology of mental illness. He seems to develop a clearer idea as to which symptoms increase his control over his environment and which receive rather short shrift. One is tempted, at times, to view the mentally ill "commuter" (that is, the highly mobile type of mentally ill individual who is always on his way into or out of a mental institution) as an adept professional.

It has also been evident from the report of researchers that situations somewhat parallel to those of Pirandello's play actually may occur in the chronic wards of mental hospitals. Individuals committed to mental institutions have at times recovered but have quietly preserved the whole symptomology and continued to participate in a patient culture which preserves them from outside influences. It will be recalled that when one patient was asked what he would do if he were released, he retorted hotly that they would never "railroad" him out of there. The investigators described what they called a sort of culture of "chronicity."

But while there are elements of learning in all three conditions, one cannot account for mental illness, alcoholism, and drug addiction by learning alone. There is another component, a contingency most clearly represented in the phenomena of drug dependence—that of getting "hooked"—that separate the problem drinker from the alcoholic and the person with many of the symptoms thereof from the truly mentally ill.

With the addicting drugs, tolerance by the body is fairly rapid, so that more and more of the drug is required to achieve the same effect. Moreover, withdrawal symptoms are severe, and the greater the dependence on the drug, the more severe the shock when it is withdrawn. The withdrawal of heroin produces vomiting, diarrhea, tremors, aches, and sweats; the withdrawal of barbiturates produces delirium tremens, and other symptoms; the withdrawal of amphetamines produces depression and apathy. Hence, on a purely physiological basis, the individual requires the drug to prevent intense physical symptoms. He is "hooked." All of the drugs of abuse tend as well to produce psychological dependence. The individual comes to use the drug as a device for not facing his psychological problems. These have a way of growing worse, the longer they are postponed. Hence, with the nonuse of drugs, the implications of his condition crash on the individual's mind.

While it is not conventional to conceive of alcoholism in these terms, it is quite clear that direct parallels are present to becoming "hooked" on drugs. But alcoholism in time also produces physiological changes in the individual. Delirium tremens and other symptoms accompany withdrawal. All students of alcoholism have tended to draw the line between problem drinking and alcoholism at that point where a "loss of control" occurs. The problem drinker may get into trouble when he is drunk, but he is still more or less in control of his drinking. Alcoholism begins where drinking is in control of the individual. The potential alcoholic is at, or at least very close to, this point when he has to have a drink to get through the hangover caused by previous drinking. This starts him on a new cycle. Psychological dependence is also quite evident in the development of alcoholism. In fact, one reason it is so hard to cure is that, as the alcoholic gains control over his condition, his social and psychological problems, which have grown worse in the meantime, have become overwhelming.

In mental illness, no chemical substance is present to create physiological dependence. There are, however, properties in the typical history of the mentally ill that seem to parallel the phenomenon of getting "hooked," or at least of "losing control." While Erving Goffman did not specifically formulate the point, his argument that the decisive element in mental illness was a career contingency calls attention to the fact that the symptomology of the mentally ill is part of the entire spectrum of behavior. It is doubtful whether there has ever been a "normal" person who did not have some of the symptoms of the "mentally ill." There is, however, a phenomenon which Goffman ignores, but one which is apparent to anyone dealing with the mentally ill in any capacity. The point at which the relatives, friends, employers or other persons involved with the individual are inclined to initiate commitment procedures (if they cannot persuade him to seek psychiatric help voluntarily) is where the balance has been tipped, and the individual's symptoms are, so to speak, in charge of him, rather than he in charge of his symptoms. This is quite the equivalent of being "hooked" by drugs or losing control over the use of alcohol.

The parallels between mental illness, alcoholism and drug dependence also extend to another point. Freud and a variety of other students have familiarized contemporary men with the idea that the symptoms of the mentally ill person often represent a solution to his personal problems. In cases of hysteria, for example, an individual may control his environment with a "paralyzed" hand. The paralysis of the trigger finger of an infantry soldier suffering from "battle fatigue" makes this quite clear. If under hypnosis one suggests that the hand is all right, the individual may regain control over it. But it was often discovered that sometime later a whole new set of hysterical symptoms appeared, worse than the original symptoms. The individual may end up, for example, psychologically blind rather than psychologically crippled. In retrospect, it sometimes seems that the hysterical patient takes the best possible path through the maze of his personal difficulties. Or again, Freud discovered that when he had eventually uncovered and brought to the surface repressed psychological material, a virtual explosion of aggressive feeling sometimes occurred. In short, when the mentally ill person is deprived of his illness, he may suffer the equivalent of "withdrawal" symptoms.

The interrelations between mental illness, alcoholism, and drug addiction are complex. A number of psychiatric syndromes result from alcoholism. The acute alcoholic psychoses include: delirium tremens, hallucinosis, and acute alcoholic intoxication.[12] In acute alcoholic psychosis, the drinker, after consuming only a small amount of alcohol, may develop total amnesia to events that follow and often carry out automatic behavior that may be violent and dangerous. Chronic alcoholic deterioration is manifest as a gradual deterioration of the moral and ethical senses and values of the patient. Korsakoff's psychosis results in extreme memory defects. Chronic alcoholic psychosis of a paranoid type and alcoholic schizophrenia appear when persons seem normal while not drinking, but manifest paranoid and schizophrenic symptoms while drinking. Wernicke's syndrome consists primarily of a clouding of consciousness and possible appearance of a stuporous or somnambulant state. Other psychopathologies from alcohol also may occur.

Among the mental complications that occur after the use of drugs are: the psychoses, paranoia, and anxiety reactions associated with the use of LSD; the psychoses ensuing from the use of barbiturates; the paranoid psychoses that are frequent manifestations of amphetamine addiction; and the probable brain damage and paranoid psychoses that appear in cases of cocaine addiction.[13]

George Thompson argues that, among the psychiatric syndromes leading to alcoholism, the manic-depressive group (comprising persons who drink to alleviate depression or in consequence of excessive psychomotor drive) is most prominent.[14] But Thompson also maintains that many patients drink because of various forms of schizophrenia, psychoneuroses (insecurity, inhibitions, anxiety, dependence, and so on), and basically psychopathic personalities. It seems likely that these psychiatric syndromes are also among the causes of drug use.

When commitment petitions for involuntary hospitalization are being prepared, it is often difficult to decide whether the patient should be committed for alcoholism, drug addiction, or mental illness. Only after intensive medical and psychiatric evaluation does the preferred diagnosis appear, and even then there may be doubt. While alcoholism and drug addiction may cause various psychiatric conditions and/or be effects of them, it is also quite possible that at times various psychiatric syndromes may be temporarily palliated by the patient's use of drugs or alcohol to solve his problems. In such cases, the removal of drugs and alcohol can lead to a worsening rather than an improvement of the individual's mental illness.

The various evidences seem to add up to the fact that mental illness, alcoholism, and drug addiction represent variations of essentially the same problem, or at least variations of a closely related group of problems. The possibility has repeatedly been raised that there may be physiological factors that make individuals differentially susceptible to mental illness and to alcoholism. Although physiological factors that might make individuals differentially susceptible to drug dependence have not yet been sought, the same reasoning should apply here. Since all human behavior rests on man's biology, and since there are considerable variations in the physiology of individuals, it is quite reasonable to expect that research may eventually establish various types of physiological factors which make their possessors especially susceptible to mental illness, alcoholism, and drug addiction. The present state of knowledge, however, seems to indicate that physiological factors are at best a contributing rather than a sole cause of any of these three conditions.

Whatever may be the eventual status of physiological causes of mental illness, alcoholism, and drug addiction, there is evidence that learned behavior plays a role in all three. When one explores the role of such social factors as social class, religion, ethnic group, peer group, differential association, and subculture in the incidence of mental illness, alcoholism and drug dependence, one may be isolating categories of differential physical and psychological risk, but certainly of differential social risk. But what one learns as a member of a society as a whole or of one subsection of it is a contributing factor for or against, not an exclusive cause.

Mental illness, alcoholism, and drug addiction are primarily contingencies of individual development. At the same time, no attempt to find any single psychological factor or unique complex of psychological factors which could be unambiguously established as the primary cause has been convincing. The only safe conclusion from the multiplicity of studies reviewed is that there are numerous routes to mental illness, alcoholism, and drug addiction. *We submit that the common property of all three problems is the general character of the psychological developmental process rather than any particular psychological content. Our theory in brief is that mental illness, alcoholism, and drug dependence represent failures of socialization.*

FACTORS IN FAILURE OF SOCIALIZATION

It is man's fate as the terminal creature in a series of species that developed its intelligence as a substitute for instincts—to be condemned to forge his own individuality and his own social life in the course of experience. In his endless explorations of the environment and the possibilities of interhuman life, man has no other guide than a sense of personal well-being and adequacy to external physical and social situations.

One of the most basic aspects of socialization—that is, of the development of a well-knit, autonomous selfhood on the part of individuals equipped with the emotional and conceptual resources adequate to the demands placed on them by the natural and social world—is the individual's acquisition of what might be described as the basic alphabet and language of emotions of his society. There is no more fundamental level of learning, with respect to the individual's capacity to get on with others in a particular society, than learning what feelings or emotions are appropriate to which life circumstances. If an individual experiences emotions that are socially appropriate to any given situation, he shares a profound subrational level of kinship with others of the society. If he does not experience the appropriate emotions, he is alienated, defensive, and uncertain. To be sure, if an individual does not possess the knowledge and skills appropriate to his various predicaments, he may experience tensions from this source as well, but if his basic feelings are in order, the knowledge and skills are usually quickly and easily acquired.

That failure of socialization at this primary level is central to mental illness, alcoholism, and drug addiction may be seen from the terms that are endlessly intoned whenever these problems are discussed. Again and again, they are said to arise from a sense of inadequacy, from immaturity, from a sense of alienation, from a lack of self-confidence, from anxiety, from an incapacity to face problems, and so forth. From this standpoint, it becomes clear why such problems appear with great frequency in ghetto areas where many individuals face lives of permanent frustration, and among individuals from broken homes or from homes where these problems are already present. Any circumstance, in short, that stands in the way of the development of a coherent and autonomous sense of self and adequacy to external situations is an open invitation to mental illness, alcoholism, or drug dependence.

From this same perspective, it is also clear why, in complex societies with a variety of underprivileged minorities and in societies with accelerated rates of change, the incidence of mental illness, alcoholism, and drug dependence increases. Thomas Szasz would undoubtedly say at this particular point that, in times of rapid change, the games of life change so rapidly that the individual is not able to keep up, that he tries to play new games with old rules no longer appropriate. This is correct if one understands by this formulation that the individual's emotional responses are not appropriate to the situations in which he is expected to perform, and that he opts out of the major games of life for a much diminished game of his own.

There is a tendency on the part of the well-knit coherent ego to explore new areas of experience, to be sensitive to new developments, to experiment. Hence, there is not, per se, anything indicative of emotional inadequacy in the use of alcohol or drugs. They have been used by man since the dawn of history. Moreover, it is quite possible that the use of alcohol and drugs has in the past usually been life-promoting, for they may release various kinds of repressed materials, acting like a safety valve.

In a series of articles on drug use in the Minneapolis *Tribune,* the possibility is raised that, if the person experimenting with drugs begins with a well-knit sense of self, the experience does not necessarily do him harm.

"Hippies are the last people in the world who should take drugs," said G. H. (Hank) Harrison III, a man who would know if anyone would.

Harrison, now a technical writer for Honeywell, Inc., spent four years in San Francisco, Calif., running what is, to the best of his knowledge, the first LSD rescue center anywhere. In the course of writing his just-completed book—"Head, The Drug User in America"—Harrison delved into the fields of pharmacology, medicine, physiology, theology, sociology and anthropology.

He also drew on his own experiences in head culture: as an acid user, manager of the rock group "The Grateful Dead," and friend of author Ken Kesey, the Hell's Angels and many other persons and groups who play roles in the drug scene.

Harrison ran LSD Rescue during the height of the influx into San Francisco's Haight-Ashbury district and handled more than 4,000 drug problem cases.

Harrison, a big, tough, fast-talking man, has little patience with what he calls the "Reader's Digest stereotype of the drug crisis."

He says the mass media are spreading massive amounts of misinformation about drugs, and is himself dedicated to spreading "solid words." He was instrumental in setting up the YES (Youth Emergency Service) phones in Minneapolis. YES handles calls from those on bad trips, those with any drug problem and those who just need to talk.

Harrison believes that the dangers of drugs lie not so much in the drugs themselves but in the minds of the people who take them.

"Strong drugs just bring out what's already there," he said.

"That's the reason I believe hippies shouldn't use drugs. Look at hippies as a whole. They're anti-social, with varying degrees of hostility, they are often adolescent with all the mental confusion that stage entails, they've got general identity problems, masculine-feminine identity probems, and an unusually high proportion of neuroses and schizoid and paranoid symptoms. And they take drugs. Ugh.

"And to the extent that these mental confusions are common to most adolescents, the same dangers in drug-taking are there for them too. They are simply not mature enough to handle them."

"Please understand that I am not anti-drug. I think it would be one of the most tremendous and socially valuable things I can think of if LSD were legalized and dispensed in clinics under psychiatric supervision. With a good hi-fi and friends thrown in, LSD was for me a religious and therapeutic experience. But I know that its use should be limited.[15]

If one disregards the missionary tone (and possible rationalization) so characteristic of the ex-drug user, this formulation still quite correctly sees the use of drugs as dangerous, when such use arises out of and contributes to emotional inadequacy. In effect, Harrison is formulating the problem of drug abuse as a failure of socialization.

The experimental and adventurous inclination of the outgoing individual with a well-knit sense of self make it doubly important to avoid mythology when one is dealing with alcohol or drugs. When at least twelve million Americans have experimented with marijuana, federal laws that treat its possession as a felony potentially do more damage to the individual than the drug. *Life* (October 31, 1969) carries the story of a young man without any previous record of criminal activity who received a twenty-year sentence (the same as the minimum sentence for first degree murder) from the state of Virginia for possession of marijuana. Operation Intercept, which drove up the price of marijuana, seems in many cases to have had the effect of turning many youthful users to the so-called hard drugs. The antidote for the inclination to use drugs experimentally is honest education.

To be effective, they must be honest.

Dr. Donald B. Louria, president of the New York State Council on Drug Addiction said:

"It should be stressed that educational programs and individual speakers must be scrupulously honest and factual. If an over-zealous lecturer, for example, states that marijuana leads to lung cancer or that it inevitably impels the user to turn to more potent drugs, he is almost certain to undermine his credibility, and end by actually performing a disservice."

And Dr. Stanley F. Yolles, director of the National Institute of Mental Health added:

"Fortunately, there is some evidence that the 'Now Generation' holds a healthy respect for the facts and for the findings of science. While parental panic and admonition are [of] little value as guidance, and tend to stoke the fires of adolescent rebellion, knowledge of the facts may help." [16]

When inappropriate legislation and scare mythologies that are provably false are raised against drug use, it only adds zest to experimentalism. Experimentalism, in turn, can operate as a kind of umbrella for individuals whose use of drugs arises out of uncertain emotional maturity. Similar reflections apply to alcohol use. Furthermore, while individuals using drugs or alcohol in this manner may not develop into alcoholics or drug addicts, they postpone facing their personal problems, which in turn may progressively worsen because of the very drug and alcohol use. In this manner, subsequent mental illness may have been aggravated by attempts to solve problems with drugs and alcohol. This appears often in the case histories of the mentally ill.

Meanwhile, it should be noted that socialization is a two-sided relation: it involves both the coherence of the individual ego, and the demands placed on the individual by the social situations in which he operates. Failures of socialization may start from either side. There are individuals who get along all right in ordinary social situations, but who, when using drugs or alcohol, undergo a radical change of personality—becoming, for example, violent or sexually aggressive. It is often difficult to decide whether the effect is actually due to the drugs or alcohol, or whether the individual is simply doing what he wanted to do all along and is now able to attribute this action to the drugs or alcohol. In any case, such behavior is indicative of serious emotional incongruities close to the surface of the individual's adjustment; in the later history of such individuals, mental illness, alcoholism, drug addiction, or some combination of these manifestations may appear. In cases of this sort, the failure of socialization primarily arises from inadequacies of the individual ego.

The case is somewhat different for individuals who get along quite well for years in ordinary life situations, but who may find themselves for a period of time in conditions of unusual stress. The most obvious examples are provided by breakdowns among combat soldiers or the inmates of concentration camps. There are, however, also occupations that may be experienced as unusually stressful. The surgeon, for example, may face many situations on an almost daily basis which may involve life and death implications to the patient. Apparently easy operations may suddenly develop complications that make tremendous demands on skill and require split-second decisions. Under such circumstances, the surgeon may resort, at first only occasionally, to drugs to help him through his crises until he becomes hooked. About one out of a hundred physicians becomes a drug addict, compared to one out of three thousand in the non-medical population. Similarly, the person who suddenly finds himself in a position of administration, without previous psychological preparation, may begin to drink more heavily to mitigate his sense of inadequacy. Students of the behavior of men under stress have come to the conclusion that every man has his breaking point.

Finally, it may be noted that powerful evidence for the character of mental illness, alcoholism, and drug addiction as failures of socialization are provided by the more successful trends in therapy. The most effective therapeutic procedures attack the problem from the standpoint of the individual's psychology and simultaneously transform the entire social context in which he operates into an ego-sustaining therapeutic community.

NOTES

1. Simon Dinitz, Russell R. Dynes, and Alfred C. Clarke, *Deviance: Studies in the Process of Stigmatization and Societal Reaction,* p. 3.

2. Ibid., p. 4.

3. Ibid., p. 20.

4. "Pop Drugs: The High as a Way of Life," *Time* (September 26, 1969): 69.

5. Paul G. Ashdown and Stanley M. Brown, "The Area Is a Narcotics Supermarket," St. Paul *Pioneer Press,* October 12, 1969, p. 1.

6. Minneapolis *Tribune,* September 2, 1969, p. 13.

7. St. Paul *Pioneer Press,* October 6, 1969, p. 7.

8. Edwin M. Schur, *Narcotic Addiction in Britain and America* (Bloomington, Indiana: Indiana University Press, 1963).

9. Donald B. Louria, *The Drug Scene,* pp. 63ff.

10. Alfred R. Lindesmith, "A Sociological Theory of Drug Addiction," *American Journal of Sociology* 43 (1938): 599ff.

11. James F. Short, Jr. and Fred L. Strodtbeck, *Group Process and Gang Delinquency* (Chicago: University of Chicago Press, 1965), pp. 63ff.
12. George N. Thompson, "The Psychiatry of Alcoholism," in George N. Thompson, ed., *Alcoholism*, pp. 464ff.
13. Sidney Cohen, *The Drug Dilemma*, p. 133.
14. Thompson, "The Psychiatry of Alcoholism," p. 460.
15. Molly Ivins, "Expert Finds Drugs 'Not for Kids,'" *Minneapolis Tribune*, October 29, 1969, p. 21.
16. Dan Wascoe, Jr., Minneapolis *Tribune*, October 31, 1969, p. 32.

BIBLIOGRAPHY

American Medical Association. *Manual on Alcoholism* 1968.

Angrist, Shirley S.; Lefton, Mark; Dinitz, Simon; and Pasamanick, Benjamin. *Women After Treatment, A Study of Former Mental Patients and Their Normal Neighbors.* New York: Appleton-Century-Crofts, 1968.

Ausubel, David P. *Drug Addiction: Physiological, Psychological, and Sociological Aspects.* New York: Random House, 1958.

Ball, J. C.; Bates, W. M.; and O'Donnell, J. A. *Characteristics of Hospitalized Narcotic Addicts.* Washington, D. C.: Dept. of Health, Education and Welfare, 1966.

Belknap, Ivan. *Human Problems of a State Mental Hospital.* New York: McGraw-Hill Book Co., Inc., 1956.

Biggs, John, Jr. *The Guilty Mind, Psychiatry and the Law of Homicide.* Baltimore, Md.: Johns Hopkins Press, 1967.

Blane, Howard T. *The Personality of the Alcoholic: Guises of Dependency.* New York: Harper & Row, 1968.

Block, Marvin A. *Alcoholism: Its Facets and Phases.* New York: John Day, 1965.

Blum, Richard H. and Associates. *Utopiates, A Study of the Use and Users of LSD-25.* New York: Atherton Press, 1964.

Bromberg, Walter. *The Mind of Man.* New York: Harper & Row, 1959.

Chafetz, Morris E. *Liquor, Servant of Man.* Boston: Little, Brown, 1965.

Chein, Isidor.; Gerard, Donald L.; Lee, Robert S.; and Rosenfeld, Eva. *The Road to H.* New York: Basic Books, 1964.

Chein, Isidor, and Rosenfeld, Eva. "Juvenile Narcotics Use." *Law and Contemporary Problems* 22.

Clinard, Marshall B. *Sociology of Deviant Behavior.* New York: Holt, Rinehart and Winston, Inc., 1968.

Cohen, Sidney. *The Drug Dilemma.* New York: McGraw-Hill, 1969.

Crabtree, Arthur P. *You and The Law.* New York: Holt, Rinehart and Winston, Inc., 1964.

Denber, Herman C. B., ed. *Research Conference on Therapeutic Community.* Springfield, Ill.: Charles C. Thomas, 1960.

Deutsch, Albert. *The Mentally Ill in America: A History of Their Care and Treatment from Colonial Times.* New York: Columbia University Press, 1949.

Dinitz, Simon; Dynes, Russell R.; and Clarke, Alfred C., eds. *Deviance, Studies in the Process of Stigmatization and Societal Reaction.* New York: Oxford University Press, 1969.

Farmer, Robert A. and Associates. *The Rights of the Mentally Ill.* New York: Arco Publishing Co., Inc., 1967.

Finestone, H. "Cats, Kicks and Color." In *Identity and Anxiety,* edited by M. Stein, A. Vidich, and M. White. Glencoe, Ill.: Free Press, 1960.

Fink, Arthur E.; Anderson, Wilson; Conover, C.; and Merrill, B. *The Field of Social Work.* New York: Holt, Rinehart and Winston, Inc., 1968.

Glasscote, Raymond M.; Plaut, Thomas F. A.; Hammersley, Donald W.; O'Neill, Francis J.; Chafetz, Morris E.; and Cumming, Elaine. *The Treatment of Alcoholism: A Study of Programs and Problems.* Washington, D. C.: American Psychiatric Association, 1967.

Glasscote, Raymond M.; Sanders, David S.; Forstenzer, H. M.; and Foley, A. R. *The Community Mental Health Center, An Analysis of Existing Models.* Washington, D. C.: American Psychiatric Association, 1964.

Glasser, William. *Mental Health or Mental Illness? Psychiatry for Practical Action.* New York: Harper & Row, 1960.

Glueck, Sheldon. *Law and Psychiatry, Cold War or Entente Cordiale?* Baltimore: Johns Hopkins Press, 1966.

Goffman, Erving. *Asylums, Essays on the Social Situation of Mental Patients and Other Inmates.* Garden City, N. Y.: Doubleday & Co., Inc., 1961.

———. *Stigma, Notes on the Management of Spoiled Identity.* Englewood Cliffs, N. J.: Prentice-Hall, Inc., 1963.

Greenblatt, Milton; York,, Richard H.; and Brown, Esther Lucile. *From Custodial to Therapeutic Care in Mental Hospitals.* New York: Russell Sage Foundation, 1955.

Hasek, Jaroslav. *The Good Soldier Schweik.* New York: Frederick Ungar, 1930.

Hollingshead, August B., and Redlich, Fredrick. *Social Class and Mental Illness: A Community Study.* New York: John Wiley & Sons, Inc., 1958.

Jellinek, E. M. *The Disease Concept of Alcoholism.* Highland Park, N. J.: Hillhouse Press, 1960.

Joint Commission on Mental Illness and Health. *Action for Mental Health: Final Report.* New York: Basic Books, Inc., 1961.

Leech, Kenneth, and Jordan, Brenda. *Drugs for Young People: Their Use and Misuse.* Oxford: Religious Education Press, Ltd., 1967.

Lindesmith, Alfred R. *Opiate Addiction.* Bloomington, Ind.: Indiana diana University Press, 1947.

———. *The Addict and the Law.* Bloomington, Ind.: Indiana University Press, 1965.

Lolli, Giorgio. *Social Drinking.* Cleveland: World, 1960.

Lolli, Giorgio; Serianni, Emidio; Golder, Grace M.; and Luzzatto-Fegiz, Pierpaolo. *Alcohol in Italian Culture.* New Brunswick, N. J.: Rutgers Center of Alcohol Studies, 1958.

Louria, Donald B. *The Drug Scene.* New York: McGraw-Hill, 1968.

Lucia, Salvatore P., ed. *Alcohol and Civilization*. New York: Mc-Graw-Hill, 1963.

Maddox, George L., and McCall, Bevode C. *Drinking Among Teen-Agers*. New Brunswick, N. J.: Rutgers Center of Alcohol Studies, 1964.

Martin, Denis V. *Adventure in Psychiatry, Social Change in a Mental Hospital*. Oxford: Bruno Cassirer, 1962.

Milt, Harry. *Basic Handbook on Alcoholism*. Fair Haven, N. J.: Scientific Aids Publications, 1967.

———. *Basic Handbook on Mental Illness*. Fair Haven, N. J.: Scientific Aids Publications, 1966.

Morris, Norval. "Psychiatry and the Dangerous Criminal." *Southern California Law Review* 41 (1968).

Mumford, Emily, and Skipper, James K., Jr. *Sociology in Hospital Care*. New York: Harper & Row, 1967.

Myers, Jerome K. and Roberts, Bertram H. *Family and Class Dynamics in Mental Illness*. New York: John Wiley & Sons, 1959.

National Conference on Social Welfare. *Mental Health and Social Welfare*. New York: Columbia University Press, 1961.

Nowlis, Helen H. *Drugs on the College Campus*. Garden City, New York: Doubleday & Co., Inc., 1969.

O'Donnell, John A. "A Follow-up of Narcotic Addicts; Morality, Relapse, and Abstinence." *American Journal of Orthopsychiatry* 34 (1964): 948–954.

———. "Narcotic Addiction and Crime." *Social Problems* 13 (1966): 374–384.

Pearlstein, Stanley. *Psychiatry, The Law and Mental Health*. New York: Oceana Publishers, Inc., 1967.

Pittman, David J. and Snyder, Charles R., eds. *Society, Culture and Drinking Patterns*. New York: Wiley, 1962.

President's Commission on Law Enforcement. *Task Force Report: Narcotics and Drug Abuse*. Washington: U. S. Government Printing Office, 1967.

Putnam, P., and Ellinwood, E. "Narcotic Addiction Among Physicians; a Ten-Year Follow Up." *American Journal of Psychiatry* 122 (1966): 745–747.

Raush, Harold L., with Raush, Charlotte L. *The Halfway House Movement: A Search for Sanity.* New York: Appleton-Century-Crofts, 1968.

Robinson, Alice M. *The Psychiatric Aide.* Philadelphia: J. B. Lippincott Co., 1964.

Robinson, Reginald; DeMarche, David F.; and Wagle, Mildred K. *Community Resources in Mental Health.* New York: Basic Books, Inc., 1960.

Ross, Martin J. *Handbook of Everyday Law.* New York: Harper & Row, 1967.

Rubenstein, Robert, and Lasswell, Harold D. *The Sharing of Power in a Psychiatric Hospital.* New Haven: Yale University Press, 1966.

Schofield, William. *Psychotherapy, The Purchase of Friendship.* Englewood Cliffs, N. J.: Prentice-Hall, Inc., 1964.

Schwartz, Morris S., and Schwartz, Charlotte Green. *Social Approaches to Mental Patient Care.* New York: Columbia University Press, 1964.

Singer, Charles, and Underwood, E. Ashworth. *A Short History of Medicine.* New York and Oxford: Oxford University Press, 1962.

Stanton, Alfred H., and Schwartz, Morris S. *The Mental Hospital, A Study of Institutional Participation in Psychiatric Illness and Treatment.* New York: Basic Books, Inc., 1954.

Stern, Edith M. *Mental Illness, A Guide for the Family.* New York: Harper & Row, 1962.

Straus, Robert, and Bacon, Selden D. *Drinking in College.* New Haven: Yale University Press, 1953.

Szasz, Thomas S. *The Myth of Mental Illness, Foundations of a Theory of Personal Conduct.* New York: Harper & Row, 1968.

Thompson, George N., ed. *Alcoholism.* Springfield, Ill: Charles C. Thomas, 1956.

U. S. Dept. of Health, Education and Welfare. *Narcotic Drug Addiction.* Mental Health Monograph no. 2. Bethesda, Md.: U. S. Dept. of Health, Education and Welfare, 1965.

Vail, David J. *The British Mental Hospital System.* Springfield, Ill.: Charles C. Thomas, 1965.

————. *Mental Health Systems in Scandinavia.* Springfield, Ill.:
Charles C. Thomas, 1968.

Williams, Roger J. *Alcoholism: The Nutritional Approach.* Austin:
University of Texas Press, 1964.

Winick, C. "Narcotics Addiction and Its Treatment." *Law and Contemporary Problems* 22 (1957): 9–33.

Zilboorg, Gregory, M.D. *The Psychology of the Criminal Act and
Punishment.* New York: Harcourt, Brace and Company, 1954.

INDEX

ABOUT THE AUTHORS

Don Martindale is Professor of Sociology at the University of Minnesota. Among his published works are *The Nature and Types of Sociological Theory, American Social Structure, American Society, Social Life and Cultural Change, Community Character and Civilization, Institutions, Organizations and Mass Society,* and, with R. Galen Hanson, *Small Town and the Nation.* He has also published various other books and monographs, and has translated and edited four books of Max Weber's. Professor Martindale serves as the series editor for Greenwood's Contributions in Sociology.

Edith Martindale has had extensive experience in the field of medical and psychiatric care. She is a registered nurse and holds a B.S. degree from the University of Wisconsin. Mrs. Martindale has served as a registered nurse in intensive psychiatric treatment and in aftercare services for the mentally ill.

The Social Dimensions
of Mental Illness, Alcoholism, and
Drug Dependence was composed in Intertype Garamond
with Optima display by Port City Press, Inc.,
Baltimore, Maryland. The entire book
was printed by offset lithography
by Litho Crafters, Inc.,
Ann Arbor, Michigan